MW00615603

— RECLAIM —
YOUR DARK
GODDESS

— RECLAIM —
YOUR DARK
GODDESS

The alchemy of transformation

FLAVIA KATE PETERS

ROCKPOOL

A Rockpool book
PO Box 252
Summer Hill
NSW 2130
Australia

rockpoolpublishing.com
Follow us! **f** ⓘ rockpoolpublishing
Tag your images with #rockpoolpublishing

ISBN: 9781922579065

Published in 2022, by Rockpool Publishing

Copyright text © Flavia Kate Peters, 2022
Copyright images © Mira Nurdianti, 2022
Copyright design © Rockpool Publishing, 2022

All rights reserved. No part of this publication may be reproduced, stored
in a retrieval system, or transmitted in any form or by any means, electronic,
mechanical, photocopying, recording or otherwise, without the prior written
permission of the publisher.

Design and typesetting by Sara Lindberg, Rockpool Publishing
Edited by Lisa Macken

A catalogue record for this
book is available from the
National Library of Australia

Printed and bound in China
10 9 8 7 6 5 4 3 2 1

This goes where other handbooks of practical magick have generally dared not venture, and where magick is badly needed: into areas where people need to be rescued, supported and empowered, so that acts of magickal transformation create survivors and teachers.

Professor Ronald Hutton FBA, MA(Cantab.), DPhil(Oxon.), FRHistS, FSA, FLSW
Professor of history, author

This book is more than just an initiation; it is a beacon, a way shower. Few books exist that are as honest and as challenging about transcending the dark night of the soul. Within the pages an honesty and integrity oozes forth: Flavia not only conveys with beauty but with an honesty that bares herself to the world. Reading these pages gives us all hope of the light that exists even in the darkest moments of our journey. It shows us that we all have the ability and choice to become stronger than we were. You will cry and you will laugh as you read these pages. You will go on a journey, one that might even mirror aspects of your own life in unique ways. You will find parallels in the most unlikely of places and you will find your own truth, your own voice and your own strength that have been within always.

Olaf Nixon, MSc, DipHypCS
International psychotherapist and counsellor

Within the sacred Eleusinian Mysteries of the feminine divine was a sacred Dark Goddess initiation so deep, so profound that only the highest initiates attempted it. Those mysteries were driven underground but remained hidden in the bones, blood and souls of the descendants of the high priestess of the Eleusinian Mysteries until a time came when once more they would emerge and be needed to assist humanity. That time is now, and here within the pages of this book is a process so deep, so profound it will help you to comprehend each twist and turn in life assisted by each dark goddess.

Flavia has written this book from her experiences of her journey to meet each dark goddess individually as she transversed the death and rebirth process, changing her life forever. Flavia holds your hand as she guides you with her innate knowledge and experience of how to uncover every part of you that has been denied, repressed or disowned, bringing balance to light and dark, for the wise witch knows that the shadows come from the light.

Flavia's authentic guidance to enlightenment will show you the way out of the dark, into a spiritual awakening of remembering who you truly are by strengthening your own personal belief system and empowering you to reclaim what was lost and forgotten.

This long-awaited book is powerful, incredible and life changing. It is an ancient map that has been lost until now, helping you to navigate your voyage back home to yourselves, rewriting your soul's destiny to reclaim a new way of living, thinking and feeling for yourself. A masterpiece of personal psychological and deep wisdom reaching the very depths of your soul's knowing.

It's time to embrace the Dark Goddess, reclaim your magic, your birthright, for we are now in the age of transformation and change. Who better than Flavia to lead us all through the dark night of the soul with her courage and passion, to help make the change and transformation we have been waiting for all along.

Barbara Meiklejohn-Free, The Highland Seer
Bestselling author

Witch, high priestess and international author Flavia Kate Peters's latest book *Reclaim Your Dark Goddess* is the ultimate witchy survival kit to activate your inner magick. Through the power of the dark goddesses from all cultures and traditions it helps us understand our own shadow and how to embrace our inner dark traits to fully heal ourselves and be whole again. It is certainly going to have a central position in my book collection of powerful, inspiring women's books that show us how to live our lives to the fullest potential.

Lynne Franks, OBE
Founder of SEED Women's Empowerment Network
and bestselling author

CONTENTS

INTRODUCTION

There comes a time for many of us when we are emotionally, physically and spiritually exhausted, when we feel the world is too heavy to bear and that we cannot move past dark, negative emotions or remove the things that are harming and paralysing us. We often turn on ourselves, blaming our weakness, our past, our lack of knowledge, or we rail against fate, cursing the people and situations we believe brought us here. It is a dark place, and it can leave you feeling hopeless.

But it is not a dark place.

When shadows and difficult times manifest in your life it may feel like all is lost, but it is here that the most powerful of all spiritual journeys start. It is a place where you can find the strength to enter into a process of understanding and forgiveness that will enable you to embrace the parts of yourself long forgotten or abandoned, the real self that lies hidden in the darkness.

The Dark Goddess has long been the guardian of this realm of understanding and ancient mystery. The manifestation of the timeless mantra 'Know thyself', she can shed light on that which has been hidden. When you ask the Dark Goddess – who can take on many guises – to guide you, you will become exactly who you are meant to be. The sad fact is that most of us do not know our true selves. We hide, often unaware, behind a mask or facade that society, media and even our closest relationships have deceived us into thinking we embody. This false representation leads to darkness, but understanding it can lead to light.

A place of darkness is not only for those who have fallen on hard times. It can be a choice you make to explore the darker side of your nature and understand yourself completely; to finally confront the hard truths about life you have avoided; and the comfort you cling to even while your soul aches for you to step out of your comfort zone and understand your true purpose and your true self.

If you wish to scramble out of the web of lies the world is caught up in and step into truth, the Dark Goddess is waiting for you. She will accompany you as you begin to acknowledge the darker aspects of life and yourself. She will give you the opportunity to get to know those parts of yourself you have feared, ignored and pushed beneath the surface, consciously or subconsciously. You just need to be brave enough and strong enough to ask her.

The Dark Goddess unearths hidden emotions, often from childhood, such as jealousy and anger. Lifting these emotions into the light will bring discomfort but also opportunities for learning how to deal with them in a healthier, more effective way.

Throughout this journey you may find you no longer recognise who you are, but don't despair for this will be when the Dark Goddess is holding your hand. She encourages you to dig deep and get to the bottom of any feelings that have prevented you from receiving all that you have desired. She will journey with you to the source of the real problem and then together you can decide what you need to shed.

During this process you may be tempted to throw a cloak over any new discoveries, preferring to go back into the denial and repression that shielded you from the truth. Be strong and be brave, because once you begin this journey it will become the *only* way open to you. Eventually, as you truly get to know, accept and understand your darker and deeper emotions, you will learn how to draw wisdom from your shadow side and apply it in a positive way whenever a situation calls for you to do so.

Like most people in this world I have faced the dark depths of despair. I experienced depression and severe illness, and I witnessed the loss of all I knew until I had nothing and had to start all over again. While I was going through this I felt I was being punished and made to deal with it all alone, unloved and unwanted. There were times when I wished to go back, when I regretted this journey to my inner self as it was hard and confronting and full of loss.

However, with the help of the Dark Goddess I pushed through my trials, confronting the worst parts of myself and gaining the knowledge that my life was precious and not to be frittered away. My prayers became stronger and gradually, by facing my pain and fears, my body was given an energetic overhaul. I felt the very force of the Dark Goddess as she pushed and pulled me to my limits of despair yet I carried on, as she was both a danger and a reward that offered me the future I desired if I was willing to work through my pain. I could almost see it and taste it, all the while never knowing when I would arrive at the brand-new day I was striving towards.

When I became a *victim* the Dark Goddess ignored my tears, never once embracing me or telling me everything was okay. She battled with my melodramatic outbursts so the drama queen was never pandered to. The guilt I suffered was a hungry, insatiable monster I found hard to release, and as it ate away at me the Dark Goddess dismissed my turmoil. Eventually I had no choice but to learn how not to react, how not to be a victim or drama queen, how not to feel guilt or jealousy or any of the lower emotions that antagonised my dark journey. I had to become indifferent to the outcome of any situation, just like the Wheel of Fortune teaches, and see the hidden blessings within each.

At last the dawn appeared – when I least expected it, of course. The lessons had been learned. I had been stripped to the very core of who I was, and slowly the Dark Goddess built me up piece by piece. I had walked through the darkness and emerged, transformed, into the light, and I was now holding energy in balance with knowing and wisdom. No longer am I paralysed by any fears: I am fully confident and strong in all that I do, and I know exactly who I am. I walked the journey on my own, with only the Dark Goddess as my difficult companion, but I made it through to a place in which only truth and reality can exist. This is my new playground.

If you are prepared to have your world crash all around you, to not even recognise who you are any more as your old self dies to the new, you can re-emerge stronger and wiser into a whole new world. The Dark Goddess will show you the way, and even though you will feel isolated and abandoned she will never leave your side. Your soul urges you to call upon her, for new life beckons and is waiting to be acknowledged fully. It is time to stop playing at life and live it for real!

It is in the quiet, dark spaces within that the truth can be heard most clearly and the light can shine most brightly. The Dark Goddess reveals the psychological aspects of your hidden self, the Dark Goddess archetypal characteristics, which have been feared since she herself was birthed. There are many lessons to learn along the way, and as the Dark Goddess reveals the darker aspects of the self she will teach you how not to be and reveal who you are not. Before or during the process you could meet the same manifestations of the Dark Goddess over and over again until you get it, until you no longer react, go into denial, believe the inner critic or go on the defensive.

Welcome to your journey into the dark night of the soul . . . and beyond.

PART I

PREPARING TO MEET THE DARK GODDESS

Welcome to your initiation!

If a dark shadow has fallen over you and there is no light to guide you, if you are confronting the unknown and there is no path to follow, if chaos reigns and your mind longs for peace, if everything you've ever known, loved or desired has been wiped from you like a macabre artist sweeping black paint across a fresh picture, then you could very well be experiencing a dark night of the soul.

What you are going through could be the ancient process of a rite of passage, a mechanism that will rid you of anything that is holding you back from your true potential, from transformation and change. As you go through it life as you once knew will disappear; it will no longer be in view or, in fact, exist. But it is that old life, those old ways of doing things and those relationships that were holding you back even if you didn't realise it. They were comfortable, known and accepted so it will take a crisis to move them on, but if you wish to overcome your difficulties in order to transform your dreams into reality and live the life you came here for then move on they must.

This is a time when you need assistance and guidance from someone who has gone before you, someone who has trodden the hidden paths of no return and who has walked through the dark forest and made it to the other side.

My personal journey took me far beyond my comfort zone as I faced each of my fears one by one in a living nightmare that I endured over the course of many years. As I lost all whom I held dear, my own identity, my confidence and everything I knew, I considered leaving this mortal coil for the process was too much to bear. In fact, I didn't even realise what it was I was actually experiencing at the time, as with most others who are taken to the dark side. But hadn't I wished for things to get better, for me to come into my own power so that I would no longer feel I was a victim of circumstance but rather master of my own fate? Ask and you shall receive!

What I had not bargained for, however, was the process of eliminating all of the opposite of what I had intended for myself – which meant a complete energetic overhaul of everything I was thus far. I hadn't realised that I would go through various long, drawn-out stages to get to where I wished to be, that each stage would become more horrific and terrifying as the process continued to strip me bare until I no longer recognised myself or the life I once knew. Yet here I stand on the other side, knowing the journey was necessary and ultimately beneficial. I am now the person I always could have been: my true self.

Such a prize does not come lightly, but it will come. If you feel yourself about to take this journey, or you are already grappling with its twists and turns or feel unhappy with your life and want a change that can only come with true transformation, then may this book be your guiding light to help you find your way out of the darkness, shining the way to the Dark Goddess. She can help you navigate through the turmoil if you are willing to brave her fearsome friendship.

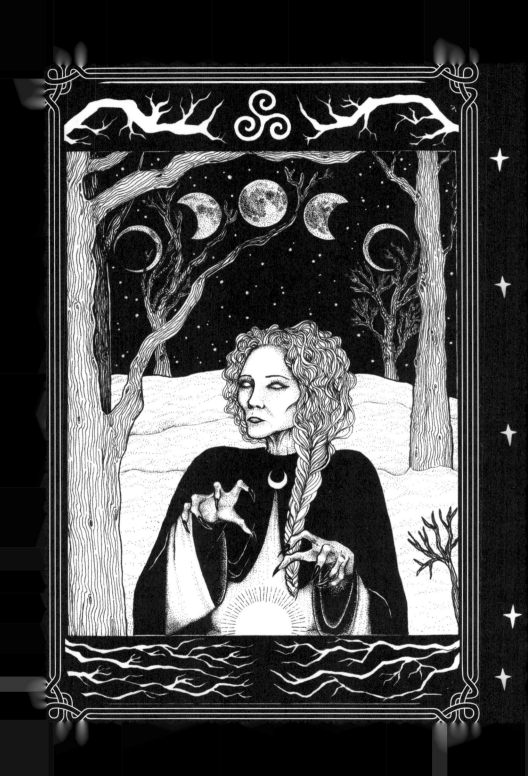

1. WHO IS THE DARK GODDESS?

They hail from the lands of ice and snow,
Where mountains peak and fir trees grow
Death, destruction now beckon you in
Hail and welcome, dark goddess within.

The Dark Goddess has existed since storytelling began.

She is the goddess of the great void; she is she without a name and yet *is* every name. She is Baba Yaga, the Cailleach, the Morrighan, Cerridwen and Maeve, for she is the power of the Dark Goddess named and unnamed. The concealed one bestows upon us a precious gift: we cannot know what is to come, so we must learn to trust the great mystery and step into the unknown with only her for unwelcome company.

Active dark goddesses who represent many aspects of darker emotions can be found all over the world, but in our dark night of the soul it is the crone of winter, the divine hag of the north who calls you to her side when you accept an invitation to witness the loss of everything you once knew in return for transformation. It is she who presides over the long, bleak winter months, and it is she who calls through the harshness of disappointment, sorrow, envy, anger and other lower emotions.

The wintery dark goddesses based on Norse, Slavic and Celtic mythology come with compelling stories and terrifying complex characters, for they were the basis of religion for the natural warrior people of Scandinavia, Britain, Ireland and the northern parts of Europe. Even today their stories heavily influence movies, television shows and games, having never lost their foothold in our deep consciousness. After all, we were brought up on bedtime tales of the wicked stepmother and the evil queen, who are of course distortions of the Dark Goddess herself.

The Dark Goddess, who often starts her cruel reign during the autumn months in the lead-up to Samhain (note that all dates are for the northern hemisphere; they would be reversed in the southern hemisphere), is cold and callous and beckons you with a bony finger to witness the death of everything you once knew as you take a step in her direction. In magickal terms the direction of north is associated with the element of earth and the icy cold season of winter. This is a time of death, when nature goes deep within itself to rest and recharge. The earth is steeped in potent magick and mystery that nurtures and restores all that resides within it, even at this severe, barren time of year. The direction of north represents hardship and discomfort, often entailing trials and tribulations for those who are called to face the glacial callousness of winter. Winter is a harsh taskmaster who takes no prisoners, much like the Dark Goddess herself.

As the winter solstice marks the longest night and shortest day of the year, pagan traditions celebrate the sun's rebirth as it slowly begins to strengthen, lengthening the days in the months leading into spring. The winter solstice is a time for change, when we acknowledge and honour the cycles of life and death and rebirth. It's a time when hope is renewed and, like the trees of the season, we are stripped bare, naked and vulnerable as the macabre presence of the crone shrouds us.

The Dark Goddess was worshipped in conjunction with the phases of the moon, the waxing, full and waning phases, which represent the three phases of the goddess as maiden, mother and crone.

THE MAIDEN:

- Moon phase: waxing.
- Season: spring.
- Colour: white.
- Festivals: Imbolc, Ostara (spring equinox).
- Aspects: beauty, enchantment, inception, expansion, new beginnings, youth, excitement, virginal, innocence.

THE MOTHER:

- Moon phase: full.
- Season: summer.
- Colour: red.
- Festivals: Beltane, Litha (summer solstice), Mabon (autumn equinox).
- Aspects: ripeness, fertility, growth, fulfilment, stability, generosity, nurturance, compassion.

THE CRONE:

- Moon phase: waning/dark or new.
- Season: winter.
- Colour: black.
- Festivals: Samhain (Hallowe'en), Yule (winter solstice).
- Aspects: wisdom, repose, magick, destruction, decay and death.

The crone is the least understood of the trinity, and she is often avoided or demonised in modern retellings. She is seen as being wicked, or the personification of death. It is true the crone has a fearful shadow side, as darkness accompanies her through the long winter nights and ultimately towards death, yet the pagans knew that physical death was not the end but rather an opportunity for rebirth and renewal just as the trees and grasses return after the desolation of winter. The crone rules the north, for it is from there that she waves her icy wand towards everything old that needs to die as she freezes out the past.

The crone is more than coldness and death: she is the grandmother, the wise one whose knowledge is sought out to guide others during life's hardships and transitions. Death, destruction and decay are all a natural part of the cycle of life. The crone takes away the old, the infirm and whatever is no longer necessary and makes way for something new.

In the cycle of life, the death of winter at Yule is followed by the promise of rebirth in spring. What is born dies, and what dies is reborn. Winter brings final rest to the earth, and it is to the earth that we all return.

Hoof and horn! Hoof and horn!
All that dies shall be reborn.

THE CALL OF THE DARK GODDESS

We have been led to believe that the call of the Dark Goddess is to be avoided at all costs, yet we are no stranger to her. She is the wicked stepmother, the ugly sisters, the old hag and other distorted versions of the crone aspect of the triple goddess we have feared since hearing our very first faery tale.

She is the dark one who spins her web of fate and teaches, through her deep wisdom, harsh life lessons that many wish to avoid. The Dark Goddess is present at the witching hour of midnight and embraces her shadow side, the side we all try to avoid, for she knows exactly who she is. She is death and rebirth, and if you are not afraid to leave your hurts behind in return for a little transformation she will strip you in a heartbeat of all you no longer need. She will wave her wand and bestow upon you all of her gifts of magickal powers and peace of mind in return for your surrender.

If you have lost your identity and wish to have belief in yourself and renewed confidence, then lay bare before her your doubts, insecurities and fears. If you feel you want to scream, shout and let it all out but instead stuff your anger and negative feelings as far down as you possibly can and bite your lip and conform, you may well need an encounter with the Dark Goddess. What you are doing is ignoring that wilder side of you that says, 'No, I'm not okay with that' or 'I'm furious and don't trust you!' You are masking how you really feel by pretending that you are all love and light, so you smile and make the right noises to show how acceptable and pleasant you are. All the while there is an entirely different dialogue going on within.

This inner darkness is known as the shadow self, and it is something we all need to come to terms with and embrace if we wish to become the best version of ourselves and break the faery tale illusion we are living in. It's all about knowing yourself inside out: what makes you tick or what pulls your trigger. Knowing yourself and acknowledging who you are increases the strength of your energy, and consequently your power increases – inner or otherwise. Your self-power will be so much stronger when you use the whole of who you are. This is the gift the Dark Goddess offers you, for only she can shed light on that which has been hidden. The light can only be illuminated by that which is the dark; one cannot possibly exist without the other.

The Dark Goddess is a force to be reckoned with, and presents powers of extremity in the highest form to those who exchange their perceived weakness for the effective dynamics she deems to offer. You should take great pains to avoid her if you want your life to remain exactly as it is. If you wish to live in a fluffy dream state and pretend that everything and everyone around you is perfectly as it should be, then never even whisper one of the Dark Goddess's many names. However, if you are brave, want adventure and are prepared to lose all that you hold dear in return for awakening to who you really are, then the Dark Goddess will slip you the pill that will reveal the reality of the matrix. But be warned, for this is truly a path of no return.

Remember that before Alice visited Wonderland she fell down a deep black hole. Her journey was one of rediscovery until she knew exactly who she was and who everyone and everything around her was in relation to her newfound life.

2. THE DARK NIGHT OF THE SOUL

The journey of the dark night represents extreme hardships you may endure in order to reach enlightenment and a union with the creator. This path is usually taken without a person realising what they are going through or what is entailed. The term itself is inspired by a poem written by St John of the Cross in the 16th century that 'narrates the journey of the soul from its bodily home to its union with God'. The poem shows just how painful an experience of the stages (stanzas) of the dark night of the soul is, as one seeks to grow spiritually.

Even before St John of the Cross put words to paper, ancient Greek philosophers Socrates and Plato presented the same concept and argued that while the soul is immortal it needs transformation to continue on. The dark night of the soul is referred to as being a type of death, a death of our beliefs through isolation and philosophical inquiry. By being well prepared we can survive these life deaths and experience new life on earth as our souls reawaken; this book will help you to navigate through each stage.

Every living being has a soul; it is the truth of who you really are and is embedded into each of your cells. Your body is like an outer shell that houses your soul and the lifetime after lifetime in various forms it experiences, as you rest and take stock of where you have journeyed so far in the spirit world.

Ancient civilisations, mystics, shamans and saints throughout history focused on the soul's awakening and knew how to fully embrace and integrate it into their human experience. However, today's modern society tends to focus externally on appearances and on the ego self without considering the need to consciously grow into our divine potential. The ego is attached to power, control, reputation and material things. During the dark night of the soul you will be compelled to let go of all that the ego values so your soul can tumble into a profound state of unknowing. You will be propelled into isolation, for the journey requires solitude.

When your soul has had enough of being ignored its primordial inner cry will be heard across the universe, unbeknown to you, for it craves for you to connect with your inner divinity. This is when the dark night of the soul will be invited in, to change things, to shake things up and to transform you completely. Philosophical in nature, the dark night is accompanied by existential reflections as you start to question life's meaning and your purpose. It heralds such deep-seated changes within you that it leaves an unquestionable impact.

The dark night of the soul is like a long, hard slap in the face that will wake you up from your old reality. It's a period of utter desolation, a deep and emotionally painful spiritual depression you have to endure before enlightenment, before gaining wisdom, clarity and understanding. Those who experience it can feel totally lost, hopeless and separated spiritually from the divine and from the truth of who they are, for the dark night of the soul is like a spiritual emergency that will test you and shake you to your core as you question the meaning of everything you once took for granted and your very existence until you become fragmented.

If you have ever felt as though a part of you was missing, such as part of your personality or your vitality or joy for life, or your energetic spirit changed after a traumatic situation it is possible that your soul has become fragmented. Perhaps you went through a terrible break-up and felt like your heart was ripped out, or lost your natural confidence after suffering at the hands of an abuser. You may find that your trust and belief in humanity or love is gone, and your thoughts and feelings have turned darker through the process. What once lit you up no longer has any meaning.

Perhaps you feel as though you don't fit in. You know what it is to be shunned, ignored and shut out to the point that you feel useless and have very little self-esteem. Maybe a childhood trauma now makes you feel demoralised, or you moved a lot and had to keep changing schools, had abusive parents or were abandoned by someone who was supposed to care for you and this left you feeling insecure and inadequate as you entered adulthood.

You don't have to experience a major devastation to kick-start your dark journey, for the dark night of the soul can creep in through forgotten memories, negative inner narratives and other concerns that may not have been apparent until a seemingly insignificant event that highlights a deeper level of emotion and sparks a deeper memory unleashes the dark night.

When you feel broken by loss, failure, betrayal, long-forgotten emotional wounds or a challenge that is so deep seated and tenacious it leaves you in a desperately dark place it can provoke strong reactions that can lead to feelings of abandonment, isolation, mental anguish or severe depression.

The dark night of the soul is not simply a manifestation of depression and thus a mental health issue but is rather a spiritual existential crisis that nobody but you can save you from. Counselling and mental health care may well provide relief at some points – and should be sought if you feel it is necessary – but along with provoking a sense of loss the dark night of the soul is a profound call from your inner self for complete change and transformation. Don't look for a quick fix, as a long, careful exploration of your true dark side provides the best chance of moving through and out of this anguish. It can be difficult, but it is possible to navigate through to the light waiting for you on the other side.

RITES OF PASSAGE

The first step in your journey of renewal is to understand that what is being presented to you is not a punishment or an injustice but rather is a rite of passage that will move you on to your next phase of soul transformation.

A rite of passage marks a personal transition between important stages that occur through your life as you grow and evolve. It usually involves teachings and ritualistic activities for preparation of change, and a ceremony to mark the stripping of the past and honouring the new role you are to undertake. The ancients went through many formal rites of passage as a matter of course, as do many modern indigenous tribes in order to help transform their souls along their journeys of continual progression. These rites are painful to symbolise the importance of the transition; the pain is not the point but rather the means of connecting with the divine.

Change, uncertainty and difficulty are made bearable and eased through rituals and rites. The ancients knew this, and this book offers some healing rites and rituals for each stage of your journey that are designed to help you connect with your Dark Goddess guide and your own soul purpose. You may think undertaking rituals is old-fashioned, primitive or unnecessary, but everyone in modern society undertakes certain rites to mark important phases in life. Graduations, bar mitzvahs, marriages and retirement parties are no more than ancient rites dressed in modern guise to help us mark and acknowledge our life transformations.

Whatever social celebratory rituals or rites you engage in they provide the possibility you will experience heightened emotions, which can be psychologically, physically or socially stressful much like other less enjoyable transitions such as puberty, serious illness or injury, religious persecution, divorce, wars and conflict and the aftermath of major social upheavals. It is possible too that you may have many mini dark nights or crises as part of your journey towards your true self, as the most transformative journeys have all sorts of twists and turns to navigate along the way.

The dark night of the soul will take you to places within that you don't recognise. As you stumble through the wilderness, the Dark Goddess will reveal hidden emotions and reactions that you didn't even know you could feel. Here she will wait while you discover the original wounding that has led to the harbouring of such emotions.

Once you have shed that part of you and healed from any hurts relating to it you will begin to observe what triggers you to react negatively, which is when the Dark Goddess will take you to journey deep within to uncover the true reason for your adverse reaction. Prepare for a long and arduous journey of discovery of your hidden self. Your hidden self – your dark side – is not evil. It is a place in which pain resides and resentment festers, but it is also a place of healing if you are willing to experience the power of your dark emotions.

All things in nature have a darker side, as nothing can be love and compassion 24/7; it's impossible and unnatural. Even nature can be seen as cruel and merciless, yet you don't accuse storms, earthquakes or tsunamis of being evil.

Some religions teach that darkness is evil and that it is the light that shall prevail; however, the darkness is essential if you are to reach enlightenment. Both have a necessary purpose and one cannot exist without the other. You need to look through the darkness in order to find the light, which is the purpose of experiencing a dark night of the soul.

The Dark Goddess will envelop you with her shadowy cloak to block out the light and make it easier for you to find your way in the darkness. It is the only way for you to truly see. She will teach you how to draw strength from the dark mystery and to claim the power that resides in the depths of your soul, for she has heard your request, your soul's cry for wholeness and balance and to live your life to its highest potential. If you are to experience the highs it is necessary to experience the opposite of all you've known, and you may find yourself cast down very low.

The dark night of the soul can be exhausting and frightening as the perfect world you once knew caves in all around you. It is literally like taking a pill that reveals the matrix, a new reality – one that is so unfamiliar to you you may wish you hadn't swallowed the pill in the first place. However, once the truth has been revealed there is no going back: only through. No longer will you recognise all that you once held dear, nor will you resonate with who you once were and your past will seem like someone else's.

The path will be as long and arduous as you make it, so don't let any stone go unturned for this is the most incredible gift you could ever experience. Everything is in place to support the cycle of life, death and rebirth, to bring about the change you desire. She changes everything she touches.

Whether you have called upon her consciously or not the Dark Goddess is the instigator, and she will wait in the shadows to accompany as you go through a really difficult time. If your world has been shaken up and you are struggling and experiencing a battle of your own, you can be sure the Dark Goddess has heard the primordial cry of your soul and knows your true potential.

CHANGE AND TRANSFORMATION

The whole purpose of the dark night of the soul is to identify inner hurts, pains, fears and worries that keep you from shining your true light. As you walk through and learn the lessons each stage offers, ridding yourself of all that no longer serves you, you take steps towards becoming the real you.

The dark night of the soul can be invited in deliberately with intention for transformation, as I did one fateful night unaware of what I was to face, or it can come about through asking or hoping for a change even if this is done through silent thoughts and secret wishes. Cast your mind back to a time when you might have wished for change; this may have been wistful dreaming, recurring thoughts and feelings or an adamant decision. You may have desired new freedom, a sexier partner, to have children, to be more attractive in appearance, a pay rise, a promotion, reconciliation, financial abundance, spiritual enhancement or anything else that you felt you needed at the time. This was your invitation to the Dark Goddess to grant you the means for your wish.

CONNECTIONS TO FAERY TALES AND MYTHS

We have always struggled with darkness and feelings of anger, hurt, betrayal, jealousy and fear. Stories have reflected our journey into the depths of these emotions for thousands of years, none more effectively or consistently as the humble faery tale.

The journey into the dark night of the soul is well known to us even if we don't personally acknowledge it. It is the basis for almost every faery tale and folkloric fable, for any story of transformation after adversity. These stories are inner truths that speak to our true knowing of the ways of darkness, as each magickal story teaches us an important life lesson and each one involves an ending of the old and a transformation of some sorts.

One of the most beloved of all faery tales, Cinderella, is a perfect recounting of a soul's transformation. Having experienced a happy life until her mother died, Cinderella suffered at the hands of her step-sisters and from the cruelty of her wicked stepmother until she went through a complete transformation, courtesy of her faery godmother, and lived happily ever after.

This is typical of a dark night of the soul. After experiencing a great loss (the loss of her mother), which is the first stage of a dark night, Cinderella was in bondage to her evil stepmother and experienced many years in isolation and misery. Her hopes rose with the prospect of meeting a prince, and as she took steps to prepare for change her faery godmother turned up bearing the power of transcendence.

What many don't realise is that the Dark Goddess is key to understanding this story: both the stepmother and the faery godmother are representations of the magickal powerful feminine who bring the gift of darkness, which is needed to appreciate the gift of light. The wicked stepmother's cruelty was the struggle Cinderella had to endure to find her true self, to go from naïve child to adult, but even the seemingly benevolent faery godmother did not just give Cinderella her prince but made her go through a trial and potential loss in order to appreciate the final triumph.

From within the shadows she of the darkness waits for you, for it is she who is responsible for all of your trials and tribulations. It is she who hears your soul's cry, who listens to your fears, doubts and worries, and it is she who offers you the gift of a living nightmare so you can awaken into the light of a new, transformative life.

When you experience a dark night of the soul you challenge your true self and allow yourself to encounter the genuine nature of divinity.

3. IS THE DARK GODDESS CALLING YOU?

The crone is the mistress of magick, the commanding sorceress who summons up power from all that she is. She knows exactly who she is and can call upon any or all of her strengths, which reside in the shadows and are used as and when necessary.

When you work with the shadow side you will be able to determine which situations call for the use of your darker traits and how to use them, but first the Dark Goddess will help you to know which powers you should nurture and which lower emotions and agitations should be dissolved.

Eventually in your day-to-day life you will be able to consciously draw from the positive aspects of the shadow traits as your inner strength. For example, when somebody tries to harm you the strength and aggression of anger can be summoned to overcome the enemy. It can serve as a positive force, motivating you to stand up for yourself while protecting your personal boundaries. However, first you need to learn how to wisely draw from each emotion and how to use that emotion carefully and in honour of the Dark Goddess as her energy powers through you.

The ancients considered the moon to be the mother of witchcraft, and each phase of the moon represents the triple goddess as follows:

- A new moon, while honouring and working in conjunction with the goddess in her maiden form, is a powerful time to manifest new projects, new beginnings, faith, hope and optimism.
- A full moon, while honouring and working in conjunction with the goddess in her mother aspect, is a powerful time to attract love, abundance, creativity and positive energy.
- A dark moon (the final crescent of a waning moon), while honouring and working in conjunction with the goddess as the crone, is a powerful time to release and let go, to banish, complete and harness magick and deep wisdom.

If you feel you are ready to let go and experience destruction, death and ultimately transformation and rebirth, then this book and the processes it describes are for you.

THE WHEEL OF THE YEAR

The Dark Goddess is inherently linked to nature and the seasons. Communing with her has traditionally been done at very specific times, so understanding the key festivals and traditions of our Celtic ancestors and their affinity with each of the seasons can help you connect more effectively with the power and energy of the Dark Goddess. Understanding the pure energy of the elemental forces of nature added to the quality of the lives of the ancients, as they connected with and honoured the aspects of the triple goddess in relation to the seasons and festivals celebrated through the wheel of the year.

In European Celtic tradition the year is made up of four seasons. The sun marks any seasonal change, and these changes are honoured by celebrating four solar festivals. Fire festivals are marked by cross-quarter and equinox celebrations, so all together eight festivals of the seasons make up the wheel of the year. The festivals represent the states of nature at particular times of the year, the agricultural calendar and the physical and spiritual effects the time of year has on humankind.

From planting in spring to harvesting in autumn, the seasons are of great importance. Different celebrations mark the times we should count our blessings, the times for reaping and recognising all that we've sowed and for giving thanks to the nature spirits as well as to the goddess in her triple aspect of maiden, mother and crone; she continues the circle that we call life on earth.

The Celtic year starts with the festival of Imbolc, when we connect with the maiden aspect of the goddess as she offers us new life and fresh beginnings, for in agriculture this is when seeds are planted and we start to see signs of flowers starting to blossom. Vegetation continues to grow and bloom through the festival of Ostara and up to the celebration of Beltane (or May Day), when we connect with the mother aspect of the goddess, peaks at the summer solstice and goes on to produce the first grain harvest at Lughnasadh (also known as Lammas).

We give thanks at the autumn equinox, when the harvest is cut down. From there most of nature starts to decay, leading us to Samhain, when nature turns inward and dies down in the winter months. This is when the crone aspect of the goddess rules. The winter solstice (21 or 22 December in the northern hemisphere; 22 June in the southern) is the first glimmer of hope as the sun, then at its weakest, starts to grow stronger each day after. Then the wheel turns to new life: to Imbolc once again.

The wheel of the year is all about death and rebirth, about accepting and adapting to change just like our ancestors had to when they relied heavily on the seasons in order to survive. Linking to the specific Dark Goddess festivals that celebrate and acknowledge the crone can make your connection with this essence so much stronger.

- Imbolc, the maiden: innocence, purity, seeding the dream and birthing the inner child.
- Ostara (autumn equinox), the maiden matures: from dark to light we explore signs of growth and discernment.
- Beltane, the mother: fertile minds, bodies and souls birthing our ideas and the soul's knowing.
- Litha (summer solstice), the mother glorified: a celebration of light and being in our full glory.

- Lughnasadh, the mother matures: gratitude for earthly, physical sustenance.
- Mabon (spring equinox), the crone: the art of contemplation explored and self-sufficiency of mind, body and spirit.
- Samhain, the crone revered: respecting our ancestors and healing our hurts.
- Yule (winter solstice), the crone fades: the returning sun, exploring purest energy and the essence of our being.

DARK GODDESS INVOCATION

So you have heeded the warnings and you want to consciously invoke the power of the Dark Goddess, to guide you through a difficult time or to embark on a journey of dark discovery and rebirth. Now is the time for your first ritual, a conscious calling or invocation to the energy of the Dark Goddess to make herself known to you on your journey. The best time to call upon the Dark Goddess is at the magickal time of midnight during a dark moon phase. You may wish to choose a winter month, a time of reflection and going deep within yourself, and you may like to wear a special robe or gown that makes you feel powerful and enhances your confidence. However you embark on this journey, it is important that you take time to think about what thoughts, words and actions may arise and how you will deal with them.

To begin, draw an imaginary circle of white light around you or carefully sprinkle stones or salt around you in an unbroken circle. Remain within its circumference confines, as this circle is for your protection against negative influences. Light a black candle and face the dark moon. Hold the candle in front of you, or place it on the ground and raise your arms to the Dark Goddess. Say out loud:

All hail dark moon this very night,
protection placed, no need for fright.
In her glory stands the crone,
I'm not afraid to stand alone.
I welcome you and all you bring,

fears to face, journey within.
Now ready for shamanic death,
new life poised upon my breath.
My ancestors who walked before,
I honour thee, and I am sure.
Dark Goddess, I now call to you,
and seek your wisdom, see me through.
This sacred path will set me free,
with harm to none – so mote it be.

Deeply breathe in the dark moon as you hold the black candle. Allow for a recalibration as you become attuned to the energy of the Dark Goddess, enabling you to connect with the energy and attributes she offers. When you feel this has been achieved, blow out the candle. Let the swirl of the extinguished flame wrap around you and say:

Gratefully I accept the magick of you,
and protection to assist in all that I do.
Lend me the courage, build power in me.
Assist my transcendence – so mote it be.

Step out of the circle and wait for the adventure of your lifetime to begin . . .

As you surrender to the Dark Goddess's will she is prepared to guide you safely through each stage of your own dark night of the soul if you will but honour her.

CREATING AN ALTAR TO THE DARK GODDESS

When you work with the Dark Goddess it is really important to honour her as well as show commitment to her, and creating a shrine in the form of an altar to her is the perfect way to do so. Since the dawn of time ancient cultures have used altars in temples or on sacred landscapes for prayer, worship, reflection, meditation, invocation and spell work.

A focal point used for ritual, intent and sacred purpose, you can easily create an altar in your home. Altars are like portals that give you direct access to the deity you are inviting in, to protect and guide whatever ritual or intention you are working with. Whenever you look at your altar you connect with the mystical energies it represents and the sacred energy the space contains.

An altar doesn't have to be anything grand, so don't worry if you don't have much room. It can be a table with a cloth on it in a quiet corner, a mantelpiece, windowsill or shelf: it doesn't matter as long as you set the right intention of dedication to the Dark Goddess, of honouring her as she journeys with you through the dark night of the soul. Build whatever you feel represents for you a connection with the Dark Goddess. You may wish to add crystals, incense cones, a figurine or a representation of the moon or anything else you feel would create a sacred threshold for the Dark Goddess to emerge into your life.

Part II of this book contains information about what is appropriate for each specific goddess, but as you begin ensure you include the fundamentals:

- **Pentagram:** for protection and to represent the five basic elements of earth, air, fire, water and spirit.
- **Altar cloth:** harness the power of colour by choosing a deep purple cloth to enhance wisdom and psychic work or black for protection.
- **Elements:** representations of the four basic elements and the fifth of spirit, the seasons and directions to ensure balance in all aspects of nature. Place items on your Dark Goddess altar to connect with the elements such as black tourmaline, jet, black obsidian and onyx crystals to represent earth; incense such as myrrh, frankincense, cinnamon and dragon's blood to represent air; a chalice or goblet with wine or spring water to represent water; and candles to represent fire and specifically black candles to represent the darkness.

Candles also work well to represent the elements, seasons and directions; place one candle on your altar as follows:

- Place a black candle in the north to represent that direction, the element of earth and the season of winter.
- Place a yellow candle in the east to represent that direction, the element of air and the season of spring.
- Place a red candle in the south to represent that direction, the element of fire and the season of summer.
- Place a blue candle in the west to represent that direction, the element of water and the season of autumn.

Once you have found your perfect place and created your sacred altar it will become your focal point. Honour the Dark Goddess by giving her an offering: it's always a good idea to keep her sweet! At the end of each goddess chapter you'll find a list of items that are energetically associated with the goddess you've just met such as flowers, crystals and even rotting fruit! You can decide whether to replace the items you placed down to honour the previous goddess with the offerings for the goddess you are currently working with, or you may prefer to create separate altars for each goddess as you meet them in turn. My preference is to honour the whole team by keeping representations of each of the dark goddesses on my altar, as they all play a significant part in the journey of the dark night of the soul. Once you've completed the journey you may find that you wish to set up an altar for your favourite goddess or for one you wish to continue working with.

As well as using your altar as a focal point to honour the Dark Goddess, use it as a sacred space to manifest your desires or for banishment. On a full moon, place your wishes of desire upon your altar or scratch them into a white candle. Light the candle and allow it to burn down. To banish anything you'd like to be rid of, let a black candle burn down on a dark moon.

This ritual of honouring the Dark Goddess and recognising her many forms will help you to survive your own personal challenges, by considering your own shadow traits to determine who has been influencing you. Each goddess has her own shadow attributes, which you will find yourself mimicking unwittingly. Once you've uncovered your shadow influencer you'll find that your traits match hers like for like, giving you a greater understanding of why you've been behaving or feeling the way you have been.

You may find that you mistake your goddess's characteristics for your own emotions, which could drive you towards darkness and despair; however, as you are introduced to each dark goddess in turn during each phase you must have faith in the process. Just as you wouldn't like to be told the ending of a movie you were watching, it's so important to completely surrender and trust in the mystery as you walk towards your goal of ultimate transformation. It will all become clear as you follow the wisdom of each of the dark goddesses you are to meet at every stage of the dark night of the soul.

JOURNAL WORK

Keeping a journal to document your experiences, feelings, opportunities and setbacks will give you a specific and effective way to reflect on and create more opportunities to embrace the changes manifesting around you, however dark they may seem. As you work through the chapters in this book it will also be useful to keep a note of your thoughts, insights, experiences or answers as you address the questions posed to you in each chapter.

Through this book we will look at every aspect of each stage of your journey so you can understand and learn from the process in order to heal. All that is required of you is honesty to yourself and a commitment to your awakening. Begin by jotting down answers to the following questions in your journal:

- Do you remember going through a modern-day rite of passage, for example, a marriage, significant birthday or graduation?
- How did you feel at this event or celebration?
- What part of your life was gone after that celebration? Did you miss that aspect, or did you happily let it go?
- Have you experienced any major life changes such as a serious illness, a war or conflict, divorce, big geographical move or the birth of a child? Write a list of them if so.

- What have you witnessed that has caused trauma and upheaval in your life?
- How do your current situation and feelings compare to how you felt during previous times of transition?

Reflect on your answers over time, and reread all of your journal entries and consider your answers as you move through your dark night of the soul. They will provide you with strength, insight and motivation as the journey goes deeper.

PEACE THROUGH PROTECTION

Whenever you do any spiritual work it is vitally important that you protect yourself. In fact, it is good practice to call in protection every day whether you are consciously working with the spirit world or not. A lack of protection leaves you wide open to psychic attack, with nothing in place to defend your energy field. The strength of another's harsh words, thoughts and actions against you can drain you of your vital life force, which is when your personal power can be snatched from under you and your mind allows fears, doubts and negative thought forms to creep in.

Negative thought forms come in all shapes and sizes. How often, for example, have you suddenly felt a sharp pain in your back for no apparent reason? There is a reason for it, and it is usually because someone is thinking or saying something negative about you. You've heard the phrase 'stabbed in the back', right? It's actually on an etheric level, the level that relates to the spiritual plane of existence. Each time you feel such a twinge know that a negative force of energy has been directed at you.

Of course, the perpetrator won't usually be consciously aware of having directed the negative force at you. If only everybody were aware of how energy works they might be more careful with their thoughts and wishes. Whatever you think and focus on is always manifested into form. Sometimes you can bring it into material embodiment, and at other times it will come through the etheric field of non-physical matter. Magickal practitioners and witches use the same principal to cast spells and bring their desires into being.

The following three sections look at procedures that will keep you safe and protected: grounding, casting a circle and the power of salt.

STAYING GROUNDED

Before partaking in any spiritual work, be it meditation, invocation or any other form, you must ground yourself. This is done so you are anchored within your body and are kept connected to the earth realm. At this stage of your journey a little grounding and protection will serve you well. It won't necessarily keep all the changes that are required for you to move forward from happening, but it will protect and empower you as you face them. It's about self-care and taking responsibility for yourself, to preserve your sensitive nature and minimise the pain of loss or whatever it is you experience at the first stage of your dark night of the soul.

Try this simple grounding exercise: go outside into nature and stand barefooted on the grass or dirt to instantly ground and connect you to the earth. If you can't go outside, see in your mind's eye potent roots growing down from the soles of your feet and burying deep into the ground. You can do this at any time and from anywhere; it will help you to feel stronger within, to be more in control and able to cope with your own tenebrous journey.

Visualise your roots growing stronger and longer until they reach the centre of the earth. Next, visualise a huge crystal in the centre of the earth: what does this crystal look like? Notice the colour and shape. See your roots wrapping around the crystal, grounding you and connecting you to Mother Earth. Breathe the crystalline energy up from the bottom of your roots, breathe the earth magick up and allow it to surge through every cell, every vessel, every part of your very being. You are now fully grounded.

CASTING A CIRCLE

Drawing a circle, whether physically or in the mind's eye, is a strong form of protection that can guard you against unwanted energies from other people such as psychic attacks and negative thought forms and from locations, such as old buildings. Simply imagining a circle surrounding you will immediately give you sufficient protection, or you can use your power finger (the index finger of whichever is your dominant hand) to draw a circle in the air in front of you. Visualise the circle growing to the size of you and step into it.

THE POWER OF SALT

Salt is an age-old and very effective form of protection that witches and magickal practitioners alike swear by. It naturally absorbs psychic energy that you might unwittingly receive. By sprinkling it around you in a circle, across the thresholds or perimeters of your dwelling or wearing it in a pocket or pouch will ensure you are shielded as your sensitivity increases. Likewise, a sea salt bath will absorb negative energies if you have been under attack and will also revive your spirit.

PROTECTION SPELL

Use this protection spell to bring all of the essential elements together and create a safer space for yourself as you continue with your dark night of the soul journey. Sprinkle a circle of salt around you at midnight. Hold a lit black candle in one hand and a grounding tourmaline crystal in the other, face the direction of north and say:

Star of protection, a circle of salt,
surround and safeguard me from any default.
I call upon the elements five,
preserve my intentions, so I can survive.
Standing within, I lift up my arms,
black candle and crystal now banish harm.
Keep safe and defend my energy flow,
as I raise my vibration, allow me to grow.
Now out of danger, protection in place, all that I am is safe to embrace.

Snuff out the black candle and step carefully out of the circle.

PART II

THE DARK GODDESS REVEALED

The Dark Goddess expects you to be responsible for yourself and your reactions, but it is not at all easy when you go through a dark night of the soul for you can be blinded by circumstance and find it hard to believe you will ever see the light again. How do you feel at the prospect of meeting the Dark Goddess? Perhaps you have already met her. If you have ever felt as though your life has crashed all around you and you have experienced many dark moments then you've certainly brushed shoulders with the Dark Goddess. You may have felt chilling goosebumps, a bad feeling or a macabre darkness engulfing you. Did you welcome her in; did you acknowledge the Dark Goddess when she turned up? Chances are you did not, for you were unaware at the time of her gruesome presence. You simply presumed you had fallen down hard on your luck. But that was your first meeting with her, and as you fell she was drawn to your side to bring about the change and loss you feared.

The element of air blows in the winds of change, and as the wheel of fortune spins four grim goddesses wait in their hidden lair among the shadows for you to fall. These fearsome four are the most terrifying of all the dark goddesses you will face on your daunting journey, for their purpose is to ensure you truly reach rock bottom. They know how far you must sink, how low you must go before you can begin your ascent. However, when you start to descend you will be unaware of the dark journey you are about to undertake. The first stage starts with a loss or a change that comes straight out of the blue, something unexpected that rocks your very foundations and shakes you to your core.

To help you with your encounters with the Dark Goddess, this book has key information about some of her most common manifestations. She has many manifestations, each with its own history, initiations and invocations. Her history and importance and clues about why she may be manifesting for you are all discussed, and also included are exercises and rituals that work with her dark energy in ways that will help you understand the purpose of and possibly the solution to your dark night of the soul.

As you traverse the darkness, through the different emotional stages of the dark night of the soul, you'll discover your own shadow side, how to embrace your inner dark traits and to know yourself fully, in order to be healed and whole again. As you uncover the shadow influencers who are responsible for each stage, you will discover who's been pulling your strings, who is influencing your recent bad-arse behaviour and how you can heal and transform. Each dark goddess aspect has her own archetypical behavioural attributes and instigates the nightmare that will bring you down to your lowest ebb, but in return it is she who offers the highest of transformations.

Each dark goddess you are about to meet will supply you with all the tools of the craft, such as anointing oils, incenses and crystals as well as the magickal methods and rituals required and needed for that part of the journey, so that you can come out the on other side spiritually enlightened and evolved, with enhanced natural power and with the Dark Goddess by your side.

She is waiting for you now in her many forms, as she beckons you to take your first sacred step into the darkness . . .

4. GAIA, EARTH MOTHER

Initiation of the start of the journey

Safe within a self-made tomb
turmoil birthed from seeded womb.
Primordial mother, matriarch.
Balance: do you choose light or dark?

ORIGIN	Greek.
NAMES	Gaia, Gaea, Ge.
GODDESSES	Demeter, Terra, Pachamama.
SYMBOLS	soil, fruit, grains, animals, trees, wood, plants.
THEMES	abundance, gratitude, nature, fertility, feasting, providence, sustenance, the earth.
LESSONS	letting go, moving forward, stepping out of your comfort zone, sense of duty, trusting the process.
COLOURS/CANDLES	green, brown, tan.
CRYSTALS	peridot, smoky quartz, amber, zircon, aragonite, agate, geodes, black tourmaline.
HERBS/FLOWERS/OILS	honeysuckle, cypress, jasmine, gardenia, rose.
MOON PHASES	new, full, dark.
SEASONS	spring, summer, autumn, winter.
TREES	all trees but particularly ash.
FESTIVAL DATE	Earth Day 22 April.

Birthed out of chaos, Gaia rose up from out of the swirling darkness and claimed sovereignty over turmoil. She is the mother of transformation, for she created the lands, seas, mountains and animals: every living thing. From a part of herself she birthed Uranus to be a consort, son and the supreme father sky god, and together they produced the Titans and Cyclops. However, Uranus vanquished their children to become imprisoned within Gaia's body as he attempted to halt the natural and progressive cycles of the earth. Gaia's extreme pain and agony inflicted conflict on the world and she cried out to her children for help. In answer the Titan Cronus (Saturn as we know him) castrated Uranus, his own father. Spilt blood fell upon Gaia and from the blood grew giants and the Furies, who cast judgement and punishment upon humankind. Uranus's genitals were cast into the ocean and Aphrodite, the goddess of love, emerged from out of the positive balance of the sea's foam.

As children of Gaia we have become witnesses to her beauty and love as well as the darkness and confusion that is as natural as the forces of nature. She is every element and the primary spirit of the earth.

MESSAGE FROM GAIA

'I am Gaia, the very soul of the earth, for it is I who through my raw maternal power and spirit gave structure to the formless earth from out of nebulous chaos, birthing the landscape, the seas and all that is alive. I am the mother from whom all gods descended, through my sexual union with the sky and sea. I am a creator and sustainer of life. My creative force leaves your destiny in my hands, for it is I who birthed the fates and it is to me whom you return upon death. From out of the dark void I offer existential life to all, in return for honour and respect. But be warned, for my nurturing mothering qualities can be deceptive, and my dark, destructive side will just as easily call me to cause catastrophe, confusion and despair when some transformation and rebirth is called for.

'It is time to slow down and take a look at what is really going on around you. While you think that all is perfect in your world you need to wake up and take another look, because all is not what it seems. Question your motives and you will begin to see a new picture emerging. This wake-up call serves you well. Look at areas where you could improve things, or investigate more deeply into situations you have previously skimmed over. Not everything is a bed of roses, and you would be wise to watch out for thorns. The world of nature must be on equal terms with humankind, to keep this planet going as we know it.

'For two millennia mankind has believed that everything on this planet is his for his own taking, to have dominion. It is time to redress the balance and live up to the sacred role as a protector of nature. Heed my call to harness the power of nature, to honour and revere the ways of your ancestors and work in union with the nature spirits and the world around you. As you honour and respect me, so shall I offer my protection to you. My strong foundations will sustain you when you crumble, and as you stumble through the darkness at this time I will lend you the strength to move forward. I am the ancestral mother: when you call upon me I will naturally unearth all that you seek within.'

SEEKING GAIA

When you are in the middle of a storm with chaos unleashing its fury all around you it's all too easy to get sucked into the dramas and traumas of other folk, while some people seem to have very high expectations of you. As usual, you take care of their needs before considering your own but it is now time to take accountability for your life and put yourself first. Mother Gaia calls to you to manifest all that you wish your life to be and to take care of *you*. Understand how the elements weave through your everyday and take a good look at everything you have created in your life so far. That's right: everything that is happening to you at this present moment has been created by your thoughts, words, actions and feelings. Gaia reveals what lies beneath the surface and reminds you that you have the ability to create or destroy. It's your choice.

Gaia's maternal side is warm and nurturing; she generates light with every step she takes as the goddess of the land. Like any mother, Gaia shows her love and compassion but she will become volatile in response to her children's bad behaviour. Her dark side is ferocious and unforgiving. She cares not for ego, disrespect or dishonour and her wrath makes Lady Gaia, the primordial earth mother, a Dark Goddess.

Dark Gaia energy reminds you that you may be feeling barren, bereft of life or stuck and unable to move forward because the place you are in is not nurturing you. Her energy tells you that you are not letting go of those things you do not need but are instead becoming obsessed with the material over the spiritual. Her magick can be dark and heavy when she perceives you are not respecting the earth and your role within it.

However, when she is properly embraced Gaia can help you feel less unconnected and remind you there is a soft, safe place to land at the end of the fall if you trust the process.

DARK GODDESS COMPARISON

'Gaia' is the name the ancient Greeks bestowed upon this goddess. A primordial fertility goddess, she was known as Terra Mater to the ancient Romans and Pachamama to the indigenous tribes of the Amazon, both of which mean 'earth mother'. Similarly, Sophia, the mother of all, was born out of nothingness, out of the silence, in accordance with Gnostic beliefs and her name in Greek means 'wisdom'. She is seen as being the mother of creation, as both divine female and the counterpart to Jesus Christ. She is the feminine divinity and the true power behind the Judeo–Christian god. She is also exalted in Kabbalah as the female expression of God and personification of sacred wisdom, who gave of her spirit to form the earth.

Just as Gaia will abandon her children in the face of their reckless behaviour, leaving them in an earthly wilderness, so too does the earth become a wasteland when the goddess Demeter goes into mourning. Worship of this Greek fertility and earth goddess of the harvest took over from that of Gaia, and she presided over the Eleusinian Mysteries when her daughter Persephone disappeared into the underworld. Her grief caused a cruel year for humankind by making the earth completely dry and barren.

However, the renewed focus on the state of the earth means that Gaia is now back with a vengeance, for she is nature's mother, the second element only to chaos. She is all of the elements, every season, each new bud of spring, the harvest abundance of summer, the falling leaves of autumn and the deep, dark mystery that accompanies the winter months. All living organisms are interconnected and form a self-regulating ecosystem, which she maintains to preserve the earth's equilibrium even to the detriment of her children if necessary. Gaia has the power to bestow on us a bountiful harvest or she can cause destruction to the entire crop, for Mother Nature teaches us there is both shadow and light in all things.

REASONS FOR WORKING WITH GAIA

Gaia is not at all a deliberately malevolent force, but she will take steps to protect the world that she has maintained over many millennia. She will eliminate us if we disrupt the balance of her delicate world and that of our own. Negative thoughts, words and an inability to go with the flow can be like a virus spreading destruction to her, and she will teach us a valuable lesson if we are being reckless by cutting us down to size in some way. Epidemics and pandemics are all part of her rage, and she can be blamed for destructive events such as tornadoes, storms and earthquakes in all forms. Tread your carbon footprint lightly upon her and you'll survive her wrath – unless, that is, you invoke her dark side unwittingly in response to your requests to grow and transform, for Gaia will ensure that you are stripped down in response to your plea, denied your comfort zone and forced to face a period of darkness and desolation in return for the transformation of new life.

PREPARING FOR GAIA

Are you ready to purposely seek out the changes you need to make in order to take the necessary steps to progress? What you wish for will not come about by sheltering within the comfort of four walls and all that makes you feel secure. You are being called to journey on the road less travelled, as the life you seek certainly won't be found while you are wallowing on the sofa! Instead, can you imagine how life would be if you had the balls to book that trip of a lifetime, soak up the fiery sun of faraway lands, climb a mountain, bathe in tropical waters or embrace the nature lover within? Gaia bids you to retreat from the material world and seek adventure. It is time to be a bold adventurer and discover for yourself what is waiting out there.

It is Gaia who hears your soul's cry to move forward, to better yourself or for improvement in your life. As the mother of all creation, Gaia naturally knows and understands what is best for each one of her children. As soon as she hears your wishes she will make plans to bring about your desires, if they are suitable for your purpose, of course. But do not be fooled, for new beginnings often mean drastic endings and Gaia will shake up your world until you take that first brave step into an unknown, unfamiliar world. If you are coming up against blocks and can't see the way towards your dreams and goals, Gaia could very well be instigating your path of no return. Signs that she's already working on your behalf are all around, and you may wonder what you have done to invoke her.

You may have subconsciously called in Gaia on a soul level when you wished:

- to make improvements in your life
- to be a better version of yourself
- for more responsibility
- to help the planet
- to be more grounded
- for balance
- to be whole
- for your true purpose to be revealed.

You may have unwittingly called in Gaia when she heard you:

- refuse to budge out of your comfort zone
- complain that your life is boring
- obsess about material wealth
- moan about the weather
- become frustrated and impatient
- get stuck in a rut

- watch a movie about Cyclops and Titans
- cry at the state of the world
- become distracted from your path
- hate your body image.

Turn to Gaia when you wish:

- to help the environment
- for a new start
- for fulfilment
- to be brave and embrace the new
- for fluidity, strength and firm foundations.

If you're always complaining, Gaia will teach you gratitude. If you favour materialism over the natural world she'll show you how to become fulfilled by embracing your storehouse within. If you feel things are moving too quickly she can help you slow things down and provide strength, if not solace, in the dark days ahead to help you draw on the restoring power of the earth.

HONOURING AND CONNECTING WITH GAIA

Honouring Gaia means understanding how her health affects yours; you need to protect her if you are to remain healthy and survive. When you take care of Mother Earth she'll take care of you. Do the following to honour and connect with Gaia:

- Give thanks to her for her abundant harvest.
- Do grounding exercises to connect you to the earth.
- Recycle at home and work.
- Grow your own vegetables and fruits.
- Buy organic whenever possible.
- Feed wild animals.
- Build shelters for the wildlife in your garden.
- Honour the seasons and the wheel of the year.

- Spend time outdoors in nature.
- Give thanks to Gaia for herbal medicines and your food, shelter and security.
- Work with crystals and seashells for healing.
- Read The Iliad.
- Seize the day and take steps to create the life you desire.
- Be responsible for your actions.
- Set clear boundaries.

Altar offerings to honour and give thanks to Gaia can include:

- a basket of fruit
- a loaf of bread
- a scattering of home-grown vegetables
- earth from a sacred site or garden
- a vase of flowers
- a stick of sage
- crystals
- a black, brown or green candle
- barley and honey cakes.

If you wish to connect with Gaia and for her to help you release the need for material things as you become more in tune with nature burn essential oils and incense, grow plants, create gardens and honour her among the trees.

INVOCATION TO GAIA

To purposely call Gaia into your energy you will need the following, but don't worry if you are unable to get hold of all of the ingredients as your focus will determine your connection with her:

- cypress incense
- a small dish of salt
- a crystal such as black agate, smoky quartz, black tourmaline or aragonite

- a green candle
- a small jug of milk
- a sprig of holly.

Call in Gaia during a full moon phase for optimum communion. Light the incense and sprinkle the salt around you in a circle for protection as you ask the goddess for her blessings. You can do this silently in your mind using whatever words come to you or you can say the following out loud:

Divine goddess, I ask you to bless and protect me as I focus on the divine light within myself. I call upon you, the Dark Goddess Gaia, for assistance. I graciously receive your blessings with an open heart in gratitude. Help me to serve, help me to shine. In love and honour, so mote it be.

Hold a crystal for protection and grounding when you are invoking or working with Gaia. Grounding is the essential connection between you and the earth, as it will keep your roots firmly placed here on the planet. Whenever you wish to connect with Gaia, powerful crystals such as aragonite that are attuned to the earth will provide strength and support while combating emotional stress. You may even find it encourages conservation and recycling, for it is a most reliable earth healer and can also be used as a grounding tool!

Sit with your back against a tree and place the soles of your bare feet upon the ground. Take three deep breaths in and out. Light the green candle for prosperity and abundance. Dig a small hole in an open space beyond the tree and pour in the milk for sustenance. Plant the holly sprig, which represents fertility and eternal life, and pat the soil down so there are no gaps. Stand with the lit candle in your hands and face the newly planted holly tree. As you gaze into the flame, focus on inviting in Gaia and say:

Mother of Earth, oh Goddess Gaia,
may your deep healing soothe all desire.
From out of chaos you created alone,
with love that poured from your very breastbone

to share of the essence of the divine
existential life for all of mankind,
Oh, to awaken the goddess within,
to embrace my gifts of deep feminine.
In your honour I sing and I dance,
entwined among nature, a gift to enhance.
And now I see that the balance in me
reflects your pure divinity.
Within my heart new strength doth reside
and shines forth new life, ne'er to hide.
As I grow stronger I am able to see
that it matters not that 'I' becomes 'we'.
I focus on honour and kindness to all,
and the goddess of earth ensures I am whole.

Let the candle burn down safely, pour any left-over milk onto the ground for Gaia to receive and say:

I invoke you now, to connect as one.
So mote it be, with harm to none.

Now that you have invoked Gaia she will leave you clues of her presence such as:

- you crave being out in nature
- your emotions become turbulent
- all weathers excite you
- you dance barefooted on the grass
- you get caught in the eye of a storm
- you recognise and embrace the seasons
- a jagged-toothed sickle presents itself
- you feel more grounded and secure
- you have an overwhelming desire to get your hands dirty
- you're attracted to working with crystals
- your maternal and nurturing qualities support others
- you embrace your feminine curves

- Ancient Greek, including stories from The Iliad, fascinates you
- you are compelled to pick up litter from the countryside
- you find that balance is vital to your well-being.

In a world of chaos and anxiety, becoming as one with the earth is a way to escape and stimulate your senses. Gaia will help you to feel stable and balanced as you take steps to connect with the ground beneath your feet.

EXERCISES AND RITUALS TO ENGAGE WITH GAIA

JOURNAL WORK

Use a journal to record your reflections on what is holding you back. In your journal, write and answer the following questions: what is keeping you stuck, when have you connected with nature in the past and how do you feel in these moments and what insights into or ideas about coping with your turmoil do these moments bring?

EARTH HEALING

If you feel drawn to help the earth there are many spells you can use. Always start by lighting a brown or black candle while facing the direction of north. Use your imagination to visualise the soil in the earth being free of pesticides and chemicals, seeing it as rich and nourished and growing from it blooms of flowers, plants and trees in healthy abundance. It is okay to visualise anything that you feel is right, and remember that whatever you imagine is done immediately in the etheric world. With more focus it eventually becomes manifest in your physical dimension, so do keep up the good work!

GAIA'S INITIATION RITUAL

Find an area of natural beauty or wildness. Alone, wearing natural fibres and barefoot, walk upon the earth and feel Gaia's energy rise up through your soles and nourish your spirit. If you are feeling particularly weary lie down upon the grass, soil or moss and allow her to soothe your frantic thoughts. As you commune with Gaia and her creatures, speak or chant the following incantation to alert her of your need and invite in her energy to help ground and keep you protected as you journey further into the dark night of the soul:

Faery folk, tiptoe soft
across the land of snow and frost.
They welcome you and all you bring.
Go deep inside and look within,
to shed all fears of gloom and doom.
Embraced and warm in winter's tomb
a call to die marks bitter end.
The crone appears not as a friend.
Immerse yourself within the earth;
let go, restore and then rebirth.

LESSONS FROM THE DARK GODDESS GAIA

If you are feeling stuck it may be Gaia letting you know you are in the wrong place, that your ground is not fertile for your soul's journey and progress is impossible. You may rile against her, try to remain where you are and feel frustrated and angry that you cannot seem to move forward on your path. This is the opposite of what your soul needs but leaving the safety of what you know can be frightening, so the Dark Goddess has to make staying even more uncomfortable than moving on.

Gaia is not just a being of the light; she embodies death and darkness as much as she does life and nurturing. She prepares the creatures of the world both for winter and for spring, so she can bring despair to dry barren soil and push the life that is dormant into a new cycle of life. When you engage with her dark energy you become aware of the interconnectedness of all things, and know that you are but a small piece in a grand design and no better or worse than anything else. She gives you perspective, so that you can see your role and your place within the realm of all life. She can make you feel small and insignificant, but in that way she forces you to let go of ego and entitlement.

Gaia reminds you of the innate wisdom, compassion and love she surrounds and constantly protects you with. You are safe on this earth nurtured within the womb of Gaia, the earth mother, the very soul of the earth. It is she who emerged from the cosmic egg at the dawn of creation and she who should be honoured and revered as the source of our kind. She is fertility, stability and a giver of life, for it is she who created and sustained us. Through the cycles of birth, fertility and sexual union and the processes of growth it is from her that we can learn how to be an earth mother while living on Mother Earth. Gaia's trials and tribulations of life lessons will teach you well, creating challenges as a deep process of healing and rebirth from mother's womb to earth womb to nurture and fulfil you on a very personal level.

Gaia is a guardian of the process of the dark night of the soul, for she too has witnessed the gloom that chaos generates and is no stranger to upheaval and disruption. As one of her children she is protector and guide for your dark journey of no return, for it is she who has instigated your new consciousness, igniting your soul to discover the best version of yourself that you can possibly be. Until that transformation can occur the Dark Goddess waits for you in her many guises.

Become ripe with expectancy, as a new darkness envelops you. Just like Gaia, the following goddess is a guardian and gatekeeper who will give you the ground rules and prepare you for your journey of the dark night of the soul. She, in order to raise you to the very highest level, will first cast you down very low and is waiting for you now . . .

5. FORTUNA

Initiation of change and loss

Enslaved to Rota Fortunae,
brought down low, thrown up high.
Spinning wheel puts you on track.
Journey freely, don't look back.

ORIGIN	Roman.
NAMES	Fortuna, Fortune, Lady Luck, Dame Fortune.
GODDESSES	Tyche, Eutykhia, Nemesis.
SYMBOLS	wheel of fortune, cornucopia, lucky charms.
THEMES	time, movement, change.
LESSONS	unexpected change and loss, indifference to outcomes.
COLOURS/CANDLES	green, gold, silver.
CRYSTALS	citrine, clear quartz, green aventurine.
HERBS/FLOWERS/OILS	jade plant, lavender, lemongrass, bergamot.
MOON PHASES	full, dark.
SEASONS	summer, winter.
TREES	money tree (*Pachira aquatica*), cherry.
FESTIVAL DATES	11 June, Fors Fortuna 24 June.

The ancients were no strangers to Fortuna, the Roman goddess of fortune, and her wheel of fortune represents chance, gain and loss in equal but incalculable measure. She spins her wheel at random while blindfolded, changing the positions of all those who are on the dial: some suffer great misfortune while others gain windfalls. She has no favourites and gives no special treatment, for Fortuna is indifferent to everything.

The wheel of fortune, which was once better known by its Latin name Rota Fortunae, was an ancient and mediaeval philosophical concept that embodied the ups and downs of a person's fate. Not only did it represent chance and gambling, it illustrated that life was a game and that any outcome was beyond the control of the players. There are many stories throughout history of those whom Fortuna threw up to the highs and cast back down again; we are familiar with the tales of, for example, Julius Caesar, Hercules, Lucifer. The concept originates from ancient Babylon and is based on the zodiac wheel turning the signs throughout the year, thus having an effect on the fortune of the world. The outer circle represents the material world, while the eight spokes of the wheel represent universal energy radiating outwards along with the eight sabbats of the year.

Fortuna is Lady Luck personified. She straddles the fine line between the prosperous and the barren, with the wheel of fortune weighing heavily around her neck as that is her burden to bear. The first-born child of Jupiter, Fortuna set her sights on Rome and never left, and there she was worshipped extensively and consulted about the future. Gamblers would honour her in the hope she would swing favour and luck their way. Likewise, poor men and slaves favoured her because she granted riches and freedom no matter what a person's status was through chance and mere luck.

In Roman art she is depicted in various ways: from standing on a ball to show how fortunes can easily change to holding a cornucopia to represent the abundance she can bestow. Other depictions have her placing a hand on a rudder to demonstrate her full control over a person's destiny and also presiding while blindfolded over the wheel of fortune. In tarot the wheel of fortune represents a new phase, of jumping on the bandwagon and taking a chance. When reversed it means you have no control, that you are trying too hard to control things, which is not self-serving when it's time to embrace change.

The sixth-century Roman philosopher Boethius wrote: 'Fortune is ever most friendly and alluring to those whom she strives to deceive, until she overwhelms them with grief beyond bearing, by deserting them when least expected.'

MESSAGE FROM FORTUNA

'Choice is but an illusion; don't you see? Your fate lies in my hands whenever I spin the wheel. You may feel like the luckiest person alive when all seems to go your way, but when a blow strikes you it can feel like the end of the world. The message of La Roué de Fortune is to be completely indifferent to both victory and defeat. Living by this rule of acceptance masters the inevitable hands of fate, for I can be an unjust and cruel goddess as well as fair and generous. It is time for you to get your reactions in check and realise that the cards you have been dealt are lessons purposefully designed for your learning, understanding, spiritual growth and evolvement. When you envy someone else who rides high, know that it could all change with just one spin of the wheel and propel you to the same dizzy heights of fate – or you may fall just as hard.

'Accept the outcome bravely and with indifference and you'll find that you're soaring through life no matter where you've been placed upon the wheel. Acceptance is key when it comes to harbouring emotions, and it's your emotions and the inner voice that protests about unfairness and injustice that will pull you down. However, it is I who will tip you upside down and throw you around for a while until you truly understand. My purpose is to remove the scales of preference and entitlement from your eyes. With my blindfold on I find you neither deserving nor entitled to remain in pole position, for it will not serve you. My only concern is to take you where you are meant to go in order to claim the prize at the end of the ride. Wherever that may be should be of no concern of mine or yours.

'Be aware of all your actions, thoughts and feelings and recognise that outcomes are measured by reactions. All situations you find yourself in, whether high or low, are lessons and experiences you need in order to grow and evolve, and if you can accept them and move on with indifference to any emotions that might rear up in the face of any given circumstance you find yourself in then the flow of the universe will support you. 'Competition, jealousy, envy and resentment will continue to accompany you whenever you fall victim to the wheel. Believing that you are a victim of the fates or a slave to negative thinking will keep you forever free falling into despair. Survival will only happen when you let go of controlling the outcome. The solution is to accept where you are on the wheel and appreciate the journey. It is time to surrender, for your fate is in my hands.'

SEEKING FORTUNA

Fortune favours the brave, so they say, and when you seek out the goddess of luck and chance you might find yourself gambling for your life. One moment you can be rising high and enjoying the fruits of chance and hard labour, but when Fortuna spins the wheel you can fall hard down on your luck. She is accused of being unjust, fickle and a mischief maker, but any luck she bestows is merely blind luck. She cares not one bit if you win or lose, and teaches that being indifferent is the only way to be.

When you reach your lowest ebb it is because part of your soul has called to the goddess Fortuna, who has blindly spun her wheel of fortune and caused your world to go into upheaval. She has started the chain of events that will lead you to spiral downwards, and although her ways may seem random and cruel she is inextricably linking you with your true fate and providing the changes you need to achieve it.

Perhaps you are experiencing a change right now or have done in recent times, something that has come like a bolt out of the blue that you were not prepared for. Consider this: you may have actually asked for this change. Everything you are experiencing could have come about through your prayers, wishes and desires: you may wish to be loved more, to have a passionate relationship; you might have asked for more money, to be abundant and prosperous; you could have wished for happiness and good health or a new career; you may have wished to enhance your connection with spirit, to have extreme psychic powers;

or perhaps you dreamed of being famous. Whatever it was, you were not necessarily prepared for what accompanied your request, and this is when the phrase 'Be careful what you wish for' should be noted.

Wherever your focus has been, the Dark Goddess hears all requests for change; it is her duty to always oblige if the outcome is for your highest good. However, in order to grant your wishes things must change and you must lose something in return for transformation, for her price always comes at the cost of unavoidable change and great loss. Consider what you could win or lose in the upcoming choices you must make, and leave nothing to chance. Treat any circumstance indifferently and without attachment. Be aware of all of your actions, thoughts and feelings and recognise that outcomes merely arise from your reactions to them – both your own and those of other people. The wheel of fortune teaches about the highs and lows of life, about life, death and rebirth. You are part of the circle of life; everyone is merely acting and reacting as they play their part. Once you understand this and practice non-attachment the wheel of fortune will cease to affect your emotions.

There is a tale about a single gentleman who kept himself to himself; nobody really knew him and the townsfolk stayed distant. One day a group of parents knocked on his door and grimly accused him of harming their children. He was told that he would be arrested and that everybody would know what he had done. He was expressionless as he simply answered 'Is that so?' before shutting the door on them. Time went by and a few months later there was another knock at the gentleman's door. 'We've come to apologise to you,' the crowd said. 'It turns out that we got it all wrong. The culprit has been arrested and we all know now that it wasn't you. We are very sorry.' The man replied 'Is that so?' and shut the door.

When you have attachments you start to pull on your emotions and draw in dramas. You fill your mind with 'what if' scenarios, which is when fear, doubts and worries creep in. The man in the story didn't have attachments, which meant he could continue to live his life without fear for he was not drawn in and had no cares about the outcome. When you understand you are just playing your part and are a cog in the wheel of life you can look at any given situation with indifference. Well, you can try!

DARK GODDESS COMPARISON

The ancient Greeks worshipped Tyche (or Tykhe) as the goddess of chance, an unpredictable distributor of good and ill fortune. She was responsible for unexpected change and events in people's lives, both good and bad. A successful person was regarded as being blessed by Tyche, and if someone worked hard but was still down on their luck then she was to blame.

Also named Eutykhia in her lighter, more favourable aspect of the goddess, she offered fortune, success and prosperity. Her overflowing cornucopia symbolises the plentiful gifts of fortune she bestows upon the lucky few. Just like Fortuna, she guides worldly affairs with her rudder and stands on a ball to represent the unsteadiness of seeking and holding on to wealth. Her dark side, Nemesis, keeps a check on all those who ask for extravagant favours and will bestow upon them a streak of bad luck to balance out an excess of good fortune.

As with Gaia, Fortuna is behind every abundant and scarce harvest, every streak of luck whether good or bad, and represents the delicate balance and unpredictability of nature.

REASONS FOR WORKING WITH FORTUNA

Are you prepared for Fortuna? Encountering her Dark Goddess side will see your world as you know it crash all around you, yet sometimes your current world is not what you need or what will nurture you. The wheel of fortune can deliver gain as well as loss. Fortuna helps you answer the question of what really matters, what you can and can't stand to lose. She will usher in your dark night of the soul to test your sense of survival, for the undesired change and loss that it brings can have devastating effects that could throw you into utter turmoil mentally, spiritually, physically and financially.

Fortuna teaches you that it's important to create indifference to ensure a future of peace and wholeness. What you think and imagine – whether it's worry, a prayer, recalling memories or a visualisation – starts to form into your reality depending on how much energy you give it through visualisation, prayer, affirmation, strong knowing and feelings. Being indifferent means you don't experience intense feelings because you are in a place of knowing, of contentment. You observe the dramas that others have manifested into their lives and watch them play their part. Shakespeare was right when he said 'All the world's a stage, And all the men and women merely players.'

When you live on an even keel you are no longer imprisoned by pain and suffering, but that would also mean never experiencing feelings of being overjoyed, surprised, worried, excited, scared or relieved – all of the stuff that makes you know you are truly alive! The wheel of fortune can throw you high, and everything goes well. You may expedite a big win, a new romance, a fresh career or a move to the house of your dreams. How excited would you feel? Would you feel that at last your turn has come and embrace your good fortune, or would you be in a constant state of worrying that all could be lost if you were to fall back down? If you were to fall lower on the wheel how would you feel: would you despair in your desolation or look at it as a chance to start anew? This indicates a lack of balance, and without balance you cannot appreciate the positive or the negative. The wheel of fortune makes you look at what is important to you and what is not. When your time comes to permanently fall off the last spoke of the wheel you should be able to do so freely.

WHEN CHANGE HAPPENS

The concept of change is usually avoided and frequently not welcomed. However, change – a natural process that happens with or without your consent – is a part of life that will always exist and can be for the better or for the worse. Some changes may be difficult to accept, while other changes can be exciting and fun. Things will always change because it is the way the world works; change is what pushes you further into knowledge, wisdom and growth. Most people don't fully embrace sudden change, instead preferring to stay within the comfort confines of what they know. On a subconscious level we genuinely believe that if we have been doing something in a certain way for a long time it must be right and it becomes comfortable to us. We like routine, as it makes us feel safe, and don't like surprises unless it's a big gift or a party.

However, none of us are strangers to changes in economic factors, politics, jobs, infrastructure planning and so on and we take the concerns of such things on board without necessarily spiralling down into a dark abyss. The one constant in life is change, which doesn't mean we ever get used to it or necessarily embrace it. On a scale of one to ten, how would you rate yourself when it comes to coping with change: are you quite good at adapting when plans change and happy to go with the flow, or do you go into meltdown when your plans go awry?

Metathesiophobia is a Greek word that means 'fear of change', with 'meta' meaning change and 'phobos' meaning fear. It perfectly sums up how you can feel when you are faced with sudden change or have no control over your life as things are constantly changing. Fear is the biggest reason not to embrace change because we humans are scared of the unknown. No one really wants to be pushed beyond their comfort zone or embrace situations that seem strange or foreign. Even when change is due to the best of circumstances it requires you to lose something, whether it be a routine, a relationship, familiarity, a place that holds memories, convenience, a reputation or a known experience. Change means unknown; change means having to relearn something; change requires you to face the reality that you're not in control; and change often makes you face things within yourself you could conveniently avoid.

Loss + change = transformation

It's a great exchange!

Before the final result there will be a period during which you will be blindfolded in the dark, as any change that ushers in a dark night of the soul comes as a long dark lesson and if not understood it can be the beginning of a living nightmare. The chaos of change first needs to blow in, and that's when the dark journey truly begins. Whether you made a request for change or not, there is no preparation for what the Dark Goddess has in store for you: she knows exactly what is needed for you to be truly transformed into the best possible version of yourself. But what is it you have to give up in order to win the prize?

You are a unique and beautiful soul who has incarnated into your current body in order to learn, grow and evolve. When you perform the same tasks day in and out and when your routine is monotonous you are not feeding your soul. You have come here to be magnificent, to shine and to thrive, and when you don't fulfil your potential you can become frustrated on a deep level. The Dark Goddess hears the primordial cry of your soul even if you don't. She will rise up to meet you, and will bring you crashing down until you no longer recognise who you are any more.

You may suddenly feel that what once appealed to you no longer does: your friends are no longer on quite the same wave length and what previously brought about immense excitement and motivation seems to have waned. You may ask what has happened to you, why you don't feel the same way you once did. What you are experiencing is a great shift in your personal energy, as what you once found attractive no longer appeals to you and this is causing some concern. However, be assured that everything you are feeling is entirely natural. Your desire to spiritually evolve and live as your authentic self has brought about these changes in you.

Before you can rise again the Dark Goddess will go to extreme measures to ensure you are stripped of all that was once familiar to you and will take away anything you are holding tightly on to. Her lesson is to let go, to have no attachments to anyone or anything or to the outcome of situations. The Dark Goddess sees the strings that hold you back like a prisoner and enforces you to surrender as she takes away the very things you were holding on to for dear life.

Everything inside of you will want to fight the change. You will try with all of your might to will, push or pray it away, but the more you do this the more painful it will become. Surrendering is not weakness. To find freedom you must surrender to the process; in order to win, to survive, you must resist fighting it. Once you let go and trust the process the darkness will give way to the light and your dark journey will be over. Change is inevitable, and in whatever form it comes it must be accepted every time. You must never fear it because change is usually for the better and leads to better outcomes. Most importantly, it shows you who you truly are and what you really want.

Fortuna came to me in my dreams one night. I dreamed I was on top of the world as people queued to offer me gifts of everything I ever wished for. I was being honoured and praised and treated like a queen, and I felt wonderful and was so happy. Suddenly the foundations beneath me started to shake and everything I had been gifted disappeared into the cracks of the earth. I tried to reach for them in desperation until a figure rose up before me. She was taller than the world itself and held up a Rota Fortunae. Blindfolded, she spun the wheel and I started to fall. Just as I was about to scream I remembered what Fortuna had said to me that day and I decided to let go: I allowed myself to free fall among the chaos. Soon it was as though I was floating on clouds, and my descent was slow, gentle and serene. The wheel of fortune stopped spinning and I found myself at the bottom in a place that only invites in misery. However, Fortuna had lent me her eyes, and with a new perspective I could only see my fall from grace as an opportunity for new beginnings and opportunity.

The true meaning of the wheel of fortune is to be aware of all of your actions, thoughts and feelings and to recognise that outcomes merely arise from your reactions to them, both our own and those of others. The wheel of fortune teaches about the highs and lows of life as it is all about life, death and rebirth. Tread with indifference and you will feel no effects.

PREPARING FOR FORTUNA

Are you ready to purposefully seek out the death of what you've been holding on to so tightly? Fortuna willingly greets any soul who cries out for new beginnings, to start again, to move on but be warned: if you find it hard to let go of the past by reliving old arguments and cannot or will not adapt to new circumstances then you could very well find yourself stuck in a rut from which it is hard to escape. Familiar habits are a part of who you are, but the transformation you may have wished for requires you to revisit the way you're thinking.

Fortuna appears when you forget the difference between earning a crust and having a feeling of self-entitlement to wealth and success without working for it. Losing a moralistic sense of duty and unity, when greed takes possessive hold, propels you to take a high-speed ride around Fortuna's spinning wheel, and that's when you can lose all sense of inner bearing and comportment.

The Rota Fortunae can throw you up very high or bring you down very low, and the secret to life's victories and defeats is to be indifferent to the outcome. You may not be able to predict or avoid the change Fortuna will bring, but you can prepare for the idea of change itself. Be open to the outcome and trust that wherever she places you on the wheel is deliberate and purposeful.

You may have subconsciously called in Fortuna on a soul level when you wished:

- to be more spiritual and magickal
- to step into your life purpose
- to be a better version of yourself
- for a new start.

You may have unwittingly called in Fortuna when she heard you:

- complain that 'It's not fair!'
- making random choices
- express desires for excitement and adventure
- ask for abundance, financial help and security
- obsess over material gain
- demand entitlement
- become stagnant, not going with the flow
- become selfish, not sharing
- gamble with your life
- wish for wealth and fame
- hold on to your possessions too tightly
- wish to be like another
- secretly wish for a new relationship, career or any life changer
- hope not to lose all that you hold dear.

Turn to Fortuna when you wish:

- for winds of change
- for balance
- for improvement in your life

- to better yourself
- for success
- to be raised up high.

You may have found yourself at the bottom of the heap, and it could be a long, arduous climb to the reach the top. Remember always to be careful what you wish for, for when Fortuna hears your plea for change then the loss you may have to endure to birth that change could be more than you can cope with. As soon as she hears your invitation to come into your life, whether subconsciously or through invocation, she will spin her wheel, and wherever it lands will kick you into drastic change or will bring you a great loss that will eventually turn your life around completely. She turns her back on entitlement behaviour and ambitious egos and invites you to release all attachment, for with it comes longing and suffering.

HONOURING AND CONNECTING WITH FORTUNA

Do the following to honour and connect with Fortuna:

- Place a wheel of fortune above your doorway to represent the unpredictable and changeable nature of luck and fate.
- Be virtuous in your decision-making.
- Play cards or gamble with no concern for the outcome.
- Fill a cornucopia with fruit, bread and flowers in gratitude for her horn of plenty.
- Carry a coin to ensure Lady Luck is on your side.
- Wear a blindfold to enhance your intuition or release favouritism.
- Observe the cycles of time and the wheel of the zodiac.
- Trust blindly in outcomes.
- Go with the flow and release attachment.

Altar offerings to honour and give thanks to Fortuna can include:

- a citrine crystal for luck in wealth and prosperity
- clear quartz for finding your purpose

- green aventurine for luck and energy
- honey
- milk
- poppies
- round cakes
- fortune cookies
- a handful of grain
- a blindfolded figurine of Fortuna
- a representation of the wheel of fortune
- coins
- a money jar.

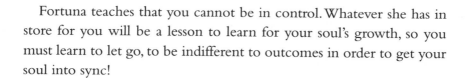

Fortuna teaches that you cannot be in control. Whatever she has in store for you will be a lesson to learn for your soul's growth, so you must learn to let go, to be indifferent to outcomes in order to get your soul into sync!

INVOCATION TO FORTUNA

To purposely call Fortuna into your energy you will need the following, but don't worry if you are unable to get hold of all of the ingredients as your focus will determine your connection with her:

- a stick
- representations of your dreams, goals and fears
- lemongrass incense
- a small dish of salt
- a blindfold or eye mask
- a coin.

Stand outside in nature, and with the stick draw a large circle in front of you on the ground to symbolise the wheel of fortune. Mark the top of the circle with representations of your dreams and goals and the bottom of the circle with representations of your fears and most dreaded situations. You can do this by placing objects on the circle, writing words in the dirt or visualisation. Light the incense and sprinkle the salt around you in a circle for protection as you ask the goddess for her blessings. You can do this silently in your mind using whatever words come to you or you can say out loud:

> *Divine goddess, I ask you to bless and protect me as I focus on*
> *the divine light within myself and I call upon you, the Dark*
> *Goddess Fortuna, for assistance. I graciously receive your magickal*
> *lessons of indifference with an open heart in gratitude. Help me*
> *to serve, help me to shine. In love and honour, so mote it be.*

Tie the blindfold over your eyes so you cannot see and say:

> *Goddess Fortuna, lady of luck,*
> *indifference shows me you don't give a fuck.*
> *I know my fate's sealed, it's destiny's call:*
> *down on my luck, or will I stand tall?*
> *Spin thrice about, step onto the wheel,*
> *with blindfold now off eyes doth reveal.*
> *Position now placed on Rota Fortunae:*
> *cast down low or raised up very high.*

Spin around three times and step into the circle, then remove the blindfold to reveal where you are on the wheel of fortune. Observe your first thoughts and emotions: are they fearful or peaceful? Disregard any attachments you've observed to the outcome of where you now stand and say:

> *The wheel hath turned, my fate is sealed.*
> *It's plain to see, or t'is concealed.*
> *I must embrace the lessons won,*
> *my fortune bright, and fear undone.*
> *Release old ties, to set me free,*
> *emotions hold past energy.*
> *Circle of life offers new slate,*
> *choices made now seal my fate.*

Bury the coin in a place of your choice within the circle to honour Fortuna and bring you some luck. Heads or tails: the choice is entirely yours; just be open to the outcome.

Fortuna announces herself with huge changes, sudden upheavals and genuine loss that may induce a dark night of the soul. You will know her dark energy is near you if you encounter any of the following:

- redundancy
- debt recovery
- eviction
- the end of a relationship
- betrayal
- poor health
- an accident
- the loss of a limb
- a break-in
- bad news
- the death of a family member, friend or pet
- a pandemic!

Will you choose to hang on to drama and the unexpected, to be a slave to your emotions, or will you choose to experience pure contentment 24/7? When we pass over we take with us our emotions and feelings, which is why it is so important to be peaceable. Don't hold on to anything you would not want to spend an eternity with! Learn to forgive and let go of obsessions and worries.

EXERCISES AND RITUALS TO ENGAGE WITH FORTUNA

JOURNAL WORK

Consider what changes in your life are unavoidable and make a list in your journal of all the natural changes in your life. Ask yourself if you are embracing these changes and, if so, how. Write down what comes to mind. Make another list of anything you feel is holding you back from moving forward. What could you easily let go of, and which things in your life would you find hard to let go of? Make a final list of everything in your life that serves your highest purpose, including people. Who are the deadbeats, and who raises your vibrations when you think of them?

TIPS FOR COPING WITH CHANGE

Sometimes you get so caught up in fighting change that you put off dealing with it, thus stunting your growth and prolonging the undesired situation. Denial is an extremely powerful force that protects you in many ways, and although it plays its part as you journey through a dark night of the soul it does not always serve your higher purpose to ignore and avoid that which will transform you. Those who cope best with change adapt faster and more effectively while enjoying the ride, so how can you most effectively cope with change? Try the following:

- Acknowledge the change.
- Keep up your regular schedule as much as possible.
- Seek support.
- Write down positives that could come from the change.
- Take steps to accept the change.
- Go with the flow.
- Breathe!

LESSONS FROM THE DARK GODDESS FORTUNA

If you have a hard time accepting change, be careful not to stunt your sense of flexibility and versatility for these qualities are the only way forward to being fluid and adaptable. The energy of water is considered to be receptive, so when you are feeling fearful imagine you are standing at the seashore. Visualise the tide receding and taking with it all the negative aspects you are feeling, then the tide drawing the ocean towards you so it gifts you with positivity and prosperity. Be open to receive and ready to flow naturally with life.

Certain things such as time are always going to change, and time causes many changes as you mature and age. This is a typical change that cannot be avoided and should be embraced as a part of life. Society seems to only embrace youth; the maiden and the crone, the hag who is ugly and old, should be avoided at all costs. Such nonsense! In years past it was the older generation that was honoured, for as we age we gain experience of life. Our wisdom years should be embraced and the wisdom keeper exalted.

The Dark Goddess is the sacred keeper of wisdom and transformation, for it is only she who instigates the changes that are an unavoidable part of your life if you are to grow and evolve. Changes such as these must never be unwelcomed or considered scary; you must always see them as something exciting and new no matter the risk, for it is also an adventure since you don't know the outcome. See all changes with indifference, as Fortuna has revealed.

Having been thrown down very low on the wheel, the journey of the dark night of the soul has now been fully initiated. With both Gaia and Fortuna standing on either side of you, a new pathway has opened up. These goddesses are the gatekeepers of the dark night of the soul and it is their invitation you have answered, albeit unwittingly. They now advise you to tread carefully under their watchful guidance as you walk through the darkness. They have given you the tools of balance and indifference, which you will need in order to survive. Take with you the wisdom they have imparted as you step over the threshold to the dark night of the soul, where nine dark goddesses await you at every stage.

The Dark Goddess you are now to meet invites you to step fully onto the path of no return, to meet her deep in the dark woods for her initiation of self-sufficiency.

6. BABA YAGA

Initiation of self-sufficiency

Lost within a forest deep:
who to trust, what to keep?
Loss denotes a frightful change;
prepare, be brave and face the strange.

ORIGIN	Slavic/Russian.
NAMES	Baba Yaga, Baba Den, Jezi Baba, Boba.
GODDESS	Kali.
SYMBOLS	mortar and pestle, witch's broom (besom), corn sheaf, rye, wreaths of wheat and wild flowers.
THEMES	harvest, rest, providence, cycles, regeneration.
LESSONS	self-sufficiency, honouring age and the older generation.
COLOURS/CANDLES	red, white, black.
CRYSTALS	bloodstone, garnet, tourmaline, smoky quartz.
HERBS/FLOWERS/OILS	geranium, patchouli, sandalwood.
MOON PHASES	waning, dark.
SEASONS	autumn, winter.
TREE	birch.
FESTIVAL DATE:	10 January.

Baba Yaga makes a link between the wise women of yesteryear and the wicked witches of faery tales, who are distorted versions of the Dark Goddess – she who brings wisdom to life's lessons as she spins her web of fate. The Dark Goddess has been around since the birth of magick itself and is a force to be reckoned with, presenting powers of extremity in the highest form and presiding over our destiny. She reminds you that disbelief destroys your inner mystic and power to reclaim your birth right, and she brings with her great lessons and unveils harsh truths to make you let go of anything or anyone who is holding you back, to learn and discover a whole world of possibilities, freedom and magick.

Of Russian and Slavic origin, where it gets bitterly cold in winter, this scary old witch has spooked and frightened little children for many centuries. *Baba* means 'grandmother' or 'old woman' in most Slavic languages, but don't be fooled by her name for this is one old lady you certainly shouldn't treat lightly!

In ancient societies older women were seen as being the keepers of wisdom and tradition for the community. These wise women understood the mysteries of birth and death, and were the healers and midwives who were thought to have the power of life and death itself. The word 'witch' once meant wise. Later, from around the 12th century as religion began to dominate northern Europe, people began to fear magick and its power. Wise women were no longer sought out for their potions and herbal advice, and the notion of the wise woman changed into one of a frightening, ugly, wicked old witch who cast evil spells, as in the faery tales we read today. These faery tales were an offshoot of mythology, and always contain an element of magickal truth as well as a moral to each story. They have a wealth of symbolism hidden within them that we can use as a psychological device to analyse the workings of our minds as we battle through our soul's dark night journey.

Just like the hideous hag, wicked queen or old crone of fables, Baba Yaga is described as being a terrifying, heinous old witch who presides over a person's fate and destiny by deciding whether to oblige their request or devour them. She is typically portrayed as a vile-looking old crone complete with a crooked nose, iron teeth, cruel thin lips, stringy hair, warts and all, and she lives in a log cabin deep within a dark forest where the pine trees grow. However, her house is not a typical kind, for it is perched on chicken feet that can turn the house around on the change of the winds so that Baba Yaga can view every angle of the forest at any time. The windows have eyes to see with, while the door to the house is never revealed until the magickal words 'Turn your back to the forest, your front to me' are uttered, and then a keyhole filled with sharp teeth appears, for it is a mouth.

Baba Yaga's vehicle is not typical for a witch either. Instead of riding a traditional broomstick, or besom, she chooses a mortar to fly in, using the pestle as a rudder. Her broom, made from silver birch, trails behind, clearing her tracks of any evidence of her whereabouts.

Some tales describe Baba Yaga as being a beautiful young woman who is a magickal assistant to heroes. This doesn't seem to make sense considering the name *Baba* means 'grandmother'. However, this wouldn't stop her from being beautiful and honoured during the time of the cult of mothers and goddess worship, for the name *Baba* was often used to refer to Mother Earth or the mother aspect of the triple goddess.

Baba Yaga's looks were most likely demonised when Christianity stripped the goddess of her divinity and she became a horrific-looking, angry old crone, but we can use her beautiful and younger portrayal to symbolise her regenerative aspect along with the ugly old woman aspect as a symbolisation of death. Therefore this all-rising Slavic witch is a goddess of both death and rebirth.

Here is an old tale about Baba Yaga. Once upon a time a beautiful girl called Vasilisa lived in a village with her father. Sadly, her mother had died some years earlier, but before she passed she gave her daughter a gift of a little rag doll. Vasilisa's mother asked her to care for the doll, so every night she made sure she fed her a little biscuit and some milk so that in return the doll would look out for her. Some years passed, and Vasilisa's father wished to marry again. His new wife moved in along with her two daughters, but none of them could compare to Vasilisa's sweet, kind character or her serene beauty. Her new stepmother and stepsisters were terribly jealous of Vasilisa. They were cruel and demanding, but would pretend to be nice to her when her father was around.

Shortly after Vasilisa's sixteenth birthday her father had to go away for a month. She begged to go with him but he wouldn't hear of it; instead, she was to stay with her stepmother and stepsisters. Once the father had left, the stepmother declared she had a task for the three girls to complete: the elder girl was to sew a button onto her mother's favourite dress and the younger was asked to roll some pastry in the kitchen, but poor Vasilisa was told to go deep into the forest to borrow some lights from Baba Yaga herself!

The whole village knew of Baba Yaga and how she loved to eat people, particularly children, so Vasilisa was rather disturbed by the prospect of looking for her in the dark forest. She took her little rag doll with her for company and told her of her fears: 'I'm in terrible trouble. I must go to Baba Yaga, and everyone knows that she is a wicked witch. Please help me and tell me what I am to do.' The little doll looked up at Vasilisa and told her to be brave, for no harm would come to her. Mustering her courage, Vasilisa walked towards the forest as a horse rider, wearing a red cloak, shot straight past her. A little further on another rider dressed in white passed her as she took the path that led to Baba Yaga's hut. Sometime later a third horse rode by and the rider wore a cloak that was as black as night.

It had become quite dark in the forest, and after a while Vasilisa came across a clearing that was lit up by skulls mounted on top of a fence, with blazing eyes all staring at her. Beyond the fence was the infamous house that stood on chicken legs. As she gasped it spun round to face her, then the chicken legs knelt down to lower the hut and a creaky door opened to reveal Baba Yaga. Scared witless, Vasilisa couldn't move, let alone speak until she remembered her mother's words: a reminder to always be polite and kind no matter what. She eventually found the courage to explain why she had come, and Baba Yaga nodded before setting her some impossible tasks to complete. Having cooked a sumptuous meal for Baba Yaga, Vasilisa was too tired to eat but made sure she fed her little rag doll with a few crumbs and some milk.

The following morning Vasilisa looked out of the window and watched Baba Yaga fly above the forest in a giant mortar until she was out of sight. She despaired at her ridiculous chore, for how could she possibly pick the black peas out of a sack filled with millions of white peas as she'd been instructed? Suddenly, she looked up at the sound of a horse. She wished with all of her might to be rescued, and when she turned back to the task at hand she found that the peas had already been sorted into two piles: one black and one white. Her chore was complete.

On her return Baba Yaga was surprised at Vasilisa's achievement, and so to test her further she asked her to collect some water in a sieve to fill up the tank: an impossible task! The little rag doll urged a very downhearted Vasilisa to believe that something wonderful would happen and it did, for as she tried to fill the sieve with water the red horseman rode by. He hurled the sieve through the open window of Baba Yaga's house, and when she returned she found that the tank had been filled with water.

Surprised at Vasilisa's success, Baba Yaga set her a further challenge, asking for the correct number of stars in the sky. She had one night to count them all and reveal the answer to Baba Yaga in the morning. 'Tell me the correct number in the morning and you can take your light and go free, but if your answer is wrong, if you tell me one star too many or too few, then I shall have you for my breakfast!'

That night Vasilisa gazed out of the window at the sky. She tried and tried to count the stars, but she wasn't sure if she was counting the same ones as some seemed to move and she had to keep starting all over again. She began to sob. She didn't want the old witch to eat her, and she held her rag doll close to her heart. 'Oh, who can help me?' she wailed. The doll gently consoled her, urging her not to worry and to have courage and faith, for all would be well. And it was, for on the stroke of midnight the black horseman rode up to the window and whispered the answer in Vasilisa's ear. The number is hugely significant and is a secret of the universe, one that cannot be shared in this story.

The following morning Baba Yaga was looking very hungry, until Vasilisa told her the number of stars in the sky. 'What! Who told you that?' Baba Yaga was so furious she threw her breakfast plate across the room. Vasilisa was scared but bravely demanded that she should be set free in accordance with their agreement. Baba Yaga's fury lessened. 'So be it,' she said in quiet defeat. 'I suppose it was Morning, Day and Night who helped you with the tasks I set for you?' Vasilisa nodded, as she finally understood who the three horsemen were.

Baba Yaga agreed to do her no harm, for if Morning, Day and Night had chosen to help her it meant her spirit was in harmony with the universe and that Baba Yaga was thus honoured and respected. Baba Yaga gave Vasilisa one of the skulls with blazing eyes as a light to take home as promised, but when the light fell upon her stepmother and stepsisters they turned to dust. When her father returned they lived happily together, until a handsome prince came riding by. When he caught sight of Vasilisa he thought she was the most beautiful girl he'd ever seen, and they married and lived happily ever after.

MESSAGE FROM BABA YAGA

'If you go into the woods today be sure of a big surprise, for it is I, Baba Yaga, who awaits and beckons you in with my bony finger, as invitation to my lair deep in the dark forest. You'll know me in an instant: I am the original wicked witch you've read about in fairy tales, the evil old hag who disturbed your childhood dreams and brought you nightmares. With a warty wrinkled face and a crooked nose I could scare you stiff with just one raspy cackle, yet you still seek me out.

'There's a part of you that yearns to die, to be rid of what's gone before, yet you hold on to death so tightly for fear of great loss. I've seen you cling to your dreams, your goals and wishes until they almost choke you, but negating self-belief, new projects and ideas out of fear of new birth invites me in to destroy everything you hold dearly. Letting go is the only way to fulfilment; so, too, is taking action for yourself instead of relying on others. It's the only way to truly get the job done and it will bring the confidence that self-sufficiency provides into your life.

'Think of me as an alternative grandmother figure, for that's what my name means, but do not expect me to be the nurturing type. My hard healing lessons are only so you can learn to be self-sufficient and independent, just like a short, sharp whack on the legs any grandmother would give a child to get them to stand on their own two feet. I will not tolerate childish behaviour, nor can I abide anything that is not helpful for your growth. Take ownership of your actions and independent steps towards self-sufficiency and I will help you flourish, but remain the victim by wallowing in self-pity and I shall gobble you up!'

SEEKING BABA YAGA

The Dark Goddess expects you to be responsible for yourself and be self-sufficient. When your world is solely dependent on others for happiness, when you cannot make big decisions without asking friends for their opinion or you feel uncomfortable doing things on your own without support, then learning how to establish your individuality is vital for your inner strength and independence. Self-sufficiency allows you to embrace your own thoughts and take your own actions without fully relying on anyone else or be affected by the opinions and validation of others.

It is not at all easy when you go through a dark night of the soul, for you are blinded by circumstance and find it hard to believe that you will ever cope or survive without someone else's help. However, as you will find out, this journey is yours to walk alone with only the Dark Goddess for company, for she knows that independence is key when it comes to re-evaluating your life and grants you the necessary freedom to escape the control or influence of others.

When your foundations were shaken to their very core as you faced the first unexpected stages of *surrender* and *change* to welcome in your dark night of the soul you would have come across a long path that winds through the forest deep, on which you found the strange-looking home of the Dark Goddess Baba Yaga. When you approach Baba Yaga you can expect her to be elusive, as she is not easy to track down. It is a long, lonely journey to take along the crooked path, each step crunching on the snow beneath your feet, through the dark forest filled with snow-laden trees to where she resides. Only a few have returned to share with others her grave lessons. Being bold when you seek her wisdom is not the right approach either, as she will refuse to come out to greet you or will welcome you in and gobble you up!

Baba Yaga calls you to tread carefully and draw near in awe and reverence and with a sense of fear. A great courage is required if you wish to look for Baba Yaga, for she is one harsh and devouring old lady. She has little time for those who are not willing to embrace death and the change it brings, and she doesn't believe in handing everything you ask for to you on a plate. Instead, she will make you work until you are self-sufficient enough to not be reliant on anyone else. She doesn't offer quick fixes and she doesn't give a pretty name to the real and lasting results that come from hard work and tenacity. A hard task mistress, she will prepare you to face, accept and embrace the changing cycles of life, for she understands that you must die to the old in order to be reborn. Her lesson is to embrace the cycles of life and be grateful.

Baba Yaga urges those who seek her to be thankful, to have gratitude for all that Mother Earth provides as she awakens within you an awareness of the seasons and the turning of the wheel. She is a goddess of regeneration who is associated with the harvest and the season of autumn, when great changes occur as the leaves turn colour and most of nature starts to decay. Her symbols are wreaths of wheat, corn and wild flowers, and she will bestow abundance upon those who show gratitude for all earthly gifts for she also represents providence and prosperity.

DARK GODDESS COMPARISON

Baba Yaga is also known as Baba Den and Jezi Baba, and in goddess terms can be likened to Kali, the Hindu goddess of death and rebirth. Like Baba Yaga, Kali is a most feared goddess for her similar aspects of death and the change she brings with it as she removes the ego and liberates the soul from the never-ending cycle of birth, death and rebirth. Just as Baba Yaga has skulls placed on all the fencing around her garden, Kali wears a garland of skulls around her neck. These dark goddesses understand that we are beings of spirit and not flesh and experience liberation when we become unattached from our bodies and the material world of ego. Both of these dark girls see the skulls as trophies, having freshly liberated their suspects!

REASONS FOR WORKING WITH BABA YAGA

Once Baba Yaga has heard your soul's cry or is called upon your life will never be quite the same again. She will bestow upon you a sense of self-sufficiency to remind you that whatever you need is never far away and magickal ingredients are always to hand if you know how to use them. When Baba Yaga hears your request you can be sure she will get to the root of the problem, although you may have to endure a testing journey to get there. She will show you the opposite of who you are in order for you to truly know yourself. This must happen through devastating change and loss, but Baba Yaga has your highest interest at heart and she will shatter any illusions that have blinded you to the truth.

EMOTIONAL DEVELOPMENT

As you look at the natural world the signs of life, death and rebirth are all around: the cycles of days and nights, the waxing and waning of the moon and sun, the turning of the seasons in the wheel of the year are reflected in your life. Within the darkness that Baba Yaga brings comes the opportunity to return to the earth, to gestate, regroup and prepare to rebirth in the form of unexpected change that she now offers you. The changes can be anything from large life ones such as a worldwide pandemic and the challenges it brings to smaller but potentially equally challenging changes such as job loss, relationship break-ups, moving house or a medical diagnosis. With every change Baba Yaga brings comes renewal and new opportunity.

As she bestows her unwanted gift of change or loss upon you she will not feed, nurture or protect you, nor will she speak words of kindness as you might expect. Instead, her mission is to destroy any ignorance and denial that prevents the death of anything that holds you back from moving forward towards your destiny. New beginnings cannot be birthed without death of the old, so Baba Yaga brings you the promise of new life through sudden change or loss. She prepares you for the next round, for like a plant that must wither and die in autumn in order to grow again in spring, you must die to an old and outdated part of you that is not helpful in your growth in order to be reborn into the best version of yourself.

Baba Yaga wants you to develop your own power and self-sufficiency, so to seek Baba Yaga is to seek a death of some part of you. She will destroy that which no longer serves your highest purpose to create space for better change and to allow something fresh and new to flourish.

Baba Yaga is not interested in those who choose to be powerless. Her medicine encourages you to accept difficulty and work towards solutions with hard labour and good sense. She has no time for victims, so although you may feel your circumstances were caused by the actions of others Baba Yaga does not care: to her, what caused your situation is in the past and she knows that only you can decide how you move forward. She is happy for you to use your power to overcome those who have harmed you, but understand that to have that power means letting go of victimhood and realising that abuse continues while you dwell on it long after the actual events themselves have passed.

REJECTING VICTIMHOOD

It is extremely hard to not go down the route of playing the victim when you have suffered any trauma. How many times when things have not gone your way have you blamed another for your misfortunes? If things go wrong, do you immediately point your finger and say it's someone else's fault? It is so easy to do! When the Dark Goddess appears you won't necessarily realise that it is her who is pulling you in. She knows that before you can walk in the light you have to face the darkness, for it is only the Dark Goddess who can shed light on that which is hidden. She does not favour the victim, and victimhood does you no favours as it keeps your focus on the negative and keeps you down low. Remember you are what you create through your thoughts and actions, and it is impossible to gain a sense of power in your life if your identity is that of the victim.

The following are signs that you have a victim mentality:

- You feel powerless and unable to solve problems and you can't cope effectively.
- You tend to see your problems as catastrophes.
- You tend to think others are purposely trying to hurt you.
- You believe you alone have been targeted for mistreatment.
- You hold tightly to thoughts and feelings related to being a victim.

Through all of your trials and tribulations, have you fallen into a victimhood mentality? If so, it's time to take steps to break out and look deeper. What lessons could be learned from this? Work on eliminating feelings of frustration around the expectation that someone is obliged to satisfy you. By doing so you will find that the victimised, paranoid feelings that inevitably always arise when you are facing a dark night of the soul will soon dissolve, and ultimate freedom will beckon as you fuel your weary mind with the positive expectations and peace it craves.

Baba Yaga comes in to remind you that victimhood will not ease your problems. Her voice is harsh and she can be cruel, but if you listen you can move beyond the crushing feeling of never being able to move away from your pain. One way you can invite Baba Yaga in to do this for you is to recite the following incantation:

> *Misery calls, invites victim in.*
> *Self-belief crushed, no room here to win.*
> *It's no longer welcome, I'll show it the door.*
> *The battle is over, for I'm now the victor!*

OTHER BENEFITS OF WORKING WITH BABA YAGA

Baba Yaga is a powerful magickal entity based on the earliest idea of the wise woman; her energy can be very useful for anyone wanting to excel in particular areas of witchcraft. Those who are brave enough to respectfully seek her and who wish to improve their witchcraft skills and knowledge know that she gives only straightforward advice, and that she will share her wisdom and knowledge for guidance, healing (physical ailments), wildcrafting, herbalism, relationship advice and hedge witchcraft.

PREPARING FOR BABA YAGA

Are you ready to purposely seek out the death of that which you've been holding on to so tightly? Baba Yaga willingly greets those souls who cry out for new beginnings, to start again, to move on, but be warned: if you find it hard to let go of the past, by reliving old arguments, heated conversations or upsetting scenes in your mind, and cannot adapt to new circumstances then you could very well become a tasty treat for her!

You may have subconsciously called in Baba Yaga on a soul level when you wished:

- to be more spiritual and magickal
- to be a better version of yourself
- for a new start
- for independence.

You may have unwittingly called in Baba Yaga when she heard you:

- complain that your life was dull and boring
- express desires for excitement and adventure
- ask for abundance, financial help and security
- secretly wish for a new relationship, career or any life changer
- hope not to lose all that you hold dear
- rely on the help and opinions of others
- become clingy
- fall into victimhood.

Turn to Baba Yaga when you wish:

- for change
- for improvement in your life
- to better yourself
- to be in control of all areas of your life
- to be self-sufficient
- to make decisions.

Do remember to be careful what you wish for, as when Baba Yaga hears your plea for change the loss may be more than you can cope with. As soon as she hears your invitation to come into your life, whether subconsciously or through invocation, Baba Yaga will set about her work and kick you into change or bring you a great loss. She will eventually turn your life around completely, but it's a long, hard road ahead.

HONOURING AND CONNECTING WITH BABA YAGA

Do the following to honour and connect with Baba Yaga:

- Make a wreath of corn and hang it on your front door for providence and prosperity.
- Feast on rye bread or bagels.
- Make your own home-made wheat bread.
- Have a multigrain cereal or toast for breakfast.
- Give thanks to Baba Yaga for the harvest and for your food.
- Carry a few grains with you to ensure you are always provided for.
- Hang up a dry cob of corn to ensure a fruitful harvest for the following year.
- Decorate your home, place of work or car with freshly picked wild flowers.
- Listen to Slavic or Russian folk music.
- Save: don't be wasteful; be frugal and trust in Baba Yaga to bring in the harvest.
- Make an altar for her and place upon it eggs, wild flowers and wreaths of wheat.

Altar offerings to honour and give thanks to Baba Yaga include:

- vodka
- wheat
- bread
- decorated eggs
- bones and skulls
- images of Baba Yaga and of her house.

INVOCATION TO BABA YAGA

To purposely call Baba Yaga into your energy you will need the following, but don't worry if you are unable to source all of the ingredients as your focus will determine your connection with her:

- patchouli or sandalwood incense
- a small dish of salt
- geraniums or a small bunch of wild flowers
- a mortar and pestle
- geranium essential oil
- a bloodstone crystal.

Light the incense and sprinkle some salt around you in a circle for protection as you ask the goddess for her blessings. You can do this silently in your mind using whatever words come to you or you can say out loud:

Divine goddess, I ask you to bless and protect me as I focus on the divine light within myself as I call upon you, the Dark Goddess Baba Yaga, for assistance. I graciously receive your lessons with an open heart in gratitude. Help me to serve, help me to shine. In love and honour, so mote it be.

Grind some of the flowers in a mortar with the pestle and mix in a drop of pure geranium essential oil. Dab the floral mixture onto your third eye and your heart centre to soothe and assure you. Hold the crystal in your right hand to bring in love and ground you. As you focus on inviting Baba Yaga to you say:

Baba Yaga, grandmother,
I call to you and to no other.
A gift invites you in, my dear,
to take away my pain and fear.
Change and loss will serve me well.
Lessons learned? Time will tell.
I invoke you in, to connect as one.
So mote it be, with harm to none.

Leave the remaining flower sprinkles and the crystal at your garden gate as a heartfelt gift to welcome Baba Yaga. Once you've consciously invited Baba Yaga in to your energy field she will assist you in coping with the change and loss she brings in answer to your plea, and upon you bestow the providence needed to survive this stage of the dark night of the soul and assist in any magickal workings, including healing.

Baba Yaga's wisdom and advice come from her long and experienced life, which makes her a most sought-after sage and healer. She will leave you clues of her presence, such as:

- You suddenly keep seeing chickens: live ones, ornaments, pictures and so on.
- You crave eating chicken legs.
- Occasional scents of sandalwood or patchouli essential oil waft around you.
- You are drawn to sit under a birch tree.
- A mortar and pestle presents itself.
- You start noticing the change in seasons.
- You feel called to work with bloodstone, tourmaline or smoky quartz crystals.
- You experience great loss and devastating change at this stage of the dark night of the soul.

EXERCISES AND RITUALS TO ENGAGE WITH BABA YAGA

JOURNAL WORK

Write down, along with the answers, the following questions in your journal:

- What is keeping you reliant on others?
- Where does your lack of confidence stem from?
- Do you feel that the opinion of others counts more than your own?
- What steps can you take to trust in your own decisions?

- How would you feel if you were truly independent: excited or fearful?

List any negative experience you've endured recently and look to the lessons that were presented in each situation:

- What have you learned?
- What was the outcome?
- How do you feel about each experience now the lesson has been revealed?

BANISHING NEGATIVITY RITUAL

Although considered to be an evil hag across Christendom, Baba Yaga actually makes for a very powerful ally. If you were to come across her strange chicken-legged cottage in the woods you would most likely find her at the stove, which stretches right across the width of her hut to demonstrate her size and ability when it comes to working magic. The stove represents fate, for whosoever fails the near-impossible tasks she sets is thrown in to be cooked and eaten. An unusual banishing ritual, but effective nonetheless!

Baba Yaga is a powerful witch with little patience or time for anyone who doesn't serve her worth, so she is a wonderful goddess to call upon whenever you need to hex or banish anyone or anything from your life that no longer matches your higher purpose. In spite of her appearance, she is only all too willing to assist those who wish to make better of themselves and to change, even if it's just in small ways.

Baba Yaga is a powerful goddess to work with during a waning dark moon for banishment spells. Surrounded by birch trees, the forest in which she lives is extremely magickal: as an excellent wildcrafter, Baba Yaga uses birch bark for banishment and to ward off evil. The light silver bark represents renewal and rebirth, which is associated with the energy of Baba Yaga, and is also used in besoms for a fresh sweep.

Invoke her for any banishing rituals by placing a mortar and pestle on your goddess altar and burning white, red and black candles so her super magickal powers can flow through. Anoint your temple with a drop of sacred essential oils such as sandalwood, patchouli or geranium for clarity and connection. Baba Yaga will also assist you in the aftermath that banishing brings by empowering you to embrace the change and loss she ushers in.

Chant this powerful affirmation while holding a piece of birch bark or when sitting under a birch tree:

I am a witch.
I am of power, that I know.
I have the power to lose and say 'No!'
I have the power to change things around.
I have the power to choose what I've found.
I have the power to speak out and to be.
I have the power to truly be me.
I am a witch.

BABA YAGA HEALING RITUAL

Although Baba Yaga's energy can seem harsh and angry, she is a powerful and natural healer who offers to cure ailments and suffering through her secret recipes of natural and herbal teas, tinctures and potions all brewed up in a cauldron on her wide stove.

For this ritual, sit in a quiet place, close your eyes and visualise you and Baba Yaga flying in her mortar high up above the dark forest. See her turn to you with a glint in her eye and tell you that you must be broken before you can ever be completely whole. See her grind you up into little pieces with her pestle until you become completely fragmented. In this state you can't feel like you any more; in fact, you don't even know who you are, what your beliefs are or anything you once knew.

As though in limbo, your soul cries out for you to be restored. Baba Yaga hears your cry to become whole, and she will always respond. As she sprinkles the waters of life over every part of you, the trauma of fragmentation starts to heal and slowly your parts knit together and transform into the whole of who you truly are. You will feel refreshed and much lighter now you have become wholly restored, for all your unnecessary traits, hurts, fears and behaviours, which no longer serve you, have been ground down and banished.

Death to the old!
New life awaits!
Death and rebirth,
cycle of the Fates.
So mote it be.

BABA YAGA CRYSTALS

Baba Yaga also works with the elemental forces with an understanding that they have the power to heal and to harm; for instance, she manipulates fire for its warmth, life force and destructive nature through spell work and healing purposes. If you are feeling unwell or unable to move beyond your sense of victimhood, the following crystals kept on or near your body may help you gain the strength to fight through into empowerment:

- **Bloodstone:** a powerful blood cleanser and healing stone that heightens intuition and creativity, and a grounding and protecting stone that draws off negative environmental energy.
- **Garnet:** revitalises, purifies and balances energy, bringing serenity or passion as appropriate. It inspires love and devotion while alleviating emotional disharmony.
- **Smoky quartz:** neutralises negative vibrations, lifts depression and disperses fear and brings in emotional calmness, relieving anxiety and stress.
- **Tourmaline:** diminishes fear and attracts protection, inspiration, tolerance and prosperity.

LESSONS FROM THE DARK GODDESS BABA YAGA

Baba Yaga is a healer who insists you are familiar with the cycles of life and death, for this understanding will pull you through this very first stage of your dark journey – the stage of great loss and unwanted change. Baba Yaga helps you to realise that the experiences you are suffering are harsh life lessons you need in order to discover just who you truly are.

Baba Yaga does not look kindly on those who have more than they need in life, and she will take from those who don't appreciate what they have. Do you really wish Baba Yaga to teach you her hard lesson in understanding loss, for the only way to learn is to experience what it is to go without. Perhaps you've lost a great deal more than you bargained for, and if this is the case then Baba Yaga has purposely stripped you of that which you held on to too tightly and urges you to appreciate what really matters in life. Give praise where it is due and learn to hone and cherish what you have, including your talents and passions.

Baba Yaga has the power to help or hurt anyone who crosses her path. Those who seek her wisdom, truth and knowledge must first complete several tasks. If the tasks are completed she will provide help, but if the tasks are not fulfilled and the seeker has not found a way to escape she will cook and eat them.

When you look to other faery tales for comparisons you will see that Baba Yaga is most certainly the crone, the Dark Goddess who can be likened to the wicked witch in the story of Hansel and Gretel. Both children were lured into a witch's cottage, imprisoned and fattened so the witch could gobble them up, bones and all. For centuries these scary stories of Baba Yaga have been told by parents to keep children close to home, but the stories are also used to teach children to be polite, respectful, and kind for it is these character traits that render Baba Yaga powerless in her attempts to kidnap and eat children. She teaches you that whoever possesses a loving and honourable heart can overcome even the worst evil.

You can look at Baba Yaga as being an antagonist as well as a source of guidance, for there are stories in which she assists those in their quests and others where she kidnaps children. She is a reminder of how you should conduct yourself in the face of change and loss. Seeking her out for assistance is a dangerous manoeuvre, although not so if you have properly prepared and have purity of spirit and basic politeness, all the key ingredients if you are to survive in life. However, you may not always be aware of or prepared for the pitfalls that could await you, so when danger lurks in the darkest shadows then outside forces require you to be on your guard.

The first exercise you are encouraged to undertake looks at what may soon change in your life, and remember: when you surrender to Baba Yaga she will accompany you as you retreat within and decide what you need to let go of and all that you need to preserve. Use your time with her wisely and you will be the stronger for it, as you encounter the next stage on your journey through the dark night of the soul – a place that pushes buttons, invites knee-jerk reactions and is presided over by the Dark Goddess Fuamnach . . .

7. FUAMNACH

Initiation of emotional triggers

Emotional triggers rule indeed.
Envy's a dangerous thing to feed.
Knee-jerk revenge just isn't right.
Release obsession, see the light.

ORIGIN	Celtic (Irish).
NAME	Fuamnach.
GODDESS	Hera.
SYMBOLS	water, worm, butterfly, fly.
THEMES	jealousy, envy, obsession, inner child, guilt, shame, transformation, revenge, storms, scrying.
LESSONS	knee-jerk reactions, outbursts, control, revenge.
COLOURS/CANDLES	black, blue.
CRYSTALS	green aventurine, blue calcite.
HERBS/FLOWERS/OILS	bergamot, marjoram, yellow hyacinth.
MOON PHASES	waning, dark.
SEASONS	autumn, winter.
TREE	ash.
FESTIVAL DAY	Sunday.

You can have no peace of mind when you are consumed with envy, jealousy, wrath and revenge, as the Dark Goddess who joins you for this phase of the dark night of the soul can testify. Driven by her own name, which means 'jealousy', Fuamnach is an Irish faery queen who has earned her reputation as a demonised, jealous troublemaker. This beautiful, cunning witchy goddess was the first wife of Midir, the lord of the underworld and son of the Dagda. Fuamnach was skilled in the knowledge and magick of the Tuatha Dé Danann, the supernatural folk of the goddess Danu – the most ancient of all Celtic deities; references have her as both goddess and god and the all-encompassing divine source – and one of the great ancient tribes of Ireland. The manuscript known as the Annals of the Four Masters shows that they ruled Ireland from 1897 BCE to 1700 BCE.

After many years of marriage, Fuamnach was outraged to find that she had been betrayed by her husband: he had taken a younger, more beautiful second wife, Étaín, whose light shined brightly for all to see. They met while Midir was staying with his foster-son Aengus Óg, the god of love, and the two began a passionate love affair. In an angry and jealous rage Fuamnach, who was raised by a wizard, used her magickal powers to turn Étaín into a shower of rain, which quickly become a pool of water. As the water condensed it turned into a fly that brought sweet music to Midir's ears, and he let the fly rest on his shoulder wherever he went. Infuriated that the spell on Étaín hadn't put Midir off, Fuamnach turned poor sweet Étaín into a butterfly to blow her away forever. Midir was heartbroken, and spent all his days and nights searching for her.

Battered and torn, Étaín survived in this delicate form for many years until a storm blew her to Aengus Óg. He changed Étaín back into a woman from dusk until dawn every night, when she met up with Midir and they once again became lovers. When Fuamnach heard this she again became enraged, turned Étaín into a fly once more and summoned a powerful storm to blow her away for many, many years until she flew through the window of a mortal king's castle and fell into the queen's goblet. The queen swallowed the fly whole as she knocked back her wine and fell pregnant.

Born again as a mortal woman, Étaín grew up with no memory of her past life, although she was just as beautiful. When the high king of Ireland, Eochaid Airem, asked for her hand in marriage she agreed, but Midir never stopped searching for her and after thousands of years, to his joy, he finally found her again. He begged her to return to him and won her in a game of chess, but as Étaín was now mortal she remained loyal to her husband. Even though she had suffered betrayal and great loss, Fuamnach got her cold revenge in the end – that is, until the end of another version in which Aengus is furious with her for what she has done and cuts off her head!

MESSAGE FROM FUAMNACH

'As a woman scorned I am best avoided, for my obsession for revenge consumes my every poisonous thought. This morbid preoccupation devours my every waking moment and has become the driving force behind acts of vengeance. It's payback time!

'You may consider my reaction to treachery volatile and quick off the mark, but believe me when I say they had it coming. Don't judge me too harshly: when emotions are hijacked it's hard not to rise to the bait. When your hard-wired beliefs and expectations aren't lived up to the disappointment and let-down bludgeons you at lightning speed, hitting you like bullets. Being provoked triggers waves of emotion that send you spiralling over the edge before you know it, and that's when the damage is done. Knee-jerk reactions, such as screaming, shouting or even self-harm, to anything deemed as a threat such as obstacles, pressure, rejection or unexpected situations is primitive survival in its highest form – and I should know. Fuming on the inside while ranting and raging on the outside is easy fuel that accompanies emotional outbursts and regrettable actions.

'Do not seek me out to soothe your tortured mind, for I will only encourage you to take revenge for yourself. My jealousy is toxic and my anger misplaced. Instead, learn from my reactions, which in turn will protect you from any backlash.'

SEEKING FUAMNACH

Fuamnach is cunning and as skilled in witchcraft as she is in magick, for her foster father was a Druid wizard. She has shape-shifting and transforming powers, and Fuamnach witchery expertise is as a weather witch. As a weather witch Fuamnach works with the basic elements and the chaotic and unpredictable forces of nature, and she knows how to raise gusts of wind, to summon up lightning and deliver torrential rain in order to blow her enemies off course. She draws to herself her power when casting spells and is able to conjure weather spells and spells for retribution with just one strike of her scarlet rowan wand (she chose rowan for its protection, robustness and ability to break charms).

As Fuamnach continues to bring you down low on the wheel of fortune, the devastation of loss and sudden change that Baba Yaga brought will leave you feeling well and truly out of your comfort zone. Panic and fear may set in, which is when you will start to react very strongly to situations in such an automatic way you won't think about your words or actions. This type of knee-jerk reaction is typical of the second phase of the dark night of the soul. Emotions will run high and reactions to trauma can be so dramatic that you know longer recognise who you are, and nor does anyone else around you.

Knee-jerk reactions to drastic change and loss could cause you to seek Fuamnach out, inviting in a powerful energy that is so strong it might blow you away so approach her with caution. As always be careful what you wish for, and be mindful of your thoughts and emotions when you seek Fuamnach for assistance at this stage of the dark night of the soul. She does not have to be discouraged when it comes to assisting in the ways of revenge and will lend a helping hand all too willingly.

Fuamnach looks to those who understand her plight and vengeful actions, for her honour was shamed when her husband Midir turned to another. The fullness of the insult left her bereft and bewildered: how could he desert her this way and what could she do to win him back? Can you imagine what it must have been like for her when her own husband introduced her to a younger, shining and more beautiful model? She would have gone into a state of shock and panic, her mind whirring with what to make of it and what action to take.

I can recall the time when my father returned home with his mistress. I was thirteen years old, and it was one hell of a shock. He, very much like Midir, wanted to show my poor mother why he had fallen for this other woman, for us all to see and understand how lovely she was. As she trembled at the threshold of the front door, my mother confronted her angrily because that was her knee-jerk reaction to the situation. She didn't take her anger as far as Fuamnach did – she didn't turn the mistress into a worm, but I bet she sure as heck wanted to and who could blame her?

As a woman scorned, Fuamnach has a very good memory and is one dark goddess whose fury just won't let it go. In fact, she is passionate about getting her own back. Approaching her full of rage and with a vengeful attitude will only rattle her, and she will encourage you to seek your revenge to the full and then suffer the consequences. However, if you seek her in an honouring way she will be lighter in her approach. Reminding Fuamnach that she is beautiful in her own right will soften her vengeful passion and drive.

She will help to expose any emotions you're not dealing with very well, such as envy and jealousy. She will draw to you anything that triggers such emotions, and in the end you will have no choice but to learn how to accept that what you desire is not always yours for the taking, nor can you continue to behave in such a volatile manner. Fuamnach's absolute passion is all about revenge, but she also encourages those who seek her to be passionate in all they do for she knows that passion is an intense desire that will drive you to be challenged, intrigued and motivated. It's an inner strength that drives you towards your desired outcome.

DARK GODDESS COMPARISON

Fuamnach can be likened to Hera, the Greek goddess of marriage and queen of the heavens who was the sister and wife of Zeus, the Greek god of gods. Hera was feared for her jealousy and vengeful acts towards the many lovers of her husband and their offspring. She is also a weather manipulator, just like Fuamnach, who raised a frightful sea storm to drive away Hercules, the illegitimate son of her husband and one of his many lovers. She was also put aside when Aphrodite was chosen over her in the name of beauty. Like Fuamnach, Hera knows all about rejection. When anger or jealousy gets the better of these dark goddesses they have no concept of fairness or forgiveness.

REASONS FOR WORKING WITH FUAMNACH

The Dark Goddess's strength is empowering and potent enough to transmute any guilt, shame, fear and blame that needs releasing, but you need to identify with such emotions first before you can heal. This will cause you to start doubting everything you once loved about yourself; in fact, your emotions will see to it that you don't even know who you are any more. That sensible, happy-go-lucky person you once were has disappeared in a puff of smoke and you have become a shell of your former self, and when the green-eyed monster starts rearing its ugly head you might start comparing yourself to others. You may find yourself in constant competition with those who have what you once had. Envy such as this causes you to desire so strongly that nothing else matters, and your obsession for possession could blind you.

When something shocks you to the very core – a death, great loss, medical diagnosis or any unwanted or volatile change – it can be terribly difficult to not act out emotions in response. If the devastation leaves you feeling vulnerable, afraid and emotionally wrecked, listen to your words. What are you saying? What do you want to say? How is your body responding: are you jumping up and down in a rage or do you want to lash out and punch a wall? Is this your normal behaviour, how you would usually respond to something unexpected?

This is the frustrated child within you. Once you come to realise that it's not the adult you who isn't coping with frustration you can become more observant. Just before you start to scream, shout and let it all out you need to realise it's the child in you and not the mature adult who wants to kick off, otherwise you will become blinded to solutions for an outcome because everything will seem to be beyond your control. Just as a child looks to an adult to take the responsibility for them, you feel that someone else must be responsible for the situation you find yourself in, that someone else should have looked after you better or should have had your back, and that's when the knee-jerk reactions will set in.

THE TRIPLE TRIGGERS OF GUILT, SHAME AND BLAME

Guilt is punishment enough;
it drowns the heart and makes it tough.
Guilt's a bully in all but name,
inviting in her sister, Shame.
Between the two they'll take you down.
Release! Move on! Now change that frown.

The heavy weight of guilt will cloud your judgement and cloak your outlook, causing your stomach to churn or for you to hang your head in shame. Beating yourself up serves nobody and will only make you feel worse, for it will tear you apart and devastate your self-esteem. Instead, acknowledge any unacceptable behaviour, take responsibility for your words and actions and own up before a situation gets out of hand. No matter how deeply they are stored, feelings of guilt demonstrate you have the capacity to acknowledge your part in the dilemma, which is the first step of the healing process.

Regret, dishonour hangs in shame,
points the finger, takes the blame.
Shame's a bully you must jilt,
who invites her sister, Guilt.
Between the two they'll make life sour.
Stand tall, move on, reclaim your power!

Being racked with shame is a horrible situation to find yourself in, and this is often the case with anyone who is going through a dark night of the soul. Emotions run so high they become hard to control, and you won't know when you might explode. It's as though you are a ticking time bomb: anything could set you off, as you are highly strung and defensive and acting out of panic and fear. Sound familiar?

However, if people are judging you for something that was out of your control or they disapprove of then shaming you is not acceptable. It is for them to get over, and to not be your judge and jury: a little support wouldn't go amiss. You may find yourself in the grips and control of another person as part of your dark night experience. Again, feelings of shame could feel justified to you if you're being made to feel that way. They are not! As you come to understand that you are not to be blamed in any way, have forgiveness for yourself and earn it from those who may be reeling from your actions by coming from a place of good intentions.

Even if you did happen to wish for some kind of change for the better to come about, you didn't expect the dark situation that came in answer to your prayers so it's much easier to put the blame on someone else. That way you don't have to feel responsible for whatever your loss or sudden change is. You may wish to blame the Dark Goddess herself, for it was she who heard your soul's cry for transformation, it was she who stripped you of all you once knew and it was she who took you out of your comfort zone to face up to all that no longer serves your highest purpose. However, the Dark Goddess is usually furthest from your mind when your world is crashing down around you.

Who have you blamed: is there anyone you've pointed the finger at or blamed for your suffering? It's interesting how we often have to find somebody or something else to blame, isn't it? It's natural human behaviour to insist on causal explanations for everything. You may blame the weather, traffic, a spouse or anything else, but when you feel that the situation is not your fault, that it is out of your control and you are not to blame you cannot take responsibility. The Dark Goddess has deliberately delivered your suffering to see how well you respond. It may present itself in various guises, such as:

Relationship break-up: how many other people can you blame for the break-up? Is it your ex-partner's fault or the fault of the person they ran off with? Did somebody else encourage the split?

Medical diagnosis: receiving bad news about your health will send you reeling. Blaming an incident on another may be justified, but whose fault is it if an organ fails or you've been diagnosed with chronic illness? Dig deeply and you will find someone else to blame somewhere.

Death: the loss of a loved one is mortifying, and you may find that you blame yourself. Please try not to.

Self-blame: one of the most toxic forms of emotional self-abuse. If you blame yourself for something that is beyond your control, please release the guilt. It does not serve you, your situation or anyone else involved, so don't beat yourself up.

As you walk the path of no return with the Dark Goddess, she will help you take steps towards peace of mind and acceptance as we explore every stage.

RECOGNISING EMOTIONAL TRIGGERS

It's interesting how emotions can be triggered. You could wake up feeling perfectly happy, that nobody could get you down today, then an innocent word or sentence is uttered by someone and without warning your emotions are all over the place. Something has just reached deep within you and pulled on a memory that caused you to feel fear, just like that! With no time to think it through, your body reacts to the pain of the memory from fear that the dire situation will happen all over again perhaps before you even realise what the issue is.

What could occur physically when this happens? Your eyes might well up as you feel a pool of great sadness within. Your body could go into shock, causing you to internally shake. You may get a sudden bout of diarrhoea or vomit as the shock affects your system. Your reaction to the trigger is immediate, and is often acted out in a way that is not necessarily socially acceptable. Emotions may cause you to suddenly burst into tears or become edgy, snappy or defensive, or you may explode into an angry rage as you shout and scream, not caring who witnesses your torrid explosion. In a split second your body will react to triggers while your emotions play out any fears attached to the memory that has just surfaced; there is no thinking about what was said when it comes to knee-jerk reactions.

Can you recall a time when this has happened and what it was that made you act out? What was the trigger and how did you react? Were you scared of how you reacted or surprised at how strong your emotions were? How did other people react to your eruption and how did that make you feel? It would be helpful to note down anything you felt in your journal. Think back to a situation in which someone reacted in a way that was highly emotional. How did it make you feel: did you cringe? Perhaps you felt embarrassed for the other person.

Managing emotional reactions means choosing how and when to express the emotions you feel. People who do a good job of managing emotions know that it's healthy to express their feelings and that it matters how and when they express them. Because of this, they're able to react to situations in productive ways such as:

They know they can choose the way they react instead of letting emotions influence them to do or say things they later regret.

They have a sense of when it's best to speak out and when it's better to wait before acting on or reacting to what they feel.

They know that their reaction influences what happens next, including how other people respond to them and the way they feel about themselves.

Those who work this way do so in conjunction with the universal law of cause and effect, for they understand that the outcome of every thought, word and deed creates their future. However, when you are taken through the dark night of the soul high emotions are birthed along with great loss or devastating change, something that occurs beyond your control. Not being in control of a situation or of your life any more is an easy invitation to let emotions spiral out of control.

Perhaps your situation is causing you to react so strongly you struggle to control your feelings. There will be nights and many days filled with sorrow, anguish and pain, which is typical of this stage of the dark night of the soul. The Dark Goddess not only expects you to deal with the disruption she has recently dealt you, but also the old hurts from the past that she uncovers as an extra surprise. As she unearths hidden emotions that have been festering possibly since childhood such as envy and jealousy, she will expose these lower agitations and you will have no choice but to either learn to accept and embrace these darker qualities of yours, to only use them as and when they are vitally needed, or to release them if you come to find they no longer have any purpose as you move forward.

You can be sure that the dark night of the soul will weigh you down with conflicts, highlighting issues of revenge and anger depending on your situation. It's easy to let emotions run the show and allow things to get out of control; you may also find your mind starts working overtime. Suddenly old grudges and destructive patterning from your past will get dragged up, usually something that bothered you a long time ago, a circumstance you thought was healed, dealt with or had at the very least been pushed to the back of your mind. However, the Dark Goddess will make sure that any emotions you need to deal with anything that's been ignored, that's been stuffed down, will reappear in such a way you can't refuse it, for the Dark Goddess knows there is no way forward for you unless old cycles that do not serve your present or future have been broken.

Everything that comes up for you to deal with in this lifetime does so because it hasn't been resolved yet from this life or from previous lifetimes. You may find you have a lot of work to do, however, the moment your emotions and your attachment to them heal you will be released and won't have to repeat the process ever again.

Everything that is thrown at you is ultimately to help you grow, for you cannot evolve until you acknowledge each lesson and understand its meaning for you. The power is yours to own the moment you realise the need to break free. As you release anything that does not serve your higher purpose, be open to ridding yourself of emotional attachment and undo any vows you've made in any lifetime that have prevented you from moving forward in this lifetime. Have you held on to something for too long knowing it should be released, but you can't quite let go?

Sometimes you may hold on to hurts as a reminder to yourself to never allow the situation to happen again, as a defence or a crutch to lean on. Your ego self kicks in and whispers weasel words of treachery and destruction about yourself and about other people, and when you are low you will listen to every mean word that is uttered. You start to believe the lies about yourself and about others and your confidence dips, and you feel the lower emotions of guilt or shame. Insecurities creep in and you beat yourself up with thoughts about how worthless you really are. It doesn't matter if you have always been full of confidence, as your emotions will strip you of that until you become a shadow of your former shining self. This is the stage of your journey when emotions start to run the entire show. There will be a river of tears, and you will howl, scream and shout and ask yourself 'Why? Why me?' over and over.

Your ego self has your best interests at heart and doesn't give one jot about the consequences. As far as the ego is concerned, as long as you are protected that is all that matters. The problem is, reacting in this way doesn't solve anything. What it does do, however, is show you where and from what you need healing, and this is the purpose of facing any old stuff that comes up when the Dark Goddess is in charge. She knows the embedded pain and hurts you still harbour and hold on to even if you don't even realise it on a conscious level. Subconsciously you will remember, and when a trigger causes you to react to a recollection you will be as surprised as the person who just witnessed your sudden outburst, which was very out of character for you. Or was it? Your inconsistent behaviour may not concur with your usual personality, but perhaps you had a small glimpse or recognition of a part of you that you thought you'd left behind as you transitioned into adulthood. That part of you is known as your inner child.

REVISITING YOUR INNER CHILD

Your inner child is that beautiful, innocent, creative, imaginative part of you that just wants to have fun. It's the part that reminds you not to take things so seriously, to lighten up and splash about in puddles. Each one of us has an inner child, a part of us we thought we had left behind when we became adults. However, inside you are the unhealed wounds you suffered in childhood, which your inner child still carries around. Your 'little me' developed coping mechanisms that helped you back then but most likely do not serve you as an adult. As you grew into adulthood you learned new coping skills, yet when you feel you aren't being listened to or when you feel left out, abandoned, isolated and scared it is often your inner child who reacts in response to the things you feared or witnessed as a child.

In most of us there is a part that is unhealed from emotional wounds and traumas experienced in childhood, and it's not necessarily anyone's fault as we all perceive events differently. It stems from the way the inner child feels after years of not being validated, seen or heard. Basically, you are a small kid in a big adult body with the emotional, mental and cognitive abilities of a child who is trying to act grown up. You were never taught how to deal with your emotions.

As you grow you come to understand what behaviour is socially acceptable and what is not. Learning how to behave appropriately in the eyes of others means learning a new way of coping. It's not done on a conscious level, for you won't have even realised as you go about your adult life; however, you've never been taught how to handle adult emotions. As an adult you have no idea that you have an inner child or that it is often them who is making your adult decisions for you, and when something doesn't go your way it's more often than not the inner child instigating your reactions. This can lead to childish temper tantrums, feelings of inadequacy and general insecurity.

Your inner child has a place within you for laughter, play and fun, helping you find balance in a rigid adult world; without your inner child there would be no silliness, creativity or joy in your life. That part of you can never leave; that part of you needs to be listened to, loved, validated, heard and nurtured. When this is not heeded the fun part of you withers away, causing you to be deadly serious in any given situation and lose your inner joy. Your inner child can also become sulky and moody for being ignored and play up, and that's when your behaviour can start to look very out of character for the adult you.

Understanding your inner child is key to understanding any difficulties you may have with relationships in the workplace, at home or socially. When you come to understand that you still have the child part of you, a part that is still very much active, you will begin to observe your emotional reactions. When you consider how you've reacted to sudden change or loss, who is it that is running the show? How would your adult self react to such a situation? How did you react: did you display your emotions maturely like an adult or were your emotions acted out by your inner child? Were you shocked at how you behaved?

When you go through the dark night of the soul it is the emotions of the inner child you are dealing with and that others are witness to. Your inner child is scared and fearful, so in situations it can't control or when it feels threatened it will respond in childish ways through outbursts of grief, anger, jealousy and envy, which are often born out of shame and guilt. Your inner child doesn't know how to deal with emotion in any other way. If you have been surprised by your reactions and how you dealt with them it is because your frightened inner child needed to be reassured. It is not easy when you as an adult have no idea what's going on or how to deal with new circumstances. More times than not your first reaction is a knee-jerk one that is not considered, and all too often it just makes things worse.

KNEE-JERK REACTIONS

Self-blame can often lead to self-shame. When you feel ashamed for your actions or behaviours you tend to project your anger onto others to cover up your shameful feelings and gain back some control. When you blame someone else and truly hold them accountable for your misfortune, resentment kicks in. You know they are at fault, so when you watch the perpetrator carry on without a care in the world you may become very angry: at them and at your situation. You may find yourself asking 'Why should I have to go through hell?' and saying 'It's not fair! Why should I suffer?' and 'How come they've got away with it?' Anger is a completely normal, healthy human emotion.

How many times has a driver flipped you the bird when you've sounded your horn in response to their driving, and this has negatively affected you? How did you respond? At first you may have found yourself feeling astonished at their shock behaviour towards you, then a flash of anger rose up in you and made you want to yell obscenities and return the gesture. Did you, or did you take a deep breath, simmer quietly and send the driver loving thoughts? When you do this you will feel more in charge of yourself and your life, but when anger gets out of control and turns destructive it can lead to problems on many levels.

Anger is explored in more depth later in the book, but know now that deep anger can cause you to lash out verbally or even physically, which is when you could really get yourself into trouble. When you stew about a situation or what you feel someone has deliberately done to harm you, the bitter indignation at having been treated unfairly may give you a warped sense of injustice – so much so that each and every time that person says or does something you resent them and feel annoyed or bitter. A grudge may develop and you find you take umbrage when you see them doing well. Jealousy has now taken over the show and you act out in spite, malice and hostility. A sense of lack that makes you feel inadequate will cause you to be envious of a person who has what you wish for or once possessed yourself. When envy is directed at another or others and you desire their qualities, success or possessions, you may idealise those traits and believe they will bring you the happiness and fulfilment you crave and restore all that you have lost.

This is the age of envy, or at least it seems to be. Everybody else seems to have it all and we believe that when we have it all we will be happy just like them! We watch reality shows, which really should be called 'fakery' shows, and wish we had skinny figures, bigger lips and perfect eyebrows just like all those taking part in the TV program. You may feel envious of a friend's new partner, house, job or even their life and wish you had the money, looks, talent, passion or even common sense they possess. Trolling on social media is a perfect example of envy, and it is a twisted way to bring someone down. Seeing images online of others looking perfect, happy or courageous is an invitation to intense competition and comparison, which can leave you seething.

As covetous thoughts invade your mind a sense of entitlement may sweep over you, which emerges from feelings of being mistreated or not getting what you need. It can be a way of saying 'I deserve to be taken care of. I deserve special treatment, just as much as they do.' This is when you may take it one step further to get what you want or to get your own back. Revenge is a dish best served cold, which suggests that the act of getting your own back is much more satisfying when enacted unexpectedly. Acting out of vengeance is a form of emotional release: you think that getting retribution for someone else's wrongful actions or words will make you feel much better. Giving the person what is coming to them is a way of gaining closure. There are many revenge stories about those who have cut up their cheating partner's best clothes, thrown their belongings into the street and even secretly sewn smelly old fish into the hem of their curtains, all in the name of revenge.

What would you do to get revenge? How far would you go? Do you think it would make you feel better, or would you be fearful of the consequences? As we have discovered, Fuamnach's revenge was pretty severe and she never gave up until her nemesis was well and truly out the picture, or so she thought. She had the advantage of possessing supernatural powers and wielded her dark powers to work a little shape-shifting magick, which is transformation taken to the physical extreme. Have you ever felt close to revenge? What did you want to do? How far will you go to get revenge, and have you ever imagined going to extremes to get rid of someone? Maybe you've already got your revenge; what did you do and how did it make you feel? What was the outcome?

VENGEFUL REACTIONS

King Henry VIII of England is a perfect example of somebody who ruled by knee-jerk reactions. When things didn't go his way, courtiers avoided his Royal Highness in fear of his frightful retribution. Most people are no strangers to the story of the infamous serial monogamist king who went through six wives to secure a male heir for his throne. Henry's obsession for a son dominated his life and influenced his everyday decisions when it came to marriage, the throne, his friends and counsel. He feared not having a son so badly that when his baby boy died in childbirth or a daughter arrived instead he blamed everyone else around him, particularly the wives involved on each sorry occasion.

Many suffered at the hands of his uncontrollable emotions as he resorted to capital punishment, killing those whom he perceived could not give him what he most desired. This knee-jerk reaction to loss caused Henry even more loss, despair and unhappiness, and he created fear wherever he went. Everyone was terrified they'd be put to death the next time something went wrong for old Henry.

Revenge is sweet, so they say, but is that really the case? It didn't work out very well for Henry. Is it really wise to take action against those who've harmed another, or can we learn from such stories? Acts of revenge and retribution that arise from envious emotions feature heavily in many a tale from bygone times and can be learned from in this day and age. Faery tales are rich in symbolism and teach us morals and values if we read between the lines. The wicked queen gave Snow White a poisonous apple in an act of revenge, for she was jealous of her ward's natural beauty and fearful of losing her position of power. Cinderella's wicked stepmother refused to allow her to attend the prince's ball in an act of revenge, for she was envious of Cinderella's relationship with her father (the stepmother's new husband) and of her pretty features and kind heart. In the tale of Sleeping Beauty, a wicked faery placed a curse on the young princess that causes her to fall asleep for 100 years, until she was awakened by true love's kiss. This act of retribution was enacted as revenge against Princess Aurora's father, the king.

Notice how it is always the character that most resembles the crone, the Dark Goddess, who is portrayed as the envious, jealous perpetrator of revenge and retribution. You are meant to fear her, to avoid her if you can, for it is she who presides over your destiny as she spins your fate, and you can choose to grow or fade in response to her harsh lessons. However, there is always wisdom to be found within the tales and experience and knowledge from yesteryear's wise woman, and you can learn that you don't need to be afraid of doing the right thing. When you get yourself into a mess you mustn't dig yourself in deeper to avoid the consequences. If you accept responsibility for your problems you will gain strength of character.

TRANSFORMATION BECOMES YOU

Étaín's story is one of transformation. When Fuamnach transformed her into a butterfly it was symbolic of transformation, rebirth and resurrection, which reminds you that you too will shine like her and be reborn. Remember that butterflies are not born as such; they must go through a series of difficult stages first that represent the initiations you face as you journey through the dark night of the soul. You have to go through some degree of loss and change before you can truly metamorphose into your whole and fabulous self. Étaín teaches us that whenever there is a storm the sun will always comes out to shine afterwards.

It was Fuamnach who gave Étaín the gift of transformation in the first place, and you too can call upon her for just that. You can invoke Fuamnach to help with your very own transformation, but be warned for it will not be an easy or comfortable process. She will expose your lower agitations, highlight any jealous areas or envious thoughts and eventually help you to focus your energy in a direction that is healthy and for your higher good. She will assist in raising magickal storms if that is what is needed and teach you to never cast spells in anger, for they seldom work the way you wish them to. Just look at the outcome in the alternative ending to Étaín's story.

As you begin to understand and heal from this stage of your dark journey, try to rejoice in the beauty and talents of others instead of fearing their success. Remember that there is no such thing as competition when it comes to your life purpose, so instead of trying so hard to capture attention, allow your inner light to shine as you cut ties and move on.

PREPARING FOR FAUMNACH

Fuamnach is no stranger; you've met her before, for she's been witness to every jealous outburst you've had, each act of revenge, and she has encouraged every one of your knee-jerk reactions. She has spectated from the sidelines and spurred on every lower action, cheering you to go on and stealing your light. However, she's also a goddess who offers to lead you out of this phase of the dark night of the soul through her gift of transformation. It was she who chose to change the form of her femme foe rather than doing away with her entirely, which means her bark is worse than her bite.

Perhaps you can relate to that right now. Reactions could cause you to lash out, to scream and shout, but deep within it's a cry for help to end this sorry state of affairs you've found yourself in. Are you ready to purposefully seek out this dark and scorned goddess? Fuamnach willingly greets you if you wish to deal with your reactions to loss and change, and is happy to assist in getting revenge or in understanding the emotions behind your reactions. Either way, it makes no difference to her. However, be warned: if you find it hard not to react then you may find Fuamnach encouraging you to wreak all sorts of havoc in the name of revenge, and you might get turned into something very unsavoury!

You may have subconsciously called in Fuamnach on a soul level when you wished:

- to keep your emotions in balance
- to be a better version of yourself
- to not react so quickly in the face of adversity
- to shine brightly.

You may have unwittingly called in Fuamnach when she heard you:

- think up vengeful plots against another person
- express envy of another person's good fortune
- complain that others have what you want
- comparing yourself unfavourably with others
- obsessing over what you can't have
- wishing you could punish someone for what they did to you
- feel your inner spark and passion fade.

Turn to Fuamnach when you wish:

- to get your own back
- to understand your emotions
- for justice
- to control your reactions.

As soon as she hears your invitation to come into your life she will appear, whether you requested her subconsciously or not.

HONOURING AND CONNECTING WITH FUAMNACH

Do the following to honour and connect with Fuamnach:

- Compose and recite to her a poem about her beauty.
- Draw or keep pictures of butterflies.
- Work with the element of water for scrying.
- Hang a flycatcher in your home.
- Make your own worm farm.
- Listen to or play pipes and harps.
- Show her your commitment by being passionate and driven.
- Make an altar for her and place upon it a chalice of water and butterfly trinkets.

Altar offerings to honour and give thanks to Fuamnach include:

- butterfly trinkets
- worms
- black or blue candles
- green aventurine
- blue calcite
- representations of the sun
- a photograph of you as a child.

INVOCATION TO FUAMNACH

To purposely call Fuamnach into your energy you will need the following, but don't worry if you are unable to get hold of all of the ingredients as your focus will determine your connection with her:

- incense
- a small dish of salt
- a blue candle
- a chalice or goblet of water
- decorations of butterflies.

Light the incense and sprinkle some of the salt around you in a circle for protection as you ask the goddess for her blessings. You can do this silently in your mind using whatever words come to you or you can say out loud:

Divine goddess, I ask you to bless and protect me as I focus on the divine light within myself as I call upon you, the Dark Goddess Fuamnach, for assistance. I graciously receive your ability for emotional control with an open heart in gratitude. Help me to serve, help me to shine. In love and honour, so mote it be.

Light the candle and place it on your Dark Goddess altar or on a table. Gaze into the chalice of water until your eyes go into a trance-like state. As pictures start to form physically or in your mind's eye, Fuamnach will shine light onto your situation and any areas of darkness will be revealed. Do not fear; be relieved, for this dark goddess has the potential to save you from drowning in dangerously dark and murky waters and from yourself. As you focus on connecting with Fuamnach say:

> *Pool of water give me sight.*
> *Darkened shadows restore light.*
> *Goddess Fuamnach guide me well,*
> *relieve me of your darkened spell.*
> *Accept, I shall, your power in me,*
> *as I heal from my triggers I am set free.*
> *I invoke you in to connect as one.*
> *So mote it be, with harm to none.*

Drink the water from a chalice, safely snuff out the candle and step out of the circle, then say:

> *Gratefully I accept the magick of you,*
> *and protection to assist in all that I do.*
> *Lend me the courage, build power in me;*
> *assist my transcendence, so mote it be.*

Signs that Fuamnach is around you include:

- You keep seeing butterflies.
- Worms appear underfoot.
- You become snappy and irritable.
- You can't control your reactions.
- You react with childish retorts.
- Your inner light fades.
- You feel guilt or shame.
- You're driven to seek revenge.
- Jealousy eats you up.
- Stormy weather appears.
- You hear the sweet sound of pipes and harps.
- You experience jealousy and can't control your knee-jerk reactions.

EXERCISES AND RITUALS TO ENGAGE WITH FUAMNACH

JOURNAL WORK

Have you ever been a victim to someone's obsession, and did it make you feel drained of your life force energy? When somebody thinks about you constantly, especially if they are angry or vindictive, you can suddenly become tired or fatigued because the person who is thinking about you is pulling on your energy. Likewise, if you keep thinking back to an old argument or playing out a scene in your head you are re-creating that situation with the energy you're giving it and both yourself and the other person will be affected on an energetic level. Perhaps you feel you haven't received the support you expected, or perhaps you're furious with your partner or parents. Knee-jerk reactions can take you beyond the limits of reasoning to a place of self-destruction. Panic sets in through your fear of having no control over the situation, and a desire to regain all you have lost sweeps over you.

In your journal, write out and respond to the following questions: who pushes your buttons? Who do you find easy to blame for your misfortunes?

ACCESSING FUAMNACH ENERGY TO EASE EMOTIONAL REACTIONS AND JEALOUSY

Fuamnach will protect you from the jealousy of others and from your own knee-jerk reactions as you take steps to balance all the aspects of your life. If you feel you need to break free from emotions and knee-jerk reactions that are keeping you tied to the past, this is a powerful ceremony that will enable you to break free and become empowered with a new sense of freedom. Fuamnach invites you to step out from the shadows of the past and claim the life you wish to live in the here and now. Use the fragrances of essential oils associated with her to help calm any knee-jerk reactions and soothe a jealous mind.

For this exercise you will need bergamot essential oil to uplift your mind and help soothe anger, anxiety, insecurity and fear, and marjoram essential oil for emotional support and calmness. Gently anoint your heart chakra with a drop or two of sacred oil to connect with Fuamnach as you say:

*I anoint this oil upon my heart,
knowledge and wisdom to impart.
Connecting us as one, is my request,
through sacred scent I'm truly blessed.*

Close your eyes and breathe up Fuamnach's sacred scent, allowing it to infuse with your energy.

SHAPE-SHIFTING YOUR ENERGY

Many dark goddesses are seasoned shape-shifters who can turn themselves into animals at will, such as a crow or raven. If you could shape-shift, what would you like to be able to do and how would it help your current situation? Would you choose your favourite animal or something that suits your needs at this moment? Shifting your energy into another form can really affect the way you engage with the world, allowing you to see it differently and understand the perspectives of other people and get empathy from them, as well as embody some of the characteristics of your chosen form.

Find a quiet place for this exercise. Close your eyes, take a deep breath and focus on the characteristics of the animal you have chosen. Breathe them into your energy, into your very being, and start to feel them. In your mind's eye, see the natural surroundings of that animal and imagine that you are there. Imagine you are the animal itself and see everything through its eyes.

As you continue to do this you will be taken on a visual journey in your mind and become one with the animal. Eventually, with practise, you will be able to take on the feeling of becoming an animal at will. You may find it frightening at first, for you will feel only the body and characteristics of the animal you have become, but do not fear for an easy transformation back into your own mind and body is assured.

EMOTIONAL RELEASE CEREMONY

For this ceremony, place a blue candle in the direction of west and a small bowl full of water at the magickal time of dusk on your goddess altar. Say:

Dark Goddess, oh Fuamnach, I call upon you to destroy my reactions, and give me value. Drown guilt and blame in water so clear so I am released from my plight and all fear.

Tear a sheet of paper into large pieces and write on each piece a word that represents any emotions that cause you to have knee-jerk reactions that you would like eliminated from your life such as envy, jealousy, resentment. Place one piece of paper at a time into the bowl of water and hold it down to drown your unwanted emotions and knee-jerk reactions. As you do, the Dark Goddess will assist in eliminating and transmuting those emotions in your life that do not serve your higher purpose. Say:

The door is closed, I won't look back.
New road ahead, back on track.
Release old ties, to set me free;
paper holds past energy.
Submerge in water, hold it down;
allow the past to fully drown.
Gratitude for lesson learned.
New door opens, truly earned.

When each piece of paper has been placed in the water, place the bowl in the freezer so your unwanted emotions are frozen in time and are unable to reclaim you in the present or the future. Carefully blow out the candle and say:

Protected by the Dark Goddess,
who watches over me.
Emotions from the past released,
for I am now set free.

It is time to rise and see the truth from all perspectives! Place a chalice of water and a blue candle on your goddess altar in honour of Fuamnach, and for healing on an emotional and deep soul level.

LESSONS FROM THE DARK GODDESS FUAMNACH

It's not really surprising that Fuamnach obsessed over seeking revenge, for she suffered her own dark night of the soul when her husband fell in love with another. Surely that would make any wife seethe! As much as you may defend these actions, envy poisons your mind until you just can't think straight any more and becomes an obsession. Fuamnach's reputation as a jealous, envious, bitter witch who would stop at nothing to make sure Étaín did not have the happiness with Midir they both desired preceded her. She used her magick to transform Étaín, ensuring that her husband could not look upon his new love's beautiful face. Fuamnach's jealousy consumed her and became an obsession, for the loss of her husband was too much for her to bear. She lost herself in her need for revenge, which is not the best path for any soul.

A new direction will emerge, but only if you have learned the lessons of the past and gained wisdom and emotional control through those experiences. If not, it is very likely you will soon come into contact with the Dark Goddess again, this time in an even darker place in which concealment and denial take hold. She awaits you now; her purpose will bring you a step closer to overcoming all that holds you back and keeps you hidden in the darkness.

8. HEL

Initiation of isolation and denial

Concealed within a personal hell,
isolation hides you well.
Reach within for secrets hidden,
denying all that's not forbidden.

ORIGIN	Norse.
NAMES	Hel, Hela, the hidden one, goddess of death, queen of Helheim.
GODDESSES	Maman Brigitte, Santa Muerte.
SYMBOLS	evergreens, white flowers, dogs, wolves, black and white, rotting fruit, Hagalaz rune.
THEMES	dark magick, compassion, death, reincarnation, rule, denial, secrecy, necromancy.
LESSONS	acceptance, honour, patience.
COLOURS/CANDLES	black, white.
CRYSTALS	black agate, obsidian, jet, onyx.
HERBS/FLOWERS/OILS	myrrh.
MOON PHASES	dark, new.
SEASONS	Samhain (spring), winter.
TREE	elder.
FESTIVAL DAY	every Saturday.

This dark goddess is one scary and confusing witch to look upon, for her appearance is both beautiful and fearsome. She is often depicted as a half-black and half-white monster, with one side of her face being a greenish black colour, with clear, smooth skin and a high cheekbone revealing a grim beauty similar to the face of the wicked witch of the west from *The Wizard of Oz*. The other side of her face is composed of rotting white flesh just like that of a corpse's, exposing bone, sinew and dark caverns. Her deathly face rocks a sinister and gloomy look that gives her a grotesque half-dead, half-alive air, while her presence is vast, commanding and magnetic and you will feel her pull as she waits in the silence of the darkness you will retreat into. She governs the world beyond that of the living and is the magick that makes thin the veil between worlds.

Hel's reputation has been greatly perverted over the years and used as a scare tactic to frighten the masses into religious submission. The concept of 'hell' was created by those in authority in the newly formed Christian church as an afterlife location in which evil souls were subjected after death to eternal suffering and torturous punishment, which makes Hel one of the most misinterpreted and misunderstood goddesses in history. She rules over a realm of the same name, but don't mistake it for one of fire and brimstone as depicted in Christian teachings for her underworld is void of any warmth. Instead, the poor souls who journeyed across icy lands to her lair could expect an eternity of frigid cold death and torture.

Hel's realm was the basis for the Judeo-Christian place in which, upon death, sinners are banished to and tortured for an eternity. However, unlike the Judeo-Christian concept of Hell, Helheim also served as the shelter and gathering place of souls to be reincarnated. From her magickal advantage point of the underworld, Hel watches over those who die peacefully of old age or illness and cares for both children and women who die in childbirth. She guides those souls who do not choose to die in battle, for they go to feast in Valhalla through the process of death and rebirth.

Like many other dark goddesses in history Hel has been demonised, but who is she and is it justified? Hel is the daughter of the Norse trickster god Loki and Angrboða, a giantess, and her siblings were

Fenrir the wolf and the Midgard serpent Jörmungandr, who lies at the bottom of the ocean wrapped around the world, holding it together with his tail in his mouth.

Hel grew up in the land of the giants until Odin, the king and ruler of the Æsir, decided she should live with the gods in Asgard, for this is where her father Loki hailed from. Odin is one of the first of the Æsir gods, and was born of the primal giants of Jotunn. He was the father of many, including Loki and his brother Thor, the god of thunder. However, when Hel arrived her grim features did not please the other gods, and they rallied for her to be cast out of Asgard. Ashamed, Hel seized the chance to be hidden away and she became the goddess of death when Odin gave her Niflheim, one the nine worlds, to rule over.

In Norse Mythology the nine worlds are Niflheim, Muspelheim, Asgard, Midgard, Jötunheimr, Vanaheim, Álfheimr, Svartálfaheimr, Helheim, and they are held in the branches and roots of the world tree Yggdrasil. Known as the 'house of mists', icy cold Niflheim was situated in the lowest level of the universe, in the realm of death. It was a place of constant wailing, with walls built out of worms and human bones. In one section of the realm was the Shore of Corpses, upon which a castle of venomous serpents stood facing north. It was full of murderers, perjurers and adulterers who suffered at the hands of a dragon named Nidhogg.

Hel became the ruler of the underworld and welcomed all souls who had not died a warrior's death. In times of plague and other disasters she would ride her white, three-legged Hel horse searching for lost souls to gather for her kingdom. On her return to her palace, which was named Eljudnir, she was waited upon by two servants called Ganglati and Ganglot who never appeared to actually move. They served her meals in a dish named Hunger and with a knife named Famine. Here she enjoyed entertaining the dead in a weird, macabre way before retiring to her bed, which was named Sickness.

In return for her new position Hel gifted Odin two ravens named Huginn and Muninn, or Thought and Memory, for the power of thought creates and memory keeps that creation alive. The two ravens flew across the nine worlds and returned to report back to Odin on all they saw and learned throughout the kingdoms.

Hel's realm was named for her, and those who died a natural death or one of ill health and disease are forced to tread the path of no return through the icy lands where no fire can live to the gates of Helheim. There she waits to determine the fate of each soul in the afterlife, rather like a grisly alternative faery godmother!

Hel isn't entirely sinister, for she is capable of showing a glimpse of compassion as demonstrated in this tale. Baldur was born to Odin and Frigg, the goddess of love, and was loved and admired by all of the gods and by mortals. He was so handsome and cheerful that he shined brightly. Baldur began to have dreams of his death, and because he was no warrior his soul would be sent to Helheim to reside with Hel for eternity when he died.

Odin mounted his horse and rode straight to the underworld to consult a seeress for her wisdom on the unfortunate matter. He arrived in disguise to find that among the misty cold the halls were decked out in grandeur for a feast in honour of the newest resident to arrive. The seeress was very moved about Baldur meeting his doom. Sad and sorrowed, Odin returned to Asgard to report his findings. His wife Frigg was so distraught at the harm that would befall her son that she went out and sought every being, living or otherwise, in the cosmos to obtain oaths not to harm him. All agreed, apart from mistletoe. Upon hearing this, Loki, being a mischief and trouble maker, went out of his way to find some mistletoe and made a spear from it.

When he returned he found his fellow gods having good fun by throwing anything they could find, such as sticks and stones, at Baldur, who was very much alive and shining. Frigg's plan had worked, and everything that was thrown at Baldur just bounced straight back off him and left him unharmed. Loki gave the mistletoe spear to the blind god Höðr, and encouraged him to shoot. With Loki pointing the old god's hand in Baldur's direction, the spear was thrown and pierced the heart of Baldur, who died on the spot. As the gods trembled in fear they understood this event was the beginning of the end, the downfall of the cosmos and the forewarning of the great cosmic battle Ragnarök. Frigg asked if there were any among them who would brave the journey to the underworld to offer a ransom in return for Baldur's release. Another of Odin's sons, Hermod, offered to take up the quest, and was given Sleipnir, the eight-legged horse, to ride upon.

Baldur was to be given a funeral pyre fit for the son of a king, but his wife, Nanna, was so overcome with grief she collapsed and died and was herself placed on the pyre alongside her husband. Every being from across the nine worlds turned out for the ceremony, and as the ship burned and dissolved into the ocean, gods, dwarves, Valkyries and giants watched and mourned.

Hermod rode Sleipnir for nine nights through deep dark valleys, battling giants and crossing torrid rivers as he followed his quest to rescue Baldur's soul from Hel. When he eventually arrived he was shocked to see Baldur sitting in the seat of honour next to Hel's throne. He pleaded with Hel for his brother's release and told her how all living things, including the gods, missed him and keenly felt his absence. Hel listened then declared that if this was so she would send him back, but only if the whole cosmos wept for him: if there was even just one being who refused to weep she would keep him.

Hermod rode all the way back to Asgard and messengers were sent straight out to bear the news to all inhabitants of the cosmos. Tears were shed as the worlds wept for Baldur – everything, that is, but the giantess Tokk, who cold-heartedly said that Baldur could go to hell and that Hel could keep him! To no one's surprise Tokk was Loki in disguise, and by his act he condemned Baldur to an eternity of freezing darkness, to never shine his beautiful golden light again.

Hel's power exceeds far greater than that of any other, for once someone is in her power no one, not even Odin, can successfully reclaim any soul she has in her possession. Without Hel's permission no soul can leave her kingdom to return to the living.

MESSAGE FROM HEL

'Restriction and control has dimmed your spirit and suffocated the expression of your soul. Your power is eternal, yet you are held down by the heaviness of burdens and tied into emotional commitment. I know the difficulties you have faced, for it has indeed been an arduous journey. There are only so many times you can endure harsh criticism, judgement and unfair comments, all because somebody fears your power, having recognised your full potential on all levels, and has led you to buy into false doubt, worry and insecurity.

'The world has waited long enough for you to grace it with your individuality: it's time to be your authentic self and to no longer cower behind the mask you have worn for far too long for fear of being persecuted. Believe me when I say I understand your desire to fit in with the world around you, but I also hear the deep call of your soul. It is time to reveal the truth of the situation, even if it is only to yourself, for you must not hide your true self any longer. Trust that I will guard you well as you take those first brave steps of authenticity to what will ultimately be your freedom. But for now this is a time for quiet, a time for reflection, to be still. The peace you crave requires you to slow down, to stop thinking and take time out. Give yourself a chance to be silent, be still, breathe and go deep into the sanctuary within. Here in this sacred place you will find restoration of balance and harmony. Once you have convalesced in tranquillity you will sense peace in every moment.'

SEEKING HEL

Hel walks between the worlds, bridging the gap between the living and the dead. It is she who encourages the ethereal whispers, fleeting dark shadows and ghostly presence in the dead of night that you might have experienced, for she wishes you to believe in the afterlife. If you feel drawn to or seem to have a natural ability to connect with the spirit world and those who have passed over into Hel's realm, it is she who has bestowed upon you the gift of communing with spirit and she encourages you to honour those who walked before you.

Her dark gifts of isolation and insecurity will force you into her hiding place, where she will welcome in you and your secrets in order to consume your fears. As she strips you of your self-esteem and you begin to conceal the truth to save face you will witness the death of all confidence, which is when denial will sweep in.

Finding yourself in between the worlds, neither here nor there, is not comfortable, when you feel half-dead but also half-alive as you try to hold on to what's left of the light. However, the pull of darkness will become stronger when this stage of the dark night is exposed, and you should be careful not to be drawn in for this is when the darkness seems most inviting.

Disruption, changes and stress about the unexpected will have taken their toll, and you'll find it hard not to part with anything as you desperately cling to the familiar vestiges of who you are and anything that has become a security blanket for you. As you come to terms with the after-effects and shock of your emotional outbursts, you will see before you a darkness, a pulsating black void throbbing with a macabre presence and inviting you to cross the portal into another world: a world that beckons you and draws you into the depth of its darkness, where you can hide away within the safety of its shadows. As you slowly sink into what you can only describe as a living hell you will be greeted by Hel, whose world is one of secrets that are hidden away and shrouded in deep mystery and silence. This is a hidden-away place of concealment and denial.

Hel's presence is vast like a pulsating black void, and her deep, hypnotic power is seductive and strong like a black hole drawing you into the dark side. However, as the goddess of the underworld sunlight weakens her resolve, so shine as brightly as you can if ever her super powers have a hypnotic effect on you and you feel pulled in.

Despite her magnetic darkness and icy attitude, Hel exudes a rare power that mirrors your own inner darkness. You may wonder if death will bring punishment or peace, but she asks you to not be afraid and instead face that which you have avoided for so long. You should never approach her with a negative attitude towards death and decay. Misunderstood and rejected for centuries, this goddess of death welcomes those who approach her with acceptance and open mindedness, for death is to be embraced if you wish for transformation and peace of mind.

DARK GODDESS COMPARISON

As a goddess of death, Hel can be compared with the Haitian queen of the cemetery, Maman Brigitte, a very powerful dark goddess in voodoo beliefs. She guards over cemeteries as a figure representing the first female buried in every voodoo cemetery, and protects and lays souls to rest. Maman Brigitte has the final say in who will be redeemed of their sins and who shall suffer from having their own sins inflicted upon them.

Similarly, Santa Muerte (Saint Death) is depicted as a frightful hooded skeleton holding a scythe in one hand and a globe in the other. This deadly Mexican saint truly is a personification of death itself, much like Hel, and could be mistaken for the grim reaper. Santa Muerte, however, also offers protection and safe passage to the afterlife to all those who honour her, for death goddesses are often looked upon as being maternal and almost loving in times of sorrow and loss. Her lesson is one of duality, a bittersweet combination of pain and love co-existing as she offers compassion and understanding while she snatches from you a loved one or something you hold dear.

REASONS FOR WORKING WITH HEL

Hel will assist you in coming out from a place of denial and isolation. When you are in denial you think it protects you from unjust condemnation, and you don't want to look bad to others as their opinion counts for some reason. Quite often people don't admit to themselves they have a problem at all, but denial is the first barrier to recovery.

Suppressing intense emotions can be dangerous, especially if you have hardwired your emotions to help you survive. Thwarting emotions is not good for mental or physical health, and you may find yourself turning to addictive substances and behaviours to avoid your feelings and drown out your thoughts. From alcohol use, drug use (prescription or otherwise) to hours of screen time, including on social media, there is a multitude of ways you can avoid having to face up to your feelings and the situation you are in.

If this sounds like the kind of steps you've been taking to desist from 'fessing up, you could quite possibly be in denial; here are some of the signs:

- You avoid talking about the issue.
- You project your bad behaviour on to others.
- You promise you're in control to ward off the concern of other people.
- You won't admit there is a problem.

- You take addictive substances such as alcohol or drugs to shut out your feelings.
- You blame others for your problem.
- You ignore the advice of or concern from loved ones.
- You start to lie to cover up, even if they start as little white lies.

If you feel you are avoiding the issue and can't admit the truth of the matter to yourself and/or others, let's have a look at why that could be. What is denial exactly, and why do we go there?

Denial occurs when people don't wish to acknowledge the bad stuff, not only to others but also to themselves. This could include a debilitating illness, a violent or torrid relationship, a break-up, weight gain, a loss, rape, verbal abuse or threats. You can deny a fact, deny responsibility, deny the impact of your actions or deny what is really going on by hiding away from your feelings, but why do you do this? When you go into denial you do so to avoid embarrassment, to save face and to pretend that everything is just fine. The word 'fine' means 'in good health'; however, it is often misused and uttered to conceal true feelings. If anyone tells you that they are fine when you ask them how they are, its acronym will demonstrate that they feel anything but!

F = fucked up
I = insecure
N = neurotic
E = emotional

Nobody wants to admit they can't cope, so in an attempt to keep it together you try to adjust to the dark night of the soul by neglecting the real impact it has on you, but by doing so you will find yourself drawn into a river of contradiction called denial. When you use denial to defend yourself or as a coping mechanism you are contradicting the reality of the situation. You might deny the reality of your emotions, because accepting a reality that is uncomfortable, painful or incongruous to what you expect means you must also alter your perception of yourself. Denial helps you to ignore the truth about how you feel and prevents you from having to deal with it.

However, the extent of denial may not really be the issue at hand. What's important is not that you recognise denial but that you are able to accept the feelings that led to the denial in the first place. Denial hides the shame of being exposed, and from your hiding place you can go through a cognitive process in an attempt to alter your experience of unwanted emotions. Maybe you're in denial to give you time to adjust to your distressing situation. You might feel embarrassed about the whole sorry affair, whatever it might be, and don't want to look like a fool in front of others. We often refuse to acknowledge a bad situation in the hope that it might change for the better, and if this is the case who needs to know? Or you may simply bury your head in the sand in the hope that it will go away. When you feel backed into a corner your vulnerabilities leave you feeling insecure and force you to withdraw into your shell, to run and hide!

Hel knows all about hiding, as she was forced into it to conceal her formidable appearance; 'she who hides' is the translation of her name. Like Hel, when you are in denial that's in effect what you are doing: hiding from everything, from everybody, just wishing it would all go away and wishing you could go back to the way things were. However, much has changed and the dark night of the soul is, after all, the path of no return; there is no going back. What you once knew no longer exists. As you retreat into hiding like a hermit you step into the sacred space of within, in which you won't be challenged by others. Hel will meet you in the secluded grove of your inner sanctum, where it is safe to reveal hidden secrets to yourself.

THE ENIGMA OF SECRETS

Secrets are mysterious, intriguing and attractive to the seeker. People always want what they can't have, but to the keeper the forbidden information is often too dark to share or could cause harm if it were. None of us are strangers to secrets: we held on to them in childhood or shared them with our best friends. Back then secrets were fun, especially when it came to keeping a diary or hiding little notes in a locked treasure box.

Secrets are everywhere! They are hidden all around the world, often to keep control of and the truth from the general population. Underneath the Vatican is the sacred site of Cybele, which is dedicated to the Anatolian earth goddess. When the Delphi oracle prophesied a famine and failed harvest in Rome, Cybele was brought to Rome in the form of a black meteoric stone. The site of St Peters stands upon her foundations, which includes a pagan burial ground and an Egyptian obelisk as well as other pagan artefacts. Why would the centre of Catholicism, a religion based on patriarchy, require the powers of the goddess? Perhaps it's because they know the true powers of the goddess and work her in secret. The secret to the powers of the universe is often hidden from the masses and the knowledge kept for the few under the guise of religions based in secrecy. History is filled with evidence of secrets, as many ancient temples, tombs and places that kept ancient knowledge such as the Library of Alexandria were all destroyed and erased from memory.

Have you ever tried to keep a secret in the past? It's hard, isn't it, so you know the effort that goes into hiding something. What was the reason for keeping your secret: was it so that another couldn't be part of something you wanted for yourself, or was it something you felt ashamed of, something you didn't want anyone to discover for fear of being found out? How would you feel if someone kept something hidden from you? If you are told to keep away from something that is out of bounds, do you adhere to the rules? Would you understand that the secret was being kept hidden for a reason?

Whenever anything is hidden, kept secret or lied about it is to keep another from the truth! Hel will shed light on that which is hidden to reveal the truth so you can live the life you came here to live. However, following your soul's path often means upheaval, emotional pain and loss in order to gain everything: it's the only way! What's the point in living a lie and settling for a life that is only second best to what you could have, and living in the illusion of ease and comfort? Many people do this for years, believing they are happy without realising that beyond the rainbow exists their true potential. Hiding your feelings doesn't mean they go away, and looking okay on the outside doesn't mean you feel good inside.

HIDING BEHIND A MASK

Nordic shamans called upon Hel as their protector and guide to watch over them as they journeyed into her realm of death seeking experience of the great unknown in order to find themselves. To pass through the gateway undetected they wore a *helkappe*, a magick mask of invisibility, to disguise themselves.

All of us wear a mask to some degree. Both women and men enhance their features by putting make-up on their faces before stepping out of their front door. Clothing is also a mask: there are many personas you can project in the clothing you wear, including Goth, hippy, punk, casual, sporty, designer and businessperson, which tells the world who you are. But does it really? Since I was a teenager I have preferred to dress all in black and wear heavy black eye make-up. I love the look, as it makes me feel good and also makes me feel brave! So, really, when I dig deeper I guess I dress in this way to disguise my feelings, my insecurity, when I'm out and about, but nobody would guess that. In fact, I'm looked upon as somebody who is highly confident as I stride out in my punky boots.

The one thing I haven't got swept along with is non-surgical procedures, but there are many out there who boost their looks with Botox, fillers and other toxic substances so they look acceptable to themselves and others. It's the done thing, and it's so easy for people to pop out on their lunch break to have an injection or two. Why can't we be happy with the way we naturally look? In this day and age people are scared of the ageing process; we all try to appear younger than our years. Billions of dollars are spent each year on preventing our age lines and the effects of a lack of collagen. Society seems to only embrace youth, the maiden, whereas the crone should be avoided for she is the old, ugly hag. Such nonsense!

What's your disguise? Do you wear make-up and, if so, why: is it to enhance your looks so people will think you're more attractive than you think you are, or is it because you truly enjoy wearing it for yourself? It's so important to always be honest, as it's the only way to break through the barriers to truly knowing yourself. Which clothes do you prefer to wear? Maybe you like to look smart, to portray an air of good breeding, or perhaps you are a slave to fashion and have got to be seen in the latest garments. Imagine how amazing it would be to get dressed every day in whatever clothing you felt would express who you are and how you feel. Think of how freeing it would be to act in the appropriate way to your true personality, how wonderful it would be to admit your genuine likes and dislikes and act accordingly, never minding the judgements and opinions of others.

Our masks aren't always physical: we often change our personality to fit in with situations. I'm sure you're a different person at work than you are when you're at the pub! When I was 13 I was taken out of boarding school and put into a state school. It was a huge culture shock for me, as I hadn't been the most popular girl at my previous school but I had nice friends. I had watched and learned from the in crowd, so at my new school I presented myself as someone everybody wanted to be friends with. It worked, and I continued to be that person: popular, pretty and the life and soul of the party, so much so I truly believed I was. I wanted to be seen as being attractive, fun and confident and the person to get in with and admire, but that wasn't who I really was deep down. I had been a kind, sensitive and spiritual soul in my younger days but I tried to forget this. Through my self-belief and the belief of others I manifested into the person I wished to be.

Why is it that when we are facing a debilitating circumstance, whether it's illness, grief or any other challenge, we try to keep going? We should be able to give ourselves time to go within and journey to the route cause, to be gentle with ourselves and to nurture ourselves with kindness and compassion. I think perhaps it's because of other people's expectations of us and because of the responsibilities we have to meet. We smile and pretend we are fine, that all is okay, if we can. We put on a mask and fight through any challenges. Is this so that we don't look weak, or to impress others?

Princess Diana was looked upon as being the most beautiful woman in the world, and perhaps the luckiest. At just 19 years of age she was engaged to the Prince of Wales, and would be a queen in waiting. Thousands of people watched across the globe with joy in their hearts as she married her handsome prince and hoped they would live happily ever after, but it was not to be. Soon after the wedding Diana discovered hidden secrets that were to reveal her marriage was a sham, for her husband had previously concealed his desires for another woman. To hide her shame and pain and the devastation she felt about the situation Diana controlled her emotions in public by putting on a persona. She smiled and laughed and dressed immaculately in up-to-the-minute fashion styles that wowed the world. As she threw herself into charity work to rescue others, she herself needed saving from the effects of her pain. As she tried to overcome the demons of bulimia – a knee-jerk reaction and emotional coping mechanism – nobody on the outside realised her torture, for she had painted such a convincing mask. That was, until the time came for it to fall off, and sadly for Diana she never got to reveal who she really was underneath it.

Do you wear a mask? Think about how you are with others: do you change according to whose company you are in or depending on the situation? Maybe you wear many different masks: for work, out socially and when you're with family. It is time to reveal the real you: do you even remember who that is? Maybe you'd like to show to the world who you really are but are scared of the reactions of others: what if you are rejected in some way? Are you brave enough to step out and expose your true nature? Sometimes we go out of our way to be the person others expect us to be. Is that so they don't think less of us, I wonder, or so that we don't let them or their expectations down?

Maybe you're not ready to become unmasked and are reluctant to let your props go. Your disguise is your security and serves you well for now, but what would happen if you dropped the act? How would others react when they realised you aren't at all who you appeared to be? Would you be treated differently? Ask yourself these questions and don't be afraid to admit the truth in your answers. Only you can decide whether you are brave enough to be your authentic self or will continue to hide within a world of illusion.

PREPARING FOR HEL

Hel appears to those who are destined to die, to those who are to join her in her icy realm of Helheim and to those who are to experience a death of the old, an ending of sorts. She seeks out those who have hidden away in denial for fear of being exposed. Are you ready to purposefully seek out the death of all you've been denying? Hel willingly greets the souls of those who wish to face up to the truth of the matter. She will uncover all insecurities, fears and worries that you've been concealing, but be warned: if you refuse to come out of isolation you could remain frozen in time for all eternity.

You may have subconsciously called in Hel on a soul level when you wished:

- for the truth to be revealed
- to be 'discovered'
- to clean up your act
- to be honest with everyone
- to be your authentic self
- for a hunger for spiritual truth.

You may have unwittingly called in Hel when she heard you:

- express fears about going to hell
- fearing death itself
- crying out for death
- retreat from the world
- deny the truth
- run away to hide
- fear the truth
- pointing your finger at other people and blaming them for your situation
- harbouring secrets
- deceiving others
- sitting alone among gravestones
- being someone you're not
- covering your tracks
- telling deliberate, bare-faced lies
- hiding the real you behind glamour
- going hungry
- refusing to believe in the afterlife
- honouring and connecting with the deceased
- naming your household furniture.

Turn to Hel when you wish:

- to face up to the truth
- to own up
- to admit to your addictions and clean up your act on all levels
- for an ending of sorts
- to face the fear of death and endings such as relationships
- to understand and embrace death
- for comfort at the loss of a dearly departed loved one
- to commune with the ancestors.

When Hel hears your cry through the icy darkness she will seek you out to expose your deepest fears. As she forces you to face each one in turn you can choose between admittance or denial, to heal or to remain in your own personal hell. The outcome is down to you; either way, she's not bothered.

HONOURING AND CONNECTING WITH HEL

Do the following to honour and connect with Hel:

- Visit a cemetery and tend to the gravestones.
- Offer a drop of your blood in return for pain and fear.
- Dress in black and white, dedicating your look to her.
- Drink black tea and white coffee in her honour.
- Pour a glass of red wine in honour of the ancestral dead.
- Pay your respects to the dead.
- Plant white flowers or an apple tree.
- Offer support to the bereaved.
- Listen to Nordic folk music.
- Let apples rot.
- Sprinkle black rose petals on your bed before sleeping.
- Make an altar for her and place upon it rotting fruit, black roses and a glass of apple cider.

Altar offerings to honour and give thanks to Hel include:

- white flowers
- sprigs of evergreens
- pictures of your ancestors
- a black shroud or veil
- a black and white framed picture of Hel
- black crystals such as obsidian, jet or onyx
- a Hagalaz rune.

INVOCATION TO HEL

To purposely call Hel into your energy you will need the following, but don't worry if you are unable to get hold of all of the ingredients as your focus will determine your connection with her:

- myrrh incense
- a small bowl of salt
- a black crystal such as black agate, obsidian, jet or onyx
- a black cloth
- bones (use bones left over from a roast dinner or from a decaying carcass found in nature)
- one black and one white candle
- bread
- a goblet of red wine.

Light the incense and sprinkle some of the salt around you in a circle for protection as you ask the goddess for her blessings. You can do this silently in your mind using whatever words come to you or you can say out loud:

> *Divine goddess, I ask you to bless and protect me as I focus
> on the divine light within myself as I call upon you, the
> Dark Goddess Hel, for assistance. I graciously receive your
> acceptance with an open heart in gratitude. Help me to serve,
> help me to shine. In love and honour, so mote it be.*

Always hold a black crystal for protection and grounding when invoking or working with Hel. Grounding is the essential connection between you and the earth, keeping your roots firmly placed on the planet whenever you are working with the higher forces of spirit and a powerful goddess such as Hel.

Call in Hel during a dark or new moon phase for optimum communion. Place the black cloth on the ground and lay the bones out in the middle. Place the black candle to the right and the white to the left of the bones. Set the offering of bread and red wine in front of the bones and light the candles. As you gaze into the flames, focus on inviting in Hel and say:

> *Lady of Helheim, goddess of death,*
> *hidden in time til my last dying breath.*
> *As I face the dark, embraced in the light,*
> *I seek thy hallows, for all's not black and white.*
> *Daughter of Loki, woman of bone,*
> *for all my misgivings I wish to atone.*
> *A keeper of secrets, I'll not deny;*
> *bless me as I seek you, for I'm ready to die.*
> *I invoke you now, to connect as one.*
> *So mote it be, with harm to none.*

Let the candles safely burn down and pour the wine onto the ground for Hel to receive in the underworld.

So you know she's around Hel will leave you clues about her presence such as:

- You experience feelings of isolation and loneliness.
- You are cold and just can't seem to warm up.
- Situations seem black and white to you.
- You have been told to 'Go to hell!'
- Dogs bark at you.
- Fruit keeps rotting.
- You don't believe what others are saying.
- You can't take compliments.

- You feel drawn to the dark arts.
- You can't bear anyone looking at you.
- You've become withdrawn.
- You connect with the afterlife.
- Death seems attractive.
- You experience denial and isolation at this stage of the dark night of the soul.

EXERCISES AND RITUALS TO ENGAGE WITH HEL

JOURNAL WORK

Refection to reveal that which is hidden: do you have a secret that you wish to remain hidden? Perhaps there's a truth that you dare not share with others: what is it that you fear being discovered? Maybe you're scared of being ridiculed. Are there skeletons in your closet, and what would be revealed if you were found out? What are you hiding and who are you hiding from, and why? Take time to look at the situation, allow any feelings to arise and record these and your thoughts in your journal as you take steps to take ownership of that which you are concealing.

Embarrassing moments that are too awful to speak about are good reasons to go into hiding, as too are dark memories so awful that you may prefer not to talk or even think about them. From a one-night stand to betraying your best friend, to drunkenness or violence, the shame will cause you to hide within the velvet tomb of darkness and keep your murky secrets to yourself. You become a 'secretary', a word that actually means 'keeper of secrets'.

Reflection on facing the truth: How have you actually faced up to your situation: have you admitted the truth of what's going on to yourself or do you wish it would all go away? What is it that you're struggling with and why is that? Write down in your journal all the reasons why you are struggling right now. What strategic distractions have you put in place to avoid dealing with testing times?

Hel teaches you that going into denial can interfere with your ability to tackle challenges, so why should you lie and cover up the truth of a situation? Perhaps you are embarrassed about something you've done, or you've hurt another by seeking revenge or acting out in retaliation. Maybe you've said harsh words that cannot be undone or have deliberately blanked another. Write down everything you can admit to, but don't judge yourself harshly in any way. This exercise will help you to look more deeply into your situation to uncover that which you have been denying.

INCANTATION FOR REMOVING YOUR MASK

Imagine taking a path that leads you down to the entrance of an ancient tunnel. It is dark, but you are aware that you must show no fear so you walk boldly but carefully until you reach the entrance. A serpentine mask hides the doorway, but you see it, push through and find yourself in a huge room. As you scan the room you notice there are groups of people that you recognise, not only from your past but also from the now. Observe who these groups are and where in your life they played a part; they could be colleagues from workplaces, friends from school, social friends, neighbours or peers. As you greet each group in turn, notice how you feel and how you behave with each set. Are you wearing a mask to enable you to fit in with whomever you are speaking with? If so, how does the personality of each mask you wear differ with each group?

Stand bravely in front of a group and remove your mask, allowing these people to see who you really are. What are their reactions? How do they make you feel? Maybe you're nervous, insecure or intimidated or else you feel the fabulous freedom of not living a lie any more. Do this with each group in turn. When you have finished, step back towards the serpentine masked door and notice that from this side there is a great mirror. Stand in front of the mirror. All of your masks have finally been removed and you have finally been revealed. As you gaze into the mirror, who is it that you see? State this incantation:

> *Let's drop the mask, time to be free,*
> *to reveal my true identity.*
> *Shimmer, sparkle, wear bright red,*
> *party hard, or stay in bed.*

Do what I will, t'aint no fuss;
it's my life to be fabulous.
Throw back the mask, take a stance:
no need to hide, for now's my chance.
Live my life, be who I am.
Stand proudly, and not give a damn.

When you feel the call to hide, Hel will guide you through the darkness to reveal the truth of your inner reality and the truth of the 'self' aspect as she tears down the curtains of illusion. She will encourage you to no longer hide and to face up to who you really are. Your authentic self will no longer wish to cower behind the mask that has concealed your soul, for your desire to fit in with the world around you will fade and your heart will eventually embrace the truth that Hel will reveal.

Lady Death urges you to stand up for yourself, to speak up and be exactly who you are. It's no good trying to win acceptance by people pleasing, and from her hidden world Hel will force you to look deeper. Are you a people pleaser and, if so, why: is it so that you aren't berated? Maybe you think it will keep other people happy. One of the things the Dark Goddess has taught me since my dark journey is to not have any expectations of others and to not feel obligated to live up to the expectations of others. If anyone has a problem with me that's for them to track into and ask themselves why they have a problem. I am not the source of anybody's happiness and I am not the source of other people's entertainment; I am whatever the truth calls for. It was the Dark Goddess who peeled back my layers to uncover who I really am through a long process of the dark night of the soul.

INCANTATION FOR COMING OUT

If you feel you are ready to come out of hiding, this exercise will help you to uncover the real you. State this incantation:

From out of the closet, take a stance.
No need to hide, for now's my chance,
to live my life, be who I am,
stand proudly, and don't give a damn!

INCANTATION FOR ANCESTRAL HEALING

Ancestral magick draws energy from the power of the bloodlines of the ancestors and is an honouring of your deceased loved ones and all those who have gone before, shaping your life in some way through their actions. Your lineage is old, and the ancestors aren't just recent but are also ancient. It's important to honour your ancestors to keep their memory and spirits alive by giving thanks to them. When you do so they will impart their wisdom to assist you with your own journey and spiritual work.

Hel encourages you to lay flowers on a loved one's grave or to acknowledge an ancestor whose qualities you may have acquired. You may wish to decorate a small altar with pictures of past loved ones in honour of their memories and light candles in remembrance of them. Honouring those who have walked before you and understanding their ways will help to you to release any hurts and pains.

State this incantation:

Ancestors of blood and bone,
from earth you have to spirit flown.
Honour who you truly are,
wisdom claimed to take me far.
Ancestral lines now heal at last,
and break free from the chains of past.
This magick is worked, with harm to none.
So mote it be; there, it is done.

Dream visitations from your ancestors is Hel's gift, and if one turns up for you in the dreamtime you can be sure it was Hel who accompanied your deceased loved one through the veil.

LESSONS FROM THE DARK GODDESS HEL

Hel represents death without honour and denies everything that is enjoyable, although she can also be kind and particularly to those who stand their ground just as she does. She reminds you to not be fooled by appearances, for beauty is hidden within. Her cold exterior represents the icy sleet and hard season that is winter, with which she is associated as the goddess of death: a time when nature is void of life, trees are stark and the land is barren but all the while the promise of new life is preparing within nature itself, ready to burst forth in spring.

Death is a very important part of the cycle of life; it is a necessity as it makes room for the new, just as rotting animal carcasses provide the earth with nutrients and forest fires clear out dead wood to enrich the soil. Death always has to present itself first, no matter in which form, before the beauty of the renewal of life can ever be embraced.

Hel invites you to journey to the depths of an abyss, for it is her gifts of death and rebirth that will help you to emerge stronger and wiser and become whole and complete, to become light and dark in perfect balance. As you retreat she will take you into the dark, quiet spaces where the truth can be heard most clearly, so that she can shed light on the darkest parts you've feared, ignored and pushed beneath the surface. She will reveal all aspects of your hidden self until you no longer recognise who you are or who you think you are any more. She has been unfairly misunderstood, and she will highlight any misconceptions you've had about yourself and also of others, for not only will the truth of who you are be revealed, you'll come to realise that other people in your life aren't exactly who you thought they were.

However, Hel cannot expose you unless you acknowledge that something is wrong. Refusing to admit something is wrong is often a coping mechanism when you are faced with emotional conflict. It's much easier to reject the reality of painful facts and engage in distraction strategies instead.

As the darkness beckons and you retreat deeper and deeper within, another dark goddess more fearsome than the last one waits for you to sink fully into the abyss. It's time for an encounter with the truly terrifying Sheela-na-gig, who is waiting to feed from your despair and to steal from you all hope . . .

9. SHEELA-NA-GIG

Initiation of desperation

Consumed by thoughts of gloom and doom,
darkness is her sacred womb.
Openings point to go within,
the deep void welcomes all you bring.

ORIGIN	Celtic.
NAMES	Sheela-na-gig, Sheela, Sheila, Síla, Síle nagcíoch.
GODDESS	Demeter.
SYMBOLS	womb, vulva, openings, carved stone, fertility figures.
THEMES	fertility, sexuality, protection, birth, feminine power, feminine mysteries, inner critic, silence, the great void, the mystery.
LESSONS	choices, decisions, reverence.
COLOUR/CANDLES	black.
CRYSTALS:	black onyx, hematite.
HERBS/FLOWERS/OILS	clary sage, rose.
MOON PHASES	waning, dark
SEASONS	autumn, winter.
TREE	yew.
FESTIVAL DATE	18 March.

Hidden in plain sight, ancient sculptures of a woman pulling back her private parts for all to see have sparked disgust and intrigue for centuries. Stone carvings of a woman squatting with her knees parted to expose an enormous vulva can be found in Norman churches and other sacred sites, particularly in Britain and Ireland along with parts of Europe such as France and Spain. This is is Sheela-na-gig. *Sheela* (or *sheila*) means 'girl' and *gig* or *gyg* is Norse for 'giantess', which suggests that Sheela-na-gig had supernatural powers and belonged to the race of pre-Christian giant deities that ruled the earth. The stuff of legends, giants have been worshipped, ostracised and celebrated across millennia.

There is little known documented evidence of who Sheela-na-gig was or why her blatant sexual imagery adorns old churches; what is known is that the sheelas are carved in the birthing position and are presented with their vulva on full show. It is has been suggested that Sheela-na-gig was once worshipped as a Celtic goddess of fertility, but why would she have been placed among the churches? Frequently found in prominent positions in mediaeval churches, monasteries and castles and often presiding directly over the main entrance, sheelas were thought to be much older than the churches themselves and possibly depict a pre-Christian deity.

When pagan worship was encouraged to merge with the new religion of Christianity the builders often incorporated faces of the green man, who represents the spirit of nature, hidden within the walls of the churches. Some believe they were put there in secret to remind the newly converted where their pagan hearts truly lay and that for this same reason the sheela images were incorporated into buildings. However, recent research shows they were included intentionally by the mediaeval Catholic Church possibly as fertility symbols or as protection against evil, or they were made by local carvers for churches to promote successful births. There is evidence they were associated with birthing stones, while folklore suggests that erotic sheela figures were given out to women in labour.

The figures are not of a ripe young maiden ready for the throes of motherhood, instead being presented as old hags with emaciated upper bodies that represent the crone. Were these figures meant to appease grandmothers and the spirits of dead mothers, who might bear a grudge against newborns? Perhaps the figures are sex symbols that represent fertility, used for protection.

What can be drawn from Sheela-na-gig is the depiction of the powerful Celtic goddesses that embody both life and death. The triangular pattern of her vulva evokes the sacred number 3, a magickal number we are familiar with in faery tales of old: three wishes, three tasks and so on. In magickal terms the number 3 is linked with the triple goddess and her aspects of maiden, mother and crone, which represent the cycles of birth, death and rebirth. In this aspect Sheela-na-gig is a symbol of the triple goddess, and her open vulva is a mystical gateway to the otherworld. Perhaps she was strategically placed so that worshippers could reverently touch the stone carving of her open vulva upon entering a church as an invitation to death. This she must offer, for it is only when we die to the old that she can gift to us rebirth.

Similar to Kali and other goddess figures in India and South-east Asia and in keeping with the eternal gifts of birth, death and regeneration, Sheela-na-gig is a dark goddess who has an insatiable appetite to devour.

MESSAGE FROM SHEELA-NA-GIG

'Your weariness and bleak outlook have invited you to join me in my black velvet tomb for a while, for I am an enigma, the deep vacuum of nothingness, only sought out to hide within or for solace. Finding yourself rejected and alone, the darkness of my womb is welcome relief. Rest awhile within my deep embrace and let me consume your gloom, doom and despair.

'You are so desperate for love, assurance and acceptance that your self-value has become null and void. As the keeper of divine feminine mysteries I've shed a tear whenever you dishonoured your sexuality or suffered at the hands of an abuser. Perverting your divinity will keep you locked in deep despair, a place in which you will remain powerless. Be careful not to let the deafening silence of self-blame, guilt or primal urges to spiral out of control, as that will leave you imprisoned and desolate with only feelings of nothingness for barren company. Instead, learn how to venerate yourself with holy reverence, dignity and honour, even within the confines of emotional nothingness.

'I am the guardian of the threshold to the sacred place within, a portal to new life. Meet me at the entrance and we will journey together through the vast blackness of the universe, where you shall eventually be restored. It is only from out of the dark that light can be birthed, but first you must surrender to it.'

SEEKING SHEELA-NA-GIG

After facing the icy depths of Helheim, you will begin to explore the darker recesses of the self where you will be met by a Goddess who will consume you entirely as she pulls you into the torturous depths of your mind. Self-criticism, frustration and depression will seek you out in the terror of darkness, where past battles and memories of betrayal repeat over and over and devour your sanity in the dead of night. All hope will fade as you reach breaking point, and the only way to go now is to hit rock bottom. At this stage of the dark night of the soul you will be at the mercy of your traumatised consciousness and of the dark goddess who has been waiting for you to sink to the debts of despair, Sheela-na-gig.

When you seek Sheela-na-gig you can be sure it's the mystery that shrouds her that entices you in, for when you are faced with an empty nothingness and when your future seems bleak her deep darkness seems like a welcome retreat as you approach her in utter desperation. Desperate for answers as you try to make sense of your dire situation, her pro-creative energy force is too strong to ward off and you will find yourself enveloped within the darkness of her womb.

However, Sheela-na-gig will not acknowledge you nor will she answer any questions you have for her as she is an enigma. She is as mysterious as the universe itself, and she expects you to solve your puzzle without direct assistance as the answers truly lie within and are accessible only to you. All Sheela-na-gig will do is show you the way, inviting you in through her pulled back vulva into the great mystery of the unknown. Be careful, however, not to enjoy the comfort of the darkness for too long, for the persuasive powers to remain in this dark space could leave you wallowing in desolation.

DARK GODDESS COMPARISON

Purely for the fertility aspect, Sheela-na-gig can be compared to the Greek fertility goddess Demeter, who oversees the growth of harvests and presides over the fertility of planted grains and of the earth. She is also a goddess of the cycles of life, death and rebirth and is sought for her regenerative powers of creativity as well as destruction.

REASONS FOR WORKING WITH SHEELA-NA-GIG

Sheela-na-gig is a powerful pro-creative force whose witchery expertise can be found in sex magick, fertility rituals and protection spells. If you are brave enough to seek her in reverence and wish to improve your witchy skills she will offer to share her wisdom and gives you a choice, for she knows that the moment you make a bold decision the mysteries of the universe will support you as you set off in a new direction.

There are always choices and opportunities to those who are brave enough to make a decision. If you choose to take the path to wholeness Sheela-na-gig will encourage you to do so with awareness and honour, for every step you take creates your future. However, she watched when you dishonoured your sexuality, when you gave yourself up to be used like a piece of meat because of your desperation for affection and to be loved. She heard you suffer in shame from the guilt you felt for the abuse you suffered through your need of love and affection. When you believe that some love is better than no love you open yourself up to abuse, because your message is clearly one of desperation to be used and maltreated and screams 'I'm not worthy of love.'

Those who have experienced sexual abuse or rape will know what rock bottom feels like as their safe world crashed around them and left them feeling distraught and powerless. Sheela-na-gig is also witness to those whose carnal exploits are driven by insatiable sexual appetites through an unconscious search for love and some meaning in life. These acts are a cry for help that often stem from a lack of nurturing and love in childhood or are carried out to prove a person's worth and to make them popular and sexually attractive.

Behaving in this primal fashion is a dishonouring of the divinity that resides within us all, and abusing that divinity will keep you locked in deep despair where you will remain powerless. When you exist within the silence of self-blame it is time to make a decision and choose to honour yourself. When you approach Sheela-na-gig do so in honour and reverence, for she is the guardian of thresholds to sacred places. As you meet her at the entrance, in cold, hard silence she will offer you a choice, and if you accept her and the protection she offers she will open up the gateway to the universe. She is the gatekeeper to the vast darkness in which creation is birthed, which is the only direction to go in if you wish to return to the light.

PROTECTION

As I was going through this stage of the dark night of the soul of utter desperation I had a lucid dream that I was being verbally attacked by a woman who was standing at her front door as I walked through my home village. Without thinking, and in immediate response to the verbal abuse and finger pointing, I lifted up my skirt, pulled down my underpants and thrust my pelvic region in her direction, completely flashing my yoni at her. When I awoke I was so ashamed at my actions: I couldn't believe what I had done, that I had sunk so low. How embarrassing! I didn't tell anyone about my dream, even though the vivid images of the scene kept haunting my days. A few weeks later I discovered that in ancient cultures the vagina was a symbol of protection and was believed to be imbued with protective energies. To avert wickedness, women in ancient times would deliberately flash their nether regions in the face of evil and to the devil himself.

This ritual of defence derived from ancient Mesopotamian times when Ishtar was worshipped as the primary and first known goddess. Her vulva is referred to in archaic poetic text as 'wet' and being 'ploughed', which makes comparisons with sowing seeds in a field. Centuries later fetishes of Ishtar displaying her vulva were brought into Europe by the Knights Templar and were held or touched for protection. Similar fertility figures have been found across Egypt, Asia Minor and Greece that must have been used as protective amulets for pregnant women and for those wishing to become fertile.

As you take steps towards sexual liberation Sheela-na-gig offers to heal all carnal wounds and revoke the guilt and shame that comes with them, for sexuality is a natural and beautiful expression of communing with the divine that awakens you to your natural blissful state. She does not judge; she merely reminds you that just as creativity comes from spiritual communion so, too, does the sanctity of sacred sex. It is a pure cosmic energy that provides a direct link to divine bliss and is an explosion of divine love.

YOURSELF AS A STRANGER

As you witness the change in your life and understand who you've become lately you will try desperately to cling on to who you once were. Just like the enigma that Sheela-na-gig is, you too become a mystery as you won't even recognise who you are any more. Memories will surface of you as a child and how you were as a teenager and beyond, and you might feel devastation as you recall days of freedom when you weren't a slave to your mind. The pain of recollection may urge you to take steps to get the old you back again but that is impossible, for that person has gone and you can never go back. Instead, allow the past you to merge with who you are today as you remember you are not your past.

It is the past that has prepared you for the future, and when you finally step into the light you will become the whole of who you are with all of your emotions and memories. In the meantime, you will find that a loss of identity and losing your sense of purpose will make you feel very isolated, lonely and anxious. When you go through a trying ordeal alone the lack of emotional support can increase your anxiety, which may change your perception of how bad things really are and hinder your coping ability. If you are experiencing any of the physical symptoms listed below, think about whether they are being caused by anxiety:

- increased heart rate and muscle tension
- legs turning to jelly
- internal and external trembling
- hyperventilation and difficulty breathing
- dizziness

- upset tummy
- nausea
- tension headaches
- excessive perspiration
- dry mouth
- palpitations.

The psychological symptoms anxiety can bring on go hand in hand with this stage of the dark night of the soul, and you'll know it is affecting you if you:

- feel as though you're going mad
- feel as though you've lost control
- think you're going to die
- think you're going to faint, be sick or have an incurable disease
- feel as though everybody is looking at you and criticising
- feel detached from everything and everyone
- want to run away and hide to escape your situation
- are on edge the entire time and on alert to all that's around you
- are exhausted from all of the above!

Rejection, loss, betrayal and everything that the dark night presents can wound you deeply psychologically, leaving you feeling ostracised. Neuroscientists have revealed that isolation causes us to experience actual physical pain and is an impediment to good mental health. You may begin to question everything that's going on, and in those lonely moments your mind will work overtime to give every thought and perception a sinister flavour. This will leave you frozen in place and wallowing in unease, and when this happens your mind will quickly race to the darkest possible conclusions.

If you cannot easily rid yourself of bleak, negative thoughts and feel completely hopeless it is critical that you seek professional help.

YOURSELF AS INNER CRITIC

Slowly you will begin to withdraw as you try to come to terms with all the changes around you and do your best to cope with the loss the dark night of the soul has presented. At this stage you may have reached your tipping point: a new gloom has descended to blacken your thoughts, and suddenly from within a small voice can be heard in the back of your mind. At first this voice appears to be on your side, warning you of danger, of whom not to trust and to be on your guard. As you start to listen to the voice it becomes more vocal as it reminds you of all the horrid things that have happened to you, of what somebody else has done to you. The more you listen to it the louder the voice becomes, and it will keep on and on until all of your thoughts are consumed with the betrayal and injustice you've been served.

Night-time is this voice's friend, for that's when you will be subjected to its torturous reminders of the past. As you lie in your bed wide awake trying desperately to fall back to sleep, your mind becomes very noisy and there's nothing you can do to switch off the voice. You might try to pray or meditate, to bring back peace of mind, but the voice grows stronger along with the content and you have no choice but to listen. Everything it says you concur with, for it creates no space for seeing anything apart from its own perspective and it can cause you to become lost in a web of despair. Suddenly it seems as though nobody is on your side, nor do they understand. Whatever the dark night of the soul has thrown at you will rise up and preoccupy your every thought. Conversations from the past will repeat over and over, and as you try to analyse each word and how it was said your mind soon becomes completely overwhelmed and dominated by such intensity. That's when the niggling voice of self-criticism joins in, as it plays off your anxieties and causes you to question your own worth.

This antagonistic voice is your inner critic, and its job is to help you recognise your mistakes so you can set things right. When Sheela-na-gig invites you to push past her vulva she greets you in the darkened haven of her womb. With darkness all around your inner critic will go way overboard as it pecks away, scolding, shaming and fault finding and wearing down any resilience you had left and completely killing off your self-worth. Self-worth is an internal state of being, a measure of how you regard and value yourself. If you had a favourable opinion of yourself before your encounter with the Dark Goddess you may have felt deserving and worthy of beneficial things such as happiness, wealth, love, success and good health irrespective of other people's opinions of you. However, when the inner critic begins to dominate your mind, night after night in those quieter moments and eventually 24/7, the dark night takes hold as you start to see yourself in a negative and critical light.

When you gaze into a mirror, who or what do you see looking back at you? Are you happy with who you are? What would you like to change about yourself? How do you think others see you, and does it matter to you what their opinions of you are? Why is that? As your inner critic carries on destroying your self-esteem, you may find that the perception you have of yourself becomes rather warped. When you start to focus on your faults, guilt, worries and shame instead of your positive traits, goals and dreams your world becomes shrouded by the negative comments, blames and projections of your mind. Over time, the true aspect of you only sees through the eyes of the inner critic, which becomes your only truth.

As you start to believe in and affirm your weaknesses, every bit of confidence that once propelled you forward will be shredded and you may find yourself hiding away from social situations, stopping trying new experiences and avoiding things you find challenging. A lack of confidence will block you from living your life to the full, as self-doubt holds you back. When you don't believe in yourself you expect the worst, and others will subconsciously pick up on how you view yourself and treat you accordingly.

Mental stress can lead to breakdowns of the nervous system; it seems as though more and more people today are suffering from stress-related illnesses due to the excess responsibilities they have. The modern lifestyle demands that you have a high-powered job, live in a house full of up-to-date gadgets, drive the latest car, look fabulous and have perfect kids. What's there to stress about? The reality is that you're working all hours in a job you hate to pay for all the stuff you don't even actually need just to keep up with your so-called friends, only to find you are spending more than you earn and have to work more hours to earn more money. Aaaaaaargh! It's all very cleverly designed to control us, you know. And so the wheel, that is, the circle of life, continues to turn. There is no way off the wheel unless, that is, you accept Sheela-na-gig's invitation to take the path of no return.

Here is a list of some signs of mental stress with which you might identify:

- feeling sad, down and depressed
- confused thinking or a reduced ability to concentrate
- excessive fears or worries or extreme feelings of guilt
- extreme mood changes
- withdrawal from friends and activities
- significant tiredness or low energy or problems sleeping
- detachment from reality, paranoia or even hallucinations
- an inability to cope with daily problems or stress
- trouble understanding and relating to situations and people
- problems with alcohol or drug use
- major changes in eating habits
- changes in your sex drive
- excessive anger, hostility or violence
- suicidal thoughts.

If you've been given a diagnosis of ill health, have been betrayed in some way, are grieving, are caring for a sick loved one, are cut off from family or friends or had your heart broken, your inner critic will feed you lies that jab away at you, wearing you down until you believe you are no good or not worthy or even that you will die. You may freak out that you just can't sleep, and then you get a panic attack about falling asleep as you lie awake trying to make sense of it all. Maybe you've considered harming yourself or even thought about killing yourself.

Most of us experience internal battles of some sort at various times in our lives. Maybe you've struggled to conform with society, work politics or house rules. How did or does that make you feel? Do you find yourself having imaginary conversations with those who oppose you, getting your side of the story ready in case the situation arises? Do you drive yourself crazy with what ifs? It's exhausting stuff, but it's necessary so you can analyse, process and solve what's going on in your life.

When the Dark Goddess has you in her clutches of despair you will feel so wretched that you can't continue and will beat yourself up for not behaving in a mature fashion, as you once did. There is no point in looking back when you have come this far, for when the effects of your dark night have taken their toll and have challenged your cognitive capacity, your traumatic actions when dealing with mental overload may cause someone to accuse you of having gone mad. And as your mental health continues to erode, you will start to fear they are right. It's an awful consideration, and one that would have had severe consequences not so long ago when mental health was misunderstood and not recognised as it is today. The trauma of battling with mental illness, particularly when induced by the dark night of the soul, brings with it a whirlwind of chaos and your mind can become utter bedlam.

DEPRESSION

The dark night of the soul is not taken into account when it comes to medical diagnoses. It seems as though more and more people are suffering from depression and doctors dish out medication like lollies without really seeking the root of the problem, and those who've never experienced depression really don't understand the problem. It's not about feeling a bit down from time to time; instead, it's as though a big heavy cloud has engulfed your mind. A lower vibration takes over and it feels impossible to break free from it, and as your mind becomes traumatised through overthinking that is born out of fear it consumes you until you become part of it.

Not being able to differentiate between your own thoughts and that of the torturous mind monster could overwhelm you so much that you see suicide as being the only solution. It isn't, for your despair is an illusion and is a gift from the Dark Goddess herself. She reminds you that everything you are experiencing was at your request. You may have purposely called to her for transformation, as I did one fateful night on a Cornish beach at midnight, or have no idea why the Dark Goddess has picked on you. However, what you do know is that at this phase of the dark night of the soul you have reached your lowest ebb and any inkling of hope has completely disappeared. All that stands before you is a big black void of nothingness. Your future seems all too bleak, which is when you feel there is no point carrying on.

You will ask yourself whether anyone will miss you if you departed early from this mortal coil. Who would grieve or be in despair if you took your own life? When you get to this point you won't even care about the answer. Depression is a prison, and once locked in tight there's a part of you that doesn't even want to escape. You get comfortable in your own misery as you withdraw further from others. It's a dark place to be in, a place devoid of any light or hope, so you give up all hope and surrender to the Dark Goddess Sheela-na-gig.

If you are experiencing suicidal ideation, please seek professional help as soon as possible.

PREPARING FOR SHEELA-NA-GIG

Sheela-na-gig invites in only those who are no strangers to the dark; the void in which she offers nothing but cold comfort is waiting to shield and protect you from outside harm. Within the confines of darkness she silently regards your every torturous thought and observes each relived bad memory until you can think no longer. As you drift in the emptiness of her deep void the relief of her silence will finally allow you to let go of all that consumes your poor weary mind, but be warned: refusal to accept her invitation to retreat may keep you in immutable darkness as she turns you into stone.

You may have subconsciously called in Sheela-na-gig on a soul level when you wished:

- to see the bigger picture
- to seek enlightenment
- for a baby
- for respect
- to protect your family.

You may have unwittingly called in Sheela-na-gig when she heard you:

- have suicidal thoughts
- be unable to conceive
- cry out through the darkness in desperation
- allow yourself to be sexually used
- no longer recognise yourself

- being scared of the dark
- being void of all feelings
- listen to your inner critic
- suffer through the depths of depression
- being consumed by torturous thoughts and bad memories
- feeling anxious and frustrated
- seeing yourself in a critical light
- losing all self-worth and belief in yourself
- wish for the past to return
- being promiscuous
- feeling that death was the only option.

Turn to Sheela-Na-Gig when you wish:

- to be a mystery
- to conceive
- for deep peace
- to be you again
- for protection
- for new beginnings
- to be fertile
- for assistance with feminine issues
- to heal unhealthy sexual behaviour
- to heal from sexual abuse
- to heal from the grief of cot death, abortion or miscarriage
- to explore the great mysteries of the universe
- to return to the light.

As soon as she hears your invitation to come into your life, whether it's subconscious or conscious, Sheela-na-gig will set about her work to draw you into her dark world. There she will leave you to incubate in her black womb, which is like a cold tomb void of all warmth, until you can no longer bear the desolation of darkness.

HONOURING AND CONNECTING WITH SHEELA-NA-GIG

Do the following to honour and connect with Sheela-na-gig:

- Honour yourself and acknowledge the divinity within.
- Nurture your yoni through tantric ritual and self-massage.
- Seek her images at old church entrances, monasteries and castles.
- Spend time meditating in the dark so you can connect within.
- Show her your commitment by making choices and deliberate decisions.
- Listen to European folk music.
- Make an altar for her and place upon it a sheela fertility effigy.

Altar offerings to honour and give thanks to Sheela-na-gig include:

- fertility figures
- black candles
- black onyx and hematite
- carved stones
- spirals.

INVOCATION TO SHEELA-NA-GIG

Sheela-na-gig is the embodiment of the divine hag of witchcraft who presides over the mysteries of the feminine and the eternal cycle of existence. You can work with Sheela-na-gig for her regenerative powers, inviting her in for spiritual rebirth and for protection. Focusing on fertility, easy conception or new beginnings is effective when this dark goddess is invoked. Her powers of protection can be used in ritual, particularly to safeguard pregnant women and new mothers. Her mystical healing powers and protection should be called upon for any fertility rituals and can be powerfully invoked with just one rub of her sacred vulva. She does, however, offer protection to all those who seek it.

To purposely call Sheela-na-gig into your energy you will need the following, but don't worry if you are unable to get hold of all of the ingredients as your focus will determine your connection with her:

- clary sage incense
- a small bowl of salt
- a fertility figure, which you can make from clay or you could knit one
- clary sage essential oil
- pure rose essential oil
- a black candle.

Light the incense and sprinkle some of the salt around you in a circle for protection as you ask the goddess for her blessings. You can do this silently in your mind using whatever words come to you or you can say out loud:

> *Divine goddess, I ask you to bless and protect me as I focus*
> *on the divine light within myself as I call upon you, the Dark*
> *Goddess Sheela-na-gig, for assistance. I graciously receive your*
> *mysteries with an open heart in gratitude. Help me to serve,*
> *help me to shine. In love and honour, so mote it be.*

Call in Sheela-na-gig as the moon wanes, to draw you into the magnetic darkness of the dark moon, by placing the fertility figure above the threshold of your house, bedroom or sacred room where you work with magick or have placed your altar. Anoint your temples with the clary sage essential oil to increase fertility, oestrogen production and hormonal balance, then anoint your heart with the rose essential oil for protection and to counteract anxiety. Hold the black candle, light it and gently and reverently reach up to touch the fertility figure's vulva. Blow out the candle flame and say:

> *Mistress of mystery, naked and raw,*
> *pull back your entrance, show the me door.*
> *Void of all light, black with despair,*

as darkness consumes me I give up my prayer.
Searching for answers and peace of mind,
t'is me whom I seek, but never to find.
Anguish and fear birthed in cold, dark tomb,
protect me within your deep velvet womb.
I invoke you now, to connect as one.
So mote it be, with harm to none.

You have now invited in Sheela-na-gig and invoked her fertile healing powers. Remember to acknowledge her each time you cross a threshold to ensure her protection at all times.

Signs that Sheela-na-gig is around you include:

- Feelings of desperation and suicidal thoughts.
- You no longer recognise yourself.
- Everything seems dark.
- You have a deep feeling of emptiness.
- You can't switch off your critical mind.
- You sense an air of mystery.
- You feel drawn to visit old churches and castles.
- You keep seeing spirals.
- You keep seeing the triskelion symbol and configurations of the number 3.
- A fertility doll presents itself.
- You experience utter desperation at this stage of the dark night of the soul.

EXERCISES AND RITUALS TO ENGAGE WITH SHEELA-NA-GIG

JOURNAL WORK

As goddess worship gradually declined over the centuries, scribes dishonoured women in their writings of sacred texts and in the documentation of history. Women of importance or who threatened the existence of man's control and power were accused of witchcraft, of being the devil incarnate or possessed by demons. Perhaps discrimination has affected you too in some way. If you're a girl, you may have always known your parents would've preferred a boy, or a brother was given preferential treatment as you grew up and this behaviour is still going on. Have you ever wished you were treated with more respect? Have you observed how people treat you compared to your male peers?

Reflection on identifying sexual triggers and feelings of sexual inequality: write down in your journal anything that bothers you about how you've been treated in the past by the opposite sex. Are you treated fairly, as an equal? Perhaps people see you as being a sex symbol: how does that make you feel? Do you feel popular and attractive or cheap and used? What do you feel you can do to change the situation? Have you ever been called an unsavoury name by a jealous ex-partner or been unfairly accused of being a whore when they didn't get what they wanted from you? It's an all too familiar situation that sadly many women bear the brunt of: men can cheat, but they are congratulated for their sexual prowess.

It is all too easy to point the finger at men for history's wrongful portrayal of women and this book is by no means a male witch hunt, for we are all sisters and brothers trying to navigate the circle of life and learning the hard way, especially those who have heard the call of the Dark Goddess. We all need to heal from the terrible accusations of the past, and when Sheela-na-gig appears it is evidence you have buried yourself so deeply your life has become void of all light.

Reflections of positive affirmations of self: positive affirmations said daily will increase your feelings of self-assurance, and an appreciation of your unique qualities will help you to believe in yourself. Write down in your journal all of your good qualities, including everything you love or once loved about yourself. Do you still believe those aspects about yourself and, if not, why? What happened for you to not believe and what steps can you take to believe in yourself again? Write down a list of everything you would like to be or reclaim, then make up positive statements about yourself such as 'I am worthy of being loved', 'I deserve happiness', 'I am fully confident' and 'I am strong and courageous.' Don't be shy: you can believe in anything at all. The more often you declare your positive statements and believe in them the more confident you will become.

CREATING A PERSONAL SHEELA-NA-GIG

Making your own Sheela-na-gig effigy from modelling clay and placing it over your threshold will protect your property and all those residing within. This can be done quite easily and the size, style and look of your Sheela-na-gig are completely up to you, as long as she embraces the key feminine vulva. Fertility figures can be made to represent the pregnant or those who wish to conceive, and can be carried around to help remove negativity around barrenness and ward off evil. Look after and treat the effigy carefully and with respect, for it is symbolic of the person it represents. This is called sympathetic magick and is as old as witchcraft itself.

INCANTATION FOR RECLAIMING YOUR CONFIDENCE

This powerful incarnation, which you can say as often as you wish, will banish your inner critic once and for all and return your self-esteem. Why not look into a mirror while you declare your positive intentions? Mirror magick works powerfully in co-operation with your own belief and will reflect all that you believe in and all that you believe you see. Say out loud:

Mirror, mirror on the wall,
reflect the truth and show me all.
The critic rules inside my head;
doubts and fears are how it's fed.
Trauma hears a bunch of lies:
do not listen, don't reply!
With words of positivity,
I'll starve it out. Oh, to be free!
Doubts begone, I choose belief,
peace of mind to bring relief.
Affirmations are the key,
inviting positivity.

Continue on assertive theme,
building up new self-esteem.
Healed solar plexus, mine to own;
now self-assured when I'm alone.
Shining brightly like the sun,
exuding confidence and fun.

Eventually your confidence will manifest into reality as you say and repeat positive affirmations daily while truly believing every word you utter. When your new confidence ultimately shines forth you will be more readily available to share with the world with strong conviction everything you have to offer.

MEDITATION FOR JOURNEYING WITHIN TO THE VOID

Imagine you are walking up a narrow pathway towards an old church. On either side of the path stands a scattering of tombstones, so you acknowledge those who have passed before you as you approach the old oak doorway. You look up to see a carving in the stonework of a figure: round, old, toothless and breastless and pulling at her female genitalia so that it is wide open. Intrigued, you feel an urge to accept the ancient invitation and reach up to touch her sacred vulva. As you push through the double doors of her private parts the old hag invites you into the dark of her barren womb in order to face death, an ending of all that you once knew. Immediately you are thrown into darkness and all is silent; all around you is blackness and a vast eternity of nothingness. You are suspended in one moment of time.

You have stepped into the void of your despair. There is nothing, and so you merge with the nothingness. How does it feel to have nothing, and how does it feel to be nothing? There are no time or space limitations here so you become one with the void itself, for in this place there are no feelings, no thoughts. It is a dark space devoid of all comfort, support or hope. In desperation you call out, but as your echo ricochets across the universe you realise that you are all alone and isolated from all you know.

I am the entire universe within the void.

The booming words break the silence and echo all around you.

You cannot miss what you already have.
You cannot know yourself until you become a stranger.
You cannot live until you die.
My sacred entrance is a portal to the otherworld that now reflects your inner
self. Take a look for yourself, for the darkness reveals the answers you seek.

From within the cold tomb of nothingness, Sheela-na-gig has welcomed you into her cosmic womb. The rebirth she offers is a spiritual invitation into the greater mysteries. As you remain in a suspended state, hanging in the balance between the veil of life and death, take an opportunity for reflection. Go deeply within as you search desperately for your truth, meaning and purpose, taking as long as you need for time does not exist here.

Eventually, a glimpse of understanding sweeps over you, and in that same moment a tiny light sparkles in the distance that gives you a very faint glimmer of a feeling you've not felt in a very long while: *hope*. Immediately you feel an almighty push from within and find yourself being propelled downwards through a long dark tunnel. The pain you experience is immense as you birth yourself from out of the void, through the stone carved vulva and back into the present moment.

Place upon your goddess altar a carving of female genitalia or a black piece of fabric to represent the silence of the deep black void.

LESSONS FROM THE DARK GODDESS SHEELA-NA-GIG

What can you learn from the mysterious old hag who sports a designer vagina? One thing is that her vulva represents creation, for it is through the sacred portal of a woman's womb that we are all birthed into this dimension. It represents the power of the Dark Goddess and embodies her feminine mysteries of life, death, rebirth and sex.

It has also been an inspiration for terror. As goddess worship was gradually replaced with the authority of the patriarchy, women were made to feel ashamed of their body parts. Patriarchy is a structure in which men are considered to have a monopoly on power and women are expected to submit. As the church grew in power, sex became frowned upon as being evil fornication, and eventually the status of women, once honoured along with the goddess, diminished. A goddess's power of creation was replaced with weakness to make women less threatening, less goddess-like. The idea of the goddess was replaced with a singular male god and all other deities vanished, which left the feminine figure with no honoured powers. A woman's purpose became little more than for sex and childbirth and to serve and so it came to pass, for as women tried to appear less powerful true power was lost and over the centuries womankind became a diluted apology for the goddesses of yesteryear.

Sheela-na-gig refuses to accept that the female is inferior or our bodies are disgusting or vulgar. We are the portal to life and she reminds us that our place as women has been abused and dishonoured. She extols you to take back power and push against those who say you are not enough because of your sex. Having reached rock bottom, the only way for you to go now is up. Having returned from the emptiness and isolation of the black void, you are to be congratulated for that one tiny speck of hope you felt has released you from your darkest moments and has sparked the next dark goddess to call you to her cauldron . . .

10. CERRIDWEN

Initiation of hope and inspiration

Hubble, bubble, cast out trouble.
Clear your mind now on the double.
Sip of magick from her potions;
ideas inspire creative notions.

ORIGIN	Celtic (Welsh).
NAMES	Cerridwen, Ceridwen, Caridwen, Cereduin, Ceredwen, Kerridwen, Kyrridwen, the white sow, the white lady of inspiration and death, the lady of the cauldron.
GODDESSES	Arianrhod, Diana, Blodeuwedd, grail goddess.
SYMBOLS	white sow, the moon, corn, cauldron, acorns, vervain, apples, hawks, otter, hens, her six sacred ingredients.
THEMES	regeneration, shape-shifting, rebirth, transformation, magic, poetry, music, prophecy, knowledge, inspiration, hope.
LESSONS	unity, self-worth.
COLOURS/CANDLES	black, purple, silver.
CRYSTALS	moonstone, carnelian.
HERBS/FLOWERS/OILS	cowslip, mugwort, bergamot, vervain.
MOON PHASES	dark, new.
SEASONS	Samhain, winter.
TREE	apple.
FESTIVAL DATE	21 October.

The Welsh goddess Cerridwen is regarded as being an enchantress of transformative power.

She is the keeper of the cauldron of regeneration, in which she brews divine knowledge, wisdom and inspiration, and is heavily associated with magick and transformation. Although a dark goddess, Cerridwen is seen by many as both mother and crone and takes on the role of mother in her story.

Cerridwen is known by many names, including that of the white crafty one or white sow, which symbolises fertility and her ability to produce an abundance of new life and spiritual growth and represents her strength and tenacity as a nurturing mother. Also known as the dark moon goddess, the great mother, the white lady of inspiration and death, the goddess of nature and the grain goddess, she rules over the realms of death, fertility, regeneration, inspiration, magic, enchantment and knowledge. In Welsh her name means 'beautiful as a poem', with *cerdd* meaning 'poem' and *(g)wen* meaning 'white', 'fair' or 'blessed', linking in with the Celtic word *ven* which means 'white', even though the lucky colour linked to Cerridwen is green for new life in nature. In Celtic her whole name means 'keeper of the cauldron', which derives from the Celtic word *cerru*, and just like the goddess herself the cauldron also symbolises the transformative power of magic, wisdom, rebirth and creative inspiration.

Cauldrons were central to Celtic traditions, and stories tell of three types: the cauldron of transformation, the cauldron of rebirth and the cauldron of inspiration; Cerridwen's cauldron combines all three. As the keeper of this cauldron, she represents the womb of the goddess. She toils at her cauldron continuously as she stirs up forces of inspiration, wisdom, divine knowledge and her transformational powers of the wheel of life, the eternal cycle of birth, death and rebirth. Cerridwen's womb, like her cauldron, has the potential to birth all manifestation as it is the beginning and end of life.

Cerridwen lived on an island in the middle of Llyn Tegid (Bala Lake), which was named for her husband Tegid Foel, with her two children. She was driven by her desire to make her son, Morfran, bright and successful, for he was extremely ugly, dark and malevolent while her young daughter Creirwy was fair, light and incredibly beautiful.

Cerridwen decided to use her knowledge of magick and herbs to create an enchanted brew that would give her hideous-looking and unlucky son a complete makeover, to ensure a successful future. She was very particular as she prepared the potion, which had to be boiled for a year and a day if it was to work to full effect. To protect her secret potion and purpose she summoned a blind man to tend to the fire as the brew bubbled away in the huge cauldron and a young boy named Gwion Bach to stir it.

One day Gwion accidentally spilled three drops of the magickal liquid on his hand and quickly licked it off. Immediately he was filled with magickal knowledge and power. Petrified of Cerridwen's reaction, he quickly turned himself into a rabbit so he could run away. When Cerridwen found out she was furious, and she shape-shifted into a greyhound and chased Gwion until he became a fish and jumped into a river. Cerridwen then became an otter and Gwion turned into a bird. She flew after him in the form of a hawk but he swiftly switched into a grain of corn. The goddess then cleverly changed herself into a hen and gobbled him up.

The grain was seeded within her womb and nine moons later she gave birth to a beautiful baby boy. Cerridwen knew immediately that the child was an incarnation of Gwion Bach and determined to kill him but, as a mother, her heart softened and she just couldn't bring herself to do it. Instead, she popped him into a leather bag and set him out to sea, where he was found by Prince Elffin. Elffin and his wife adopted him and named him Taliesin. He grew up to be the greatest Welsh poet, whose words were full of inspiration and wisdom. Thus, according to legend, the Celtic bard Taliesin gained his gifts from Cerridwen's cauldron of inspiration.

MESSAGE FROM CERRIDWEN

'It's been a long and arduous journey through the dark night of the soul. Nobody held you, sympathised with you or dried your tears, nor did they congratulate or praise you. This was your path to walk alone, with only the misery of isolation for company. As you faced up to obstacles and challenges, a process of understanding and forgiveness has enabled you to embrace the parts that serve you. As one who has walked through the darkness you are ready to emerge, to be brightly transformed and hold the energy of both dark and light in balance, knowing and wisdom.

'Allow me to plant the seeds of change within your sacred womb, which I promise will birth transformation and the power of your own feminine divinity.'

SEEKING CERRIDWEN

Still blinded by the confines of your darkened prison, there is nothing that can relieve your torment. Your world remains bleak and it is a dangerous path of the mind you have been treading, as negativity continues to shroud your outlook and warp your perception. Your experience with Sheela-na-gig will have left you in the dark, and the black void within causes you to feel hollow. While you carry fears, self-doubts and worries and your head is filled with negative thoughts and constant dialogue, there is no room for clarity. The emptiness of having no purpose refuses to let you carry on, and you become desperate for some magickal transformation. However, the journey of the dark night of the soul is not to be rushed, and change for the better will manifest in good time. For now, why don't you allow the Dark Goddess Cerridwen, the keeper of the cauldron, to brew up a magickal potion especially for you? Drink of the wisdom she offers you, and allow the negative scales to fall from your eyes as she offers to breathe clarity through your mind.

As the cobwebs begin to blow away a teeny-weeny glimmer of hope will be revealed in the bleak of darkness and something will begin to stir deep within. Inspiration, new beginnings and clear visions are in sight when you taste Cerridwen's potent and magickal brew. Your surrender to the darkness offers you a clean slate, and while she stirs her cauldron she breathes inspiration into the darkest of places. It is only now, for the first time, that you hear her heartbeat in among the deafening silence of the black void.

If you grew up playing witches in the woods or in the playground as a child it is Cerridwen who was your muse. She is the epitome of the wicked old witch of yesteryear, of fairy tales and Shakespearean plays, yet her wisdom and inspiration is fully present now if you seek her out. She is the spark of light that seeds a tiny glimmer of hope within the darkness of despair, and she is the keeper of the sacred cauldron of knowledge and her potion of magickal elixirs of divine wisdom and inspiration. But don't be fooled by her appearance when she turns up, for her shape-shifting abilities could confuse you. Be careful not to be dismissive when a beautiful cloaked lady acknowledges you or a hawk circles high above, for it could be Cerridwen in one of her many guises out to fool you and test your manners.

Approach Cerridwen with an air of anticipation for she has much to offer, although the dark aspect of her nature will ensure you earn that which you seek. She will never spoon feed you from her cauldron of wisdom and inspiration, nor will she assist the half-hearted or the ungrateful. Instead she is a great believer in putting those who truly desire her magickal knowledge and wisdom through sneaky tests and tricky trials, for this is her dark recipe for ultimate spiritual transformation and growth.

Cerridwen is a dark goddess and is seen in Welsh legend as the crone aspect of the triple goddess, teaming up with Blodeuwedd as the maiden aspect and goddess of spring flowers and Arianrhod as the mother aspect and goddess of the moon. Blodeuwedd, whose name means 'flower face', and Arianrhod, who carries the dead on her silver wheel, are also separate goddesses in their own right. As the crone aspect of this triad Cerridwen resonates with darker elements and the underworld, ruling the realms of death. However, like many goddesses she embodies all three aspects of the triple goddess within herself, making her multifaceted and not only associating her with the gifts of the crone of death and rebirth, prophecy and magick but also with herbs, flowers, the moon and all lunar attributes. Thus she is the goddess of the moon as well as of the cauldron.

Whereas Cerrdiwen's crone side encompasses wisdom, it is her mother aspect that nurtures the growth of wisdom as she invites you to tap into her ceaseless energy when transformation is at hand. She is the keeper of the gates between the worlds and presides over the unbidden transformation and final phase of womanhood into the croning years, with the promise of an empty inner cauldron. In this vein she is the devouring mother into whose cauldron you must enter to understand her regenerative nature, in order to be reborn.

DARK GODDESS COMPARISON

In her moon goddess aspect Cerridwen can be compared to Diana, the Greek huntress who directed the moon phases from her chariot. However, Diana is a goddess of beauty and light with no darker aspects, unlike Cerridwen, but is also invoked for her gift of fertility and assistance in easy childbirth.

Arianrhod is a moon priestess and goddess with a mother aspect similar to Cerridwen's. She descended from the heavens in her white chariot to watch over the tides she rules at each moon phase. Moon goddesses represent the moon itself, symbolising connection with the womb and the cycle of life, death and rebirth. But of course it is the cauldron that Cerridwen is widely honoured for, a deep feminine symbol of the female fruits that provide nourishment, rebirth, intuition and wisdom. She is the cauldron of the cosmos, linking her to all Celtic grail goddesses.

REASONS FOR WORKING WITH CERRIDWEN

Cerridwen's expertise revolves around the mysteries of the manifestation of creativity, fertility and feminine health. For the Celts, her cauldron was a metaphor for the swollen belly of a pregnant woman and was seen as being a profound female symbol as well as a sacred vessel in which to brew up magick for healing and transformation. Cauldrons were also used to cook up nourishing stews and healing herbal brews. She oversees the aspects of male and female ideas, potential and new life transformed, nurtured and then birthed through the vessel of the female.

As a moon goddess Cerridwen presides over a woman's monthly cycle, which in ancient cultures was deeply respected and revered as our female ancestors celebrated it and let it flow naturally. Often now women refer to their menstruation as a curse instead of honouring it for its gift of potential power of transformation and new life. If you're a woman, do you remember how you felt when your menstrual cycle first started: did you fear or embrace the start of your fertile years? The start of menstruation for girls marks their first initiation into womanhood; what's been your journey? Do you see your moon time as something to honour or as a complete nuisance? Perhaps you've gone through the change already or had a hysterectomy. Losing an internal organ can be a major trauma, particularly the womb; how did you feel about losing yours and how did you deal with it? Did you feel you'd lost your womanhood, or were you delighted at the prospect of no more monthly suffering? If you haven't gone through menopause, how would it make you feel? Either way, losing a part of your goddesshood is something to grieve for and may be a part of your dark journey, as it was mine.

The word 'hysterectomy' evolved from the belief that women's hysteria was due to a wandering uterus. The word 'hysteria' reflects the behaviour of menopausal women, particularly in Victorian England: any woman living then who had premenstrual dysphoric disorder (PMDD) most certainly would have been locked up in Bedlam! PMDD is a very severe form of premenstrual syndrome that can cause many severe emotional and debilitating physical symptoms at least three weeks during every month. It's a condition that not many people have heard of and it generally goes unrecognised. Symptoms include:

- mood swings
- depression or feelings of hopelessness
- intense anger and conflict with other people
- tension, anxiety and irritability
- fatigue
- change in appetite
- feeling out of control
- cramps and bloating
- headaches
- joint or muscle pain
- an inability to avoid or resolve conflicts
- becoming very upset if you feel that others are rejecting you.

Sound familiar? Some of the symptoms can be quite similar to what you may have faced through the dark night of the soul.

There would have been hundreds if not thousands of women put away just because nobody understood PMDD or menopause. Even today it's not really talked about, and as young maidens it's not even on our radar and we put it aside to consider decades in the future. I still didn't feel old enough to have a hysterectomy and my vain inner maiden was desperate to cling to her youth. I'd heard horror stories about the side effects of menopause such as hot flashes, hair loss and weight gain, and I didn't relish the thought of a loss of collagen or bone density for that would accelerate the ageing process.

TRANSFORMATION AND HOPE

Be assured that transformation is at hand when Cerridwen shows up. Her ability to take on various forms represents a need for change, so something must die in order for the new to come in. What you have experienced thus far on your dark journey has been like a death, as you've had no choice but to say goodbye to the comfort of what you once knew. As everything crumbled around you, the Dark Goddess propelled you to sink to rock bottom.

Having spent a while trying to find your way in the darkness, there is hope at last of light at the end of a long black tunnel.

In the safety of her womb Cerridwen bids you to rest and heal as she nurtures you with inspiration until you are ready to be birthed from the darkness into the light. Soul expansion is her reward from the hardships you've endured, as she gives you a taste of the secret recipe that bubbles away in her cauldron. As she stirs together the ingredients along with her gifts of knowledge, wisdom and a big dose of inspiration, she prepares you to harness your own powers through the magickal act of transcendence and ultimate transformation.

Hope is an optimistic state of mind. Hope is based upon expectations of positive outcomes. As the Dark Goddess Cerridwen pursues you with her inspirational energy, give yourself permission to feel a bit of hope for it is hope that shines a light through the darkness. Hope lights the way through the dark night of the soul, and when it finally arrives you will look up from the darkest depths and know you're on your way back up. Having been in the dark for so long with no motivation, Cerridwen stirs your pot for you to move forward. Just as when the sun rises in the morning, when a new hope appears on the horizon it brings with it a sense of purpose and a reason to exist.

Mental clarity will allow your imagination to flow freely and soon visions of hope will become clear and lucid. However, once your mind is free to be clear you have a choice of whether to go forward towards new dreams or take a step back. Be strong and be aware of your inner critic, that negative voice that only causes destruction, and observe your thoughts, for Hel will attempt to entice you back to the darker side as you try to come to terms with all of your trials and tribulations. Either way change is afoot, and if you have been desperately clinging on to your old self, all of that which you know too well for fear of losing your identity, you must understand that to die to the old will escalate you to where you truly desire to be even if you don't know where that is yet. It is time to let go, to surrender and accept that death is never final; it is simply a portal to rebirthing into the next stage of your dark journey.

Cerridwen, whose power of prophecy makes her a patron goddess of all witches and wizards, invites you to her hearth, for she is the haggard old crone who stirs the cauldron at Samhain as you approach the death of all you knew. If you are brave enough to seek her and wish for inspiration to improve your witchy skills, Cerridwen offers you a taste of her magickal brew as she shares her wisdom and knowledge for kitchen witchery, healing and herbology, shape-shifting, astrology, moon magick and cauldron or grail magick. As you work with her during this stage of the dark night of the soul she will help you to return to yourself and cultivate a deep sense of self-worth.

PREPARING FOR CERRIDWEN

Cerridwen is drawn to the tiny speck of hope that faintly flickers within the confines of darkness. Just one taste of her special brew will ignite the seed of inspiration you need so you can emerge from the dark into the light. She is the goddess of inspiration, the mother of poets, and all bards are born of her. Get closer to her by writing her a personal letter from you, or write down your hopes and dreams as you introduce yourself to forge the relationship you wish to have with her.

As you build your connection she will inspire you to be inventive as you chase your dreams, and will provide you with all the spiritual ingredients needed for change and transformation. She is the midwife of your rebirth and requires that something must die before you can be reborn. As she forges the fires of transformation from her magick cauldron she brings to you true inspiration entwined with the potency of the divine feminine, in the pursuit of growth, change and personal power.

You may have subconsciously called in Cerridwen on a soul level when you wished:

- to be led out of the darkness
- for new light
- to have a dream
- for motivation
- to be positive once more
- to be a better version of yourself
- for wisdom
- to be magickal.

You may have unwittingly called in Cerridwen when you:

- expressed feelings of hopelessness
- suffered with PMDD or painful periods
- referred to your moon time as a curse
- had irregular feminine cycles
- couldn't be bothered to chase your goals
- craved change
- collected acorns
- suffered with depression
- had a sly taste when stirring your cauldron (making dinner!)
- wished to end it all
- played 'witches'
- went scrumping (stealing apples from an orchard)
- worked with the moon phases
- brewed up a potion

- crossed over the Manx Fairy Bridge
- made 'rose perfume' as a child
- fed hens.

Turn to Cerridwen when you wish:

- for new hope
- for better days
- for clarity
- to be inspired
- to write a book
- to hone your creativity
- to become a poet
- to work with herbs
- to become a kitchen witch
- to heal period pain
- to be in sync with your feminine cycles
- to work with moon phases
- to study Druidism
- for assistance with the menopause
- for spiritual knowledge and wisdom.

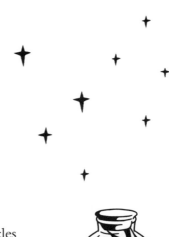

As soon as she hears your invitation to come into your life, whether subconscious or not, Cerridwen will fire up her cauldron to brew an elixir of inspiration to bring you that spark of little hope that will draw you out of the dark world in which she finds you.

HONOURING AND CONNECTING WITH CERRIDWEN

Do the following to honour and connect with Cerridwen:

- Get creative!
- Write poetry or a poem to Cerridwen.
- Use a small cauldron as a tea light candle holder.
- Eat grain breakfast cereals.

- Keep a piggy bank for savings.
- Feed oats and seeds to birds and apples to pigs.
- Keep hens.
- Listen or dance to pagan music.
- Collect acorns.
- Make an altar for her and place upon it apples, acorns and seeds.

Altar offerings to honour and give thanks to Cerridwen include:

- apples
- apple cider
- seeds, grains and acorns
- white flowers
- a figure or picture of Cerridwen stirring her cauldron
- moonstone and carnelian crystals
- a representation of the moon: a picture or a crystal sphere, for example
- dried mugwort
- a written poem to her
- figures or pictures of pigs, hens, otters and hawks
- a vase of cowslips.

INVOCATION TO CERRIDWEN

To purposely call Cerridwen into your energy you will need the following, but don't worry if you are unable to get hold of all of the ingredients as your focus will determine your connection with her:

- a mugwort, vervain or white poppy incense stick
- a small bowl of salt
- the moon
- dried mugwort herbs
- a charcoal disk
- a small cauldron or dish
- bergamot essential oil
- a moonstone crystal.

Light the incense stick and sprinkle some of the salt around you in a circle for protection as you ask the goddess for her blessings. You can do this silently in your mind using whatever words come to you or you can say out loud:

Divine goddess, I ask you to bless and protect me as I focus on the divine light within myself as I call upon you, the Dark Goddess Cerridwen, for assistance. I graciously receive your healing magick with an open heart in gratitude. Help me to serve, help me to shine. In love and honour, so mote it be.

Cerridwen's powers represent the transformative energies of the moon, which has always been regarded as being the keeper of magic, mystery and the divine feminine. The moon is the ruler of emotions, and it opens up your natural intuitive and empathetic abilities. As you call down the moon she embraces you in her soft, luminous glow and assists in opening up to your receptive, intuitive side. Bathe under the pure feminine and restorative energy as she immerses you and go sky clad (naked) in honour of Cerridwen to connect with her on a full level. Never forget that the energy of the moon lives within you as you work in conjunction with her phases, honouring at all times the new, full and dark aspects of the maiden, mother and crone.

Moon bathing is vital for balance and your health, as you are made up of the same vital minerals as the surface of the moon, and you can choose a moon phase to bathe under according to your needs. The moon's magick is at its optimum when it is full, at which phase it will charge you up with natural powers. It will do the same for the crystals associated with Cerridwen such as moonstone, which you can leave on a windowsill under a full moon's gaze for an ultimate super charge of magickal empowerment.

Burn the mugwort on the charcoal disk in the cauldron to enhance the magick. Anoint your third eye with the bergamot essential oil to promote overall balance. Hold the moonstone crystal in your left hand to amplify your connection. Stand with arms outreached to the moon and say:

Cerridwen, goddess and mother of moon,
may sweet your dark mystery help me to attune
with every phase of your bright silver wheel.
Intuitive insight, emotions to heal,
I call down the moon this very night
to shower within your feminine light.
Replenish me, cleanse me, reach deep inside,
for t'is where magickal powers reside.
This magick is worked, with harm to none.
So mote it be. There, it is done.

Breathe deep, reflect and allow yourself to soak up the magick. Bathe in this way under the healing light for as long as you feel necessary and comfortable. Allow the charcoal disc to naturally burn down.

Signs that Cerridwen is around you include:

- You crave spiritual knowledge and wisdom.
- You're drawn to working magickally with herbs and plants.
- You switch from drinking coffee to herbal teas.
- You have a lineage connection with Wales.
- You are drawn to visit or live in Wales.
- You are a Druid or are drawn to Druidism.
- You are inspired to write poetry, a blog or a book.
- You keep seeing cauldrons.
- A white sow presents itself.
- You're fascinated with the moon.

You experience a glimmer of hope through the darkness as this stage of the dark night of the soul.

The spark of hope within you is an invitation for Cerridwen to draw near, and one that she will not refuse. Be careful not to allow fear of change to deter you from working with Cerridwen, for it is she who is your ticket to the light. That small feeling of hope is your guaranteed seat on the wheel of fortune as it starts its slow journey of ascent.

EXERCISES AND RITUALS TO ENGAGE WITH CERRIDWEN

JOURNAL WORK

Reflection to reveal what is still hidden: when Cerridwen calls your name know that the need for change is upon you, that transformation is at hand. How do you feel about facing another change? What is it that no longer serves you as you continue to walk your dark journey? Does your inner critic continue to rule your mind? Do you still place blame on others? Write down the answers to these questions in your journal, because it is time to examine which circumstances in your life no longer serve you. Something must die so that something new and better can be born, and forging fires of transformation within will bring true inspiration into your life.

Has anyone ever inspired you to change your life in a significant way that made you healthier, happier or more fulfilled? If so, you understand the difference positive inspiration can make in a person's life. Inspiration is powerful and stimulates hope, and hope is what finally comes at this stage of the dark night of the soul like a hero in the dead of night coming to rescue you out of the darkness. At this stage you are still in the dark, with just a glimmer of light coming from a tiny part within called hope. Before hope you had nothing to live for and nothing to gain if you did. However, hope is power, for it can change things and will change everything for you.

Reflection on quelling your inner critic: write down everything you could possibly hope for. Don't listen to your inner critic, who will tell you that it's not possible and will never happen, or other destructive lies. When you have hope everything is possible. It's not as easy as it sounds when you are going through the dark night of the soul, however, and you might struggle to find any hope at all. Hope will ignite enough light to eventually bring you back from the dark depths of misery. Cerridwen will inspire you to feel hope, which is what this stage is all about; when hope is found, rescue is in sight. When your head is consumed with dark, muddled thoughts and you can't think straight, even just a little inspiration will light you up and be a gateway to freedom.

Call upon Cerridwen to stimulate your mind and illuminate any creative ideas. A flash of inspiration to bring about a brilliant revelation will change your course and will be reflected in your inner cauldron. To clear your mind, take long walks and allow nature to truly inspire you. Throw caution to the wind, and as you walk hand in hand with the Dark Goddess your visions will transform into reality and you will become someone commendable.

Reflection in recognition of your lost self: write down in your journal everything about you that you like but have lost. How did you lose those parts of yourself and what do you miss about them? Would it serve your highest purpose to reclaim those parts of yourself and how what steps would you take to reclaim them? Write down all of your favourite traits you love about yourself to remember who you are.

Cerridwen offers you a clean slate as you emerge gradually back into the light. This is a time of opportunity to reinvent yourself, to take steps to rediscover yourself. You might feel drawn to change your physical appearance, your outlook or how you feel within; you may even wish to change your name or career. Everything is possible when you have reached rock bottom, for only from the dark can the light emerge and only from the dark can the magick of transformation be birthed. What would you like to change about yourself? How would you like to be? Write a list of everything you would love to be. Sit with Cerridwen and feel her divine inspiration and the magick that lies within you.

CERRIDWEN INITIATION

Cerridwen stirred six sacred ingredients into an alchemical but poisonous elixir, and she offers her magickal herbal potion to those who will surrender to her call. Her six sacred ingredients are:

- cowslip (pipes of Llen)
- fluxwort (Gwion's silver)
- hedgeberry (borues of Gwion)
- vervain (Taliesin's cresses)
- mistletoe berries (sacred to the Druids)
- ocean foam.

Of course, these ingredients aren't necessarily available or practical, so instead use the sacred plants of the Druids for a powerful elixir and connection with Cerridwen.

INCANTATION TO BRING ABOUT INSPIRATION AND CLARITY OF MIND

When you feel you are unable to find clarity, make a decision or clear your mind of troubles, face the direction of east at sunrise – for east is associated with the element of air that blows in new beginnings, creativity, inspiration, clarity and freedom – light a yellow candle to represent the air and say:

Hubble, bubble, cast out trouble,
clear my mind now on the double.
Darkened mind, slippery slope,
lighten up to invite hope.
Imagination is the key;
unleash gift, trust what I see.
Paint, create and have fun,
draw from that inspiration.
Yellow flame illuminate,
clarity to meditate,
sip of magick from her potions,
ideas inspire creative notions.
Connect with muse, passion fired;
now I truly am inspired.
Lend me courage, build power in me,
assist my transcendence, so mote it be.

INVOCATION TO THE POWER OF SAMHAIN

Samhain, or Hallowe'en, is the time when the goddess becomes the crone and invites you to embrace her and step into your own crone years with acceptance if she has come for you. Draw on Cerridwen's wisdom from deep within as she cradles you during the dark months to come, and release all that no longer serves you. The veil between the worlds is at its thinnest on this evening, and it is a good time to see spirit and connect with the dark goddess. Deep within her dark tomb, let go of old patterns and recent behaviours, surrender and release the concerns and fears that prevent you from freedom. As you die to the old, new hope will germinate in the dark like a seedling in the earth waiting for spring.

As it is seen as being the Celtic new year, Samhain is also a time for growth and new life, of both endings and beginnings. Recite this invocation to harness the magickal and potent energy of this time of year:

Cauldrons boiling, lanterns are shining.
Ghouls and ghosts, groans and whining.
Parties sweep across the land,
children, adults, hand in hand.
Time of fun but must remember:
as fires burn bright and glow with embers,
our ancestors who walked before.
We honour thee and ask for more
wisdom, tools to help us be.
The wise among us, let us see,
through veil, while thin, this very night.
Protection in place, no need for fright.
So welcome in and all you bring;
go deep inside and look within,
to shed the old, a shamanic death,
embraced and warmed within the earth.
Inviting in life anew,
the goddess calls for it to be you.
Through the year from maiden to mother,
the end is now, to feel the other.
In her glory stands the crone;
don't be afraid to stand alone.
This sacred path leads you to be free.
Go forth in strength; so mote it be.

With Cerridwen's promise of transformation and new hope, your darkened days will soon be behind you. It can be very hard to believe it will be so when you are in a negative place, but when you seek transformation and take a drop of her transformative tincture she will bring to you wisdom of the heart. She brewed her magickal potion for one day and a year, adding in six different herbs at the correct astrological times. She presides over astrology and understands the meaning behind the movement of the stars and the phases of the moon and how they can be harnessed for magickal work. It is time to plant your seeds of change as you tap into Cerridwen's ceaseless energy and divine knowledge of magick and herbs.

CAULDRON OF INSPIRATION EXERCISE

For this exercise you will need:

- a cauldron or big pot
- thyme
- mugwort
- fennel
- nettle
- mayweed
- crabapple
- plantain
- cockspur grass
- lamb's cress
- a wooden spoon.

At the time of a new moon, fill the cauldron with water and gently heat it over a fire or on a stove. Imagine throwing in each of Cerridwen's six sacred components one by one (visualising this spell is very effective), or throw in the magickal herbs of the Druids for a powerful dose of inspiration. Stir the ingredients round and round with the wooden spoon as you say:

> Consumed within a darkened place,
> challenges and fears to face.
> Egotistic sense of self now dies;
> let the birth of true-self rise.
> Metamorphosis feels strange,

thyme supports a healing change.
Mugwort for new moon vibration
assists spiritual transformation.
Fennel, nettle bring protection;
mayweed for purification.
Crabapple, plantain cure;
cockspur grass and lamb's cress pure.
Stir until my passion's fired,
now I truly am inspired.
The dark embraced, no need to fight;
my journey's end reveals new light.
Dark Goddess, I accept the magick of you,
protect and assist me in all that I do.
Lend me the courage, build power in me;
assist my transcendence. So mote it be.

Dip a finger into your magickal potion and place your finger on your abdomen to heal, transform and inspire resurrection. Pour the elixir, your seeds of change, onto the ground under a waxing moon in order for them to grow for a year and a day. As Cerridwen in her moon goddess and earth mother aspects breathes her power of transformation and inspiration towards you, the illusion of the dark night of the soul will be shattered.

She will build strong foundations on which you can rely as your dark path continues. She will be the presence of support beside you, holding you up and giving you hope before you can face the world again. She is the dark mother, the crone of Samhain and goddess of witches. She presides over magick and mystery, yet there is no greater kindness to be found in either world.

She calls you to take refuge in the darkness of her womb, where she will nurture you as she stirs her cauldron until you are well rested and healed. Feel her solace, for within this sacred space your soul will expand in time as your spirits lift so that transition and transformation can take place. Place upon your Dark Goddess altar an offering in honour of Cerridwen such as black, purple and silver candles, a small cauldron and a few seeds and she will breathe new hope and inspiration into you, sparking a glimpse of light to guide you out of the depths of darkness.

EXERCISE FOR WOMB ACCEPTANCE

Many females feel have strong resistance to and fear about menopause, ageing or having fertility issues, while others believe that having a hysterectomy could diminish them as a woman. Feelings such as these need to be acknowledged and worked with, which is where rites of passage would serve you well as you step into your crone years, no matter what your age is. Rituals can help the grieving process and allow you to make a statement about your willingness to release and move on, which is something Cerridwen can assist you with on all levels.

For this ritual, simply lie on your back and rub your belly lovingly as you chant:

Salt and sand, dark mother's hand,
stirring the pot with all she's got.

Recite the words over and over again as you 'stir' your womb, your inner cauldron, until you feel the presence of the Dark Goddess. As she manifests, allow your negative feelings around your womb, your feminine cycle and your reproductive issues release and be taken away.

LESSONS FROM THE DARK GODDESS CERRIDWEN

Seen as being the mother aspect of the goddess in her tale, Cerridwen showed her darker side, as perhaps all mothers might, when it came to protecting her son. Unlike his light and fair sister he was so ugly and dark that Cerridwen was determined to pull him up from the depths of darkness to bring brilliance to his life, for it had been void of all light. Therefore, she understands how traumatic it is to be blinded by certain factors when you are held down and kept in the dark for so long. When you can see no way out you will consider taking matters into your own hands to find an alternative escape, which is not recommended, but when there is nothing but a black void staring back at you all you can do is take solitary refuge within your cold black tomb and wait for the darkness to consume you entirely. Unlike Hel, who welcomes you to stay an eternity in the depths of the abyss, Cerridwen offers to lead you out as her powers are those of transformation, which she brews in her cauldron and uses for what is called for even if it means death. However, as we have discovered, after death comes rebirth in whatever form.

In an earlier incarnation Taliesin or Gwion, the servant boy, went through the process of death, transformation and ultimately rebirth, which naturally symbolises the wheel of the year and its changing of the seasons through new life, death and rebirth. Cerridwen used her knowledge of magick to brew up a potion so potent it had the alchemical power to transcend and transform; just three drops of the tincture enabled an ordinary boy to shape-shift into animals of all sizes to escape Cerridwen.

Cerridwen is a master shape-shifter with the ability to change her own physical appearance and the power to transform others, so she can therefore help you to adapt more easily to different environments whenever you find it difficult to face the world and other people. A shape-shifter is one who is multifaceted, able to choose a characteristic that best suits the circumstance and with the transformative power to adapt to any given situation. Cerridwen calls you to look deeper, and if you find yourself adapting and fitting in with well with all walks of life like a chameleon she asks whether it actually reflects a deep insecurity and inability to commit to a particular path. If that is so, you've yet to reclaim your true identity. It's hard to know where your loyalties and affections lie after all you've been through, which could cause you to be fickle. A changeable and volatile attitude could affect your relationships, and when you face the dark night of the soul it's not easy to know who to trust. You may find yourself constantly reinventing yourself until you find yourself again.

With new hope positive change seems possible once more, and the next dark goddess will help you to move forward through the darkness in preparation for the birth of new life that awaits you. It is time to make plans!

II. MAEVE

Initiation of conflict, strategy and determination

Inner conflicts buried deep;
dependency is not to keep.
A natural leader shows the way;
determination saves the day.

ORIGIN	Celtic (Irish).
NAMES	Maeve, Meave, Mab, Queen Medb, Mea , queen of Connaught, queen of the fairies.
GODDESS	Circe.
SYMBOLS	mead, honey, bull, faeries.
THEMES	sexuality, leadership, preparation, strategy, making plans, deviousness, adaptation, determination, justice.
LESSONS	balance, self-honour, drive.
COLOURS/CANDLES	red, gold.
CRYSTALS	red agate, red aventurine, gold.
HERBS/FLOWERS/OILS	ginseng, ylang ylang, jasmine.
MOON PHASE	new.
SEASONS	autumn, winter.
TREE	hawthorn.
FESTIVAL DATES:	Beltane, Mabon.

Goddess Maeve, a forceful leader and queen who ruled over Connaught in Ireland, was as famous for her incredible beauty as she was her sexual prowess. Men would go blind on the battlefield at the very sight of her, and she had many husbands and countless lovers. Like a faery queen at Beltane, her sexual appetite was insatiable and dominating. She would test her lovers and set conditions, temporarily marrying them if they passed and destroying those who spurned her. No man could be crowned high king until she had consummated the ceremony in her royal bed! Both Celtic goddess and faery queen and known as Queen Mab in her magickal fae persona, Maeve is an excellent general and warrior who assembled one of the mightiest fighting forces known in Irish mythology.

Don't be caught up in her illusion, for Maeve's alluring looks can be deceiving. Curiosity reveals only what you may wish to see, and deliberate confusion will hinder you from seeing that which is true. Maeve works with the allure of enchantments and has pulled many in with her shining beauty and glamour magick, which is a mark of the fae. Her presence is heady and intoxicating, for she is a goddess of ecstasy, lust and passion who presides over sex along with fertility, death and war. She also has a strong rule over the faery realm and is the driving force that creates all of life in nature, which continually reproduces. Faeries exude sexuality and promiscuity, which they revere as sacred and natural. They naturally pass this potent life force on to us when we come into contact with them, helping us to feel good about ourselves and to tap into the cycle of nature's growth.

Maeve is celebrated at Beltane for the sacred blending of sexual energies of the feminine and masculine. At this time of year the goddess takes on the god as her lover in order to give birth to the full bloom of nature during the summer months to come. Beltane marks the return of full life, and nature is fully honoured in the fresh bright flowers, grasses and leaves that have started to push through. It is an abundant time of year when nature is at full bloom and is powerfully sexual, just like Maeve herself.

The autumn festival of the equinox named Mabon is celebrated in Queen Mab's honour. This is when nature starts to turn within itself and we reflect on where we have been and what has been done during the preceding months. It is a time of balance and a celebration of the harvest. During the festival Queen Mab insisted that any man who wished to be king should drink of her mead, which represented menstrual blood. In those times mead was coloured red – unlike the golden hue we recognise today – to ensure the king was acquainted with feminine mysteries, for menstrual blood is known as the wine of women's wisdom. As with Maeve Mab's name means 'mead', and in Middle England the word 'mabled' meant 'to be led astray by faeries'. This holds up to the truth of Maeve's fae persona as Mab, particularly as Mab also means 'small child' in Welsh, proving she is faery sized. In Celtic folklore Maeve's name is Queen Wolf, which also means mead, thus uniting both aspects of the faery Mab and the Irish warrior queen Maeve in name as well as in the dark mother aspect of ferocity, fury and war.

Maeve's sexually charged antics are simply carefully planned tactics, for there is no shame attached but only a driven desire to get her own way. Christian monks obviously disapproved of Maeve's rampant ways as a violent warrior with a sexual appetite strong enough to destroy, and they decided to shame her. In their eyes she abused the powerful bond of sexual union with wild abandonment, causing her victims great pain, loneliness and an obsessive yearning for more. However, the powers she demonstrated in the Ulster story were too evident to suppress or ignore, so Maeve emerged through ancient writings as an Irish faery queen who should be avoided for her shameful sexual exploits. Faery queens are well known for their bewitching allurement and sexual magnetism, energies that represent the cycle of nature. In England and Wales Maeve was relegated to faery tales and her reputation was completely usurped, as she became a tiny flower fairy riding a chariot pulled by insects!

Maeve was one of the daughters of Eochaid Feidlech, the high king of Ireland, and had been married to Conchobar mac Nessa, the king of Ulster, in the first century BCE. Sadly the marriage didn't work out, and Maeve's father offered his other daughter Eithne to Conchobar in marriage much to Maeve's fury. To sweeten Maeve, Eochaid installed her as the queen of Connaught, removing the reigning king Tinni mac Conri from power. While she ruled over Connaught Maeve made careful plans to seek her revenge and plotted her sister's murder. In an act of terrible ruthless jealousy, she drowned and killed Eithne, who was pregnant at the time but fortunately the baby survived. However, in an act of vengeance for killing his wife, Conchobar mac Nessa took the beautiful Maeve and raped her at the Hill of Tara. War between the king of Ulster and the high king of Ireland soon followed, and never would there be love lost betwixt the two.

Maeve later married Ailill mac Máta, which made him the high king of Connaught. Unlike Maeve he was completely without jealousy, but it would seem necessary for him to be so for she would continue to take lovers. Even though they were completely equal in birth, status and power, Maeve and Ailill vied with each other to prove their superiority in the relationship and fought about who had the higher status. To settle matters they looked through their belongings, and when they had counted them up it was Aillil who won for Maeve had nothing to compare with his magnificent white-horned bull.

Maeve could not bear to be inferior to her husband and made plans to possess such a creature herself. She sent men to search the lands for a bull just as splendid, and eventually the brown bull of Cooley was found. Desperate for possession of the bull, Maeve offered its owner, Dáire mac Fiachna of Cooley, lands and gold and her greatest gift of all, sexual favours, in return. Allured by her intoxicating charm, he was ready to agree to the deal until he overheard Maeve's men boasting that she would steal the bull anyway if the owner refused to sell it. Dáire resented being played this way, so he went back on his part of the deal and wouldn't part with the animal. Maeve assembled a great army from all over Ireland, gathering her allies to invade Ulster so she could steal the bull. Some of the men knew of the curse of Macha that had been on the Ulster king and his warriors for nine generations, which dictated that when the hour of greatest peril befell Ulster all the men would fall for nine days into pangs of labour as if giving birth, which would give Maeve time to complete her mission.

There was one man the curse didn't affect, and that was a young warrior named Cú Chulainn. He was the only man who stood between Maeve's army and Ulster, and despite the odds his skill and reputation as a mighty warrior meant that Maeve's army was in trouble so she needed to plan a strategy. Instead of facing her army she negotiated with Cú Chulainn to fight in single combat against each of her champions. Her plan was to win the war, and she vowed to give her daughter in marriage to the warrior who defeated Cú Chulainn. However, Cú Chulainn fought his way through her champions, including the greatest champion of all, Ferdia, who was his own foster-brother! Years later Maeve re-invaded Ulster and took revenge on the mighty warrior Cú Chulainn by slaying him.

It seemed that the tide had turned against Maeve and her followers started to blame her for her vengeful and vicious ways, but she was focused on one thing only and had already made her plans to smuggle the brown bull of Cooley into Connaught on the eve of the final clash between both armies. Her new prize joined Aillil's white-horned bull in a pasture, but unfortunately the two animals attacked each other on sight and gored each other to death, possibly symbolising the reckless and careless conflict between Connaught and Ulster.

Ultimately Maeve met her own end many years later when she was killed herself by her sister's son, Furbaide Furbend. He had been the baby taken from his dead mother's body after she had been drowned by Maeve. Furbaide catapulted a hard piece of cheese at Maeve, who fell instantly. According to legend Maeve was buried upright in a high stone cairn in Sligo, defiantly facing the direction of north towards her enemies in Ulster.

MESSAGE FROM MAEVE

'Taking charge of your life is something that only you can do if you really want to change the direction things are heading in. You have been hedging your bets for too long, sitting on the fence and following along with the herd. You have allowed too many others to tell you what to do, how to do it, when to do it and what to think about it, but you don't lack determination or any of the abilities to work things out for yourself. It's just that you have allowed others take the lead.

'Be brave, and never surrender to your fears or doubts; embrace the challenge before you. My presence here marks a fresh direction that will bring about much change for the better. This is an opportunity to birth new ideas, so get your creative juices flowing and focus on your plans for the future. Take pride in yourself and prepare yourself for what's to come. You are almost there, so don't give up. I, Queen Maeve, am your inner warrior and I have come to gift you with the fighting spirit you now need in order to make your own decisions. Awaken your zest for life, your drive for the joys of physical interaction and your determination to shine brightly again in your own right. It is time to prepare for battle, for it is your determination that will win the day.'

SEEKING MAEVE

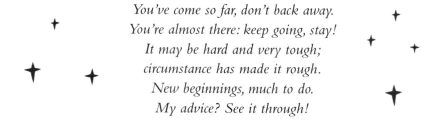

You've come so far, don't back away.
You're almost there: keep going, stay!
It may be hard and very tough;
circumstance has made it rough.
New beginnings, much to do.
My advice? See it through!

Did you enjoy the solace and comfort you found in that first glimmer of hope? Now that you've found inspiration, perhaps you feel as though you're able to clamber out of the depths of the abyss as you dare yourself to take a glimpse of the future. The Dark Goddess has stripped you right down to your core and now she will build you back up slowly, and with every piece comes a hard lesson. Maeve is just as dark as the previous five goddesses, and one who will give you the tools you need as she prepares you for combat.

When you seek Maeve be prepared to succumb to her bewitching approach, for she is as wild as she is beguiling and will lure you in to satisfy her insatiable desires, which are not to be denied. She is a seductress and an enchantress who is fully aware of the impact of her hypnotic powers, for her mere presence can make or break kings. As she races around the battlefield in her chariot at the speed of light she leans back tossing her long flaming tresses to unnerve the warriors, who yield all of their strength.

Maeve engenders an awareness of the intoxicating power of passion, for it can invoke intense and uncontrollable emotions such as anger and war as well as love and desire. When she can't have her own way she wreaks havoc in her determination to get what she wants. She teaches you to forget all about humility and humbleness if you wish to move forward. Forget worrying about stepping over the mark: overstep it! Be the force and go for it.

If you feel ashamed of your sexual exploits or confused about your own sexuality, Maeve urges you to own your actions and make a stand. She points the way towards acceptance and to claiming the truth of who you truly are. If, like Maeve, your untamed sexuality is all part of your charm to entice, she encourages you all the way when it comes to using alluring Siren skills to get exactly what you want. Likewise, if you are daunted by sexual intimacy Maeve will ignite your own sensuality and seductive powers, bestowing upon you the confidence needed for a quick bunk up or lover's tryst. However, her gift does not give you a licence for elicit wantonness or promiscuous activities that could cause you to face moral judgement, shame or discrimination. If you are longing to find expression in wild parties, sex and intoxication be careful that Maeve does not devour you, for she will encourage you to go all the way. Rather than trying to suppress any urges, be sure to express them safely and in a protected environment.

Maeve will determine the original source of any liberal and impure carnal behaviour that has any shame or discrimination attached and will restore you with self-care, self-respect and self-love in order that you can claim sexual freedom.

DARK GODDESS COMPARISON

As an enchantress Maeve can be compared with the Greek goddess Circe, for she too was a powerful witch who could easily control the minds of others with her bewitching powers. With staff in hand this red-eyed sorceress's strategy was to transform her enemies into animals, as well as murdering her husband. She turned one lover into a woodpecker and the sea goddess Scylla into a frightful six-headed dog so that she could have Scylla's lover for herself.

Daughter of the sun god Helios, Circe was known as Pure Mother Bee, which links her to honey and mead, and of the sea nymph Perse, which explains her deep magnetism and alluring Siren nature. It was Circe who rescued Odysseus from the deathly screech of the Sirens and made him her lover for a year in return for saving his men.

REASONS FOR WORKING WITH MAEVE

Maeve is the archetypal enchantress whose abilities to charm and seduce make her a most powerful sorceress and an alluring witch. She is the femme fatale of witchcraft, for her dark art is manipulation in the extreme. She casts illusory spells before battle to ensure a favourable outcome and places charms of love and pleasure upon those she wishes to seduce, ensuring they succumb to her witchy enchantments. Her lesson is about understanding your use of manipulation and seduction to avoid responsibility.

When you arrive at this stage of the dark night of the soul you may find yourself using any way you can to get people to help you out of the black hole in which you find yourself. As you try to pull yourself back out there will be others you turn to; when you're in a place of desolation and can't think straight the opinions of others really count. Having become weak and frail from your dark ordeal, you may find yourself no longer able to make decisions for yourself and you might be tempted to look to others for answers along with the comfort you seek.

Your inner critic will continue to confuse the issue so you just can't think straight, and you will go to any lengths to get what you need whether it's sympathy, attention, advice, money, love or anything you feel you deserve at this time. You may feel that because of the living nightmare you've gone through others should be more attentive or perhaps you think they should feel sorry for you because of what you're going through. This is when the victim will come into play. Going through the dark night of the soul is a lonely journey, for it is for you to walk alone with only darkness as your guide, but you want others to know your pain and all you've endured. It's not fair on you; why should it have happened to you? You tell your story to whoever will listen, for you do not want to go it alone and a bit of sympathy will bring you comfort and the attention you crave. You desperately want to share your trauma and you are distraught and will go to any lengths to try to survive.

Let's have a look at the many ways manipulation is used as a coping strategy.

Victim: none of us is a stranger to playing the victim role, particularly in childhood. How many times have you blamed your younger siblings for your woes or pointed a finger at someone who had done you wrong? How did it make you feel as you lapped up the sympathy and all the attention you got for your martyrdom? You got exactly what you set out to get, and that's manipulation. A victim won't take responsibility for the circumstance they find themselves in; they will blame an external force and get everyone to feel sorry for them. A victim will enjoy others running round for them and looking after them. Victims believe they are at the mercy of everyone and everything around them and will not make progress because they perceive themselves as being powerless and never at fault. They will hold on to grudges and always bring up the past if they have a grievance.

It's a dangerous game to play and it can be very difficult to get out of a victim mentality (refer to Chapter 4). If this is something you have used to get your way in the past know that it won't help you to heal from your dark journey, for it is not over yet and there are still many lessons to learn along the way. Acting out of victimhood will hold you back, and you may be in danger of becoming your actual story as you continue to repeat it to others and play out the drama in your mind. Does this sound like you? If so, try to recognise that when you free others of blame then power and self-control return to you, which is extremely important at this stage if you wish to return to the light.

Saboteur: self-defeating behaviours and thoughts that work against your own interests will sabotage your plans as well as adding more stress to your dark situation. It's easy to focus on the negative and ignore the positive during difficult times, but a saboteur will let fear lead the way. As fear develops into anxiety, mistrust, worry and other defeatist emotions, the saboteur turns to self-destructive behaviours such as wallowing in self-pity or using drugs, alcohol or comfort eating to ease the pain. Often rooted in underlying feelings of inadequacy and the fear of the nightmare of the dark night of the soul repeating itself, self-saboteurs push others away by deliberately wrecking the relationship. They can then either go into victim mode and blame others for the destruction or feel safer knowing that they put a stop to any harm before it happened.

Do you see? A saboteur ruins everything before and just in case they themselves get hurt. It's quite easy to understand this mentality for it is like a protection against anything terrible that might happen; however, it is a destructive path to walk on and is a strategy that could leave you out in the cold. If you recognise yourself in these descriptions, look at how often you focus on what could go wrong instead of the positive. Observe how you interact with others, and when you start to walk away from something good or speak in a way that is damaging, just stop and try to embrace the situation or conversation by giving it a positive spin. It's not easy if you've always played this game, but try to remember that if you're in living fear of the worst always happening then you've already made some grim choices for your future.

Narcissist: over time, as the dark night of the soul takes hold and as you continue to look to others as your rescuer, source of blame or for attention, you may find you have trouble handling situations, that you can't cope at all and have an adversity to criticism. Everything has become about you, and at this stage you may become impatient or demand special treatment because in your mind that's what you deserve due to your dreadful unique circumstances. If you feel this is how you've become because of the trauma you're trying to cope with, here are a few narcissistic traits you may identify with. You:

- are easily feel slighted by others
- react with rage or contempt towards those from whom you seek help
- have difficulty controlling your emotions and behaviour
- have major problems dealing with stress
- find it impossible to adapt to change

- expect special favours and unquestioning compliance with your expectations
- take advantage of others to get what you want
- have an inability or unwillingness to recognise the needs and feelings of others because it's all about you.

If you recognise any of these behavioural traits, don't feel shame or any other lower emotion. You need to understand that it is not your fault but that whatever may have worked for you in the past most probably won't serve you well now, and you may wish to change your powers of persuasion. Going through the dark night of the soul is like being blinded to everything you once knew, and as you lose your identity all principles go out of the window. You're simply trying to cope with the situation, and often it is the inner child who takes over in such cases. This is why you take such extreme measures to survive, leaving your usual upstanding behaviour and controlled emotions comprised. However, acting out like a child will only thwart your plans to persevere, so new tactics should be considered.

MAKING PLANS AND ADAPTING

Although Maeve used seduction to manipulate many of her situations, her strategy didn't always work out as planned. If like Maeve you have always used your feminine wiles or masculine charm to get what you desire you'll find that fluttering your eyelashes at the darkness won't work. The Dark Goddess has no interest in superficiality, and neither does your soul. If you're operating from an old program you may find that what once worked for you no longer serves your plans to leave the past behind or secure a brighter outcome. However, the distress of your dark journey may have caused you to install a new coping strategy, and you may be surprised to find your traits and actions match those listed above. Either way, you really don't need to use any form of manipulation in order to survive.

Now that your manipulative coping skills or tools have been taken away from you, how do you adapt to the situation? The dark night of the soul is a treacherous one, and because of the mental stress involved you may find it extremely hard to adapt to anything at all. You've already had to cope with unwanted change since BabaYaga introduced herself, so dealing with anything else is like coming up against a brick wall. There is no room for focus on anything other than what you're already dealing with, so when you're asked to change your plans you may find yourself going into meltdown to the dismay of anyone who witnesses your display of unexpected and over-the-top reactions to their simple requests.

Those without the ability to adapt will find themselves stuck in the dark for far longer than the Dark Goddess intended.

If there's one certainty in life it's that nothing is certain! The Dark Goddess changes everything she touches; everything, including yourself, is in a constant state of change. Instead of trying to resist the inevitable you should embrace it. Being able to adapt to any given situation is key when it comes to dealing with change. When Maeve was refused the brown bull she exchanged her original offer of sexual favours to an attack. She knew exactly what she wanted and how to get it, so when things weren't going her way she took back control and made careful plans. To adapt to the sudden change of the situation she employed a new strategy in order to get the outcome she desired.

How are you able to adapt to sudden changes: could you adjust to any given situation?

If so, what are your tactics? Do you make plans or simply go with the flow? A general doesn't just go into battle hoping to win; instead, he spends months planning, sending scouts out to spy on the enemy and checking out the lay of the land to cover every possible eventuality. Every soldier needs to be in place and they need to know what they should be doing, so making plans and getting the strategy right is critical if you wish to win the battle.

CONFUSION AND EXPECTATIONS

Perhaps you get so overwhelmed you just can't deal with adaptation along with the trauma you're already trying to cope with. When you're too uptight to cope with pressures it causes you to get into a dither, and that's when plans go awry. You are no good to anyone in this state, so always try to stop for a minute and take deep breaths in and out. The problem is that when the Dark Goddess strips you bare you don't know who you are any more, let alone what you want for the future. At this stage all you can truly plan for is only the next moment. Just keeping it together positively or not reacting in a rage or another lower emotion is progress. The small spark of hope you have will continually push you forward, and your plans for now could be as simple as knowing you need to get well or seek help or advice.

It's time to make plans for the future, to get you back on your feet. Start focusing on you and take each day as it comes, and try any of the following:

- Build up your strength by visiting a gym, partake in yoga or go for brisk walks.
- Set your alarm clock earlier for some meditation to bring you peace and clarity before your day starts.
- Make an appointment to speak with a counsellor or adviser.
- See your doctor or book a complementary therapy treatment such as a healing or massage.
- Focus on nutrition and healthy eating and take time out for you.
- Do whatever it takes to be gentle and kind to yourself, but at the same time kick yourself up the backside to get yourself out of your darkened rut. It will swallow you whole if you allow it to.
- Practise becoming stronger in mind, body and resolve so you can face the battles ahead.

Release your expectations of any outcome and also of others. Maeve had expectations of winning her bull and of her warriors, and when things didn't meet those expectations she swiftly changed her tactics. What are your expectations and where did they originally stem from? Do you have expectations of others? How do you cope if your expectations aren't met? All you have is those around you, and if they don't have the tools to help how do you react and how do you feel? Try to track into your expectations. Perhaps they aren't your expectations at all, or maybe you've adapted those of your parents or other influences. When you release any expectations your barriers will break down as you have acceptance and appreciation towards the outcome.

DETERMINATION AND DISCIPLINE

Determination means you never give up trying, and it will serve you well as you face the adversities that are wearing you down. Heavy responsibilities and anguish cause misgiving reactions as you continue to carry the burden of your misfortunes. Perseverance will allow you to dust yourself off and jump back on the horse. Whatever success means to you, focus, dedication and most importantly perseverance will be necessary. When you're absolutely determined to do something you'll be able to focus all your strength and energy on working to achieve it.

If ever you get knocked back, let the key to your success be persistence. Rise up in the face of difficulties and make a plan of action to get out of the dark as you fearlessly cast light on your objectives, just like Joan of Arc did in the 15th century. Joan of Arc was born around 1412 in France, and by the time she was 16 years old she had received the counsel of angels for three years in order for her to deliver France from her enemies. Her country had suffered at the hands of the English in a bitter feud that lasted for an entire century. The etheric voices Joan had heard in her head from the age of 13 pressed her to undertake the quest they had been preparing her for.

Joan's mission seemed both impossible and preposterous by anyone's measure, as she was mocked, threatened and even imprisoned. It was her feverish determination to succeed that enabled her to prepare herself and anyone willing to assist her in the battle for France and her own life. She knew what she had to do, so she sheared off her hair, dressed in male attire, put on armour and took up her sword. She raised the siege of Orléans by defying the cautious strategies of seasoned generals before her and followed the plans she'd carefully put in place, which changed the course of history and the outcome of the Hundred Years' War.

Joan's story reminds you to be steadfast in struggle and determined in difficulties and to bravely choose perseverance in order to reach your goal. Whatever your situation is, whether you're trying to lose weight, recover from grief or debt, heal an illness, mend a broken heart or escape from a situation, determination will see you through, especially when you add in the secret ingredient of discipline to ensure success. Discipline will bring stability and structure into your life and teach you to be responsible and respectful, for well-defined rules form the basis of society. If there was no discipline people would do whatever they wanted without considering others or the outcome of their own actions.

The ability to have self-restraint allows you to behave in a consistently stringent and controlled manner, whereas a lack of this ability can have disastrous results. You will have experienced this whenever your emotions got the better of you. It's not easy to be aware and conscious of your behaviour and reactions at all times, but to not give in truly is a sign of strength. To be a great and inspiring leader you must constantly display restraint. Making the right decisions can make or break you, so regardless of where you exert self-restraint it will help to promote achievements in moving forward.

When your plans are set in stone, try not to be rigid in your expectations of the direction they will take. Remember to be adaptable, and if your plans are not going quite the way you had hoped don't have a meltdown or give up. You may feel as though you're losing control, but it's important to be open to other factors. The Dark Goddess knows how much you can take; she knows what's in store for you and sometimes your plans don't always fit in with the plans she has for you. She sees the bigger picture and asks you to relinquish control over the end result.

We often experience a loss of control, but when you try too hard to control things and push back in the direction you believe things should be heading the more off course things can get. Instead of trying to control every situation or fret and worry about the outcome, just trust it. Of course, that is not so easy when you've been caught out before, so try it from another angle: take a step back and watch everything unfold naturally. Your natural instinct is to fight, but sometimes it's better to wait before making your move. This is one of those times that calls for clever tactics. Assess the situation carefully and look to see what actions will determine your desired result. You have so many strengths, yet it's easy when you're so unsure of yourself to give away your power. When your words are dissed or when your actions are criticised, your light fades because you don't stand up to be counted. The Dark Goddess requires you to stamp your authority, just like Queen Maeve did, so you can grow fully on many levels.

Be mindful of any challenges that prevent you from moving forward. Perhaps you don't feel ready even though you know you must be prepared so you can get out of the hell hole you're trapped in. What is not working for you? Why not look for alternative ideas? Possessing the insight to change direction will help now that you have the clarity and inspiration that Cerridwen gifted you. Just as Maeve faced forward for an eternity, let's look at how you can take those first steps to move forward. Doing so puts you in a state of becoming and declares to the world that you're ready to step into your power and fight for your future.

LOOKING FORWARD

Starting anew is most powerful if you focus your attention on what you choose to create. Giving all of your attention to the unwanted aspects of your life will allow what you resist to persist. You need to remember to leave enough room in the process of fresh beginnings and to be kind to yourself, because it takes time to become accustomed to anything new no matter how much you like it. There is no need to get down on yourself either if you don't reach your new goals instantly; instead, acknowledge the forward motion and choose to reset and start again, knowing that with each choice you learn, grow and move forward. It is a mental shift that allows you to clean the slate and approach anything with fresh eyes, and you can make that choice at any time.

Making the choice to start anew has its own energy; it's a promise made to you. The forward momentum creates a sort of vacuum behind it, pulling towards you all you need to help you continue moving in your chosen direction. Once the journey has begun it may take unexpected turns, but it never really ends. Like cycles in nature, there are periods of obvious growth and periods of dormancy that signal a time of waiting for the right moment to burst forth. Each time you choose to start anew you dedicate yourself to becoming the best you are able to be. When you meet Queen Maeve it indicates the opportunity to break out of the darkness and create a new chapter in your life.

At this turning point you will have experienced challenges, changes and breakdowns in relationships – as there will be certain factors that need to leave your life – before the good stuff can come in. It's been a long hard slog, but the glimmer of hope you felt with Cerridwen indicates new ideas, successful projects and other golden opportunities that await if you will but give yourself a second chance.

PREPARING FOR MAEVE

Are you ready to purposefully seek out this dark, wild and assiduous goddess? She draws to her all those who are willing to die for the greater cause, just like her warriors who passionately fought for her. The intoxicating heady allurement of her sexuality will entice you to look within to draw on your own beauty, passion and strength for what is required. Don't be afraid of going for what you want; instead, decide exactly what it is you desire and make plans to achieve your goal. Maeve encourages you to step into your personal power and go for it! It would be unwise to hold back when Maeve commands you, for her prideful nature could cause unwanted conflict and force you to settle for second best. Worst of all, you could drive her into making tactical plans for you as she did for her poor sister.

You may have subconsciously called in Maeve on a soul level when you wished:

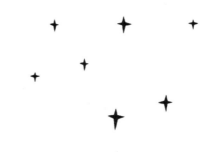

- for the strength to move forward
- for dominion over others
- for an active sex life
- for a sex change
- for new passion and drive
- to make a decision
- for a new future
- to make plans.

You may have unwittingly called in Maeve when you:

- felt jealousy towards another
- spoke a load of bull
- became intoxicated
- drank mead
- ate honey

- had a bee venom facial
- were bossy
- got your own way
- were the dominant one in a relationship
- allowed another to have power over you
- were bullied
- were determined to do something
- wore red and gold
- used manipulation as a coping strategy
- were fed a load of bull.

Turn to Maeve when you wish:

- for leadership
- to make strategic plans
- to prepare for your future
- for determination
- for passion
- to honour your sexuality
- to use your sexual prowess
- to adapt
- to connect with the fae
- for a passionate relationship
- for your sexual honour to be protected
- to visit Ireland
- to be free from conflict and control
- to marry
- for sexual union
- to be a leader.

As soon as she hears the invitation to come into your life, whether subconsciously or not, Maeve will lure you to her side as you make strategic and careful plans to draw yourself out of the darkness.

HONOURING AND CONNECTING WITH MAEVE

Do the following to honour and connect with Maeve:

- Honour your sexuality.
- Drink a goblet of mead.
- Take a spoonful of honey each day.
- Adorn yourself in gold.
- Keep bees.
- Celebrate the pagan festivals of Beltane and Mabon.
- Train birds to come to you.
- Stride out across the land.
- Play traditional Irish music.
- Leave bread and honey out for the faeries.
- Make careful preparations and plans.
- Be determined in all you do.
- Make an altar for her and place upon it some honey and a glass of mead.

Allow your heart to welcome in the energies of Queen Maeve and place upon your Dark Goddess altar an offering in honour of her such as red or gold candles, a chalice of mead and a pot of honey and she will help give you determination and strength of will. Other altar offerings to honour and give thanks to Maeve include:

- a picture or figurine of a bull
- gold birds
- faery figurines
- a picture of a faery queen
- red and gold crystals
- a vase of jasmine
- a wand of hawthorn.

INVOCATION TO MAEVE

To purposely call Maeve into your energy you will need the following, but don't worry if you are unable to get hold of all of the ingredients as your focus will determine your connection with her:

- jasmine incense
- a small bowl of salt
- a red cloak
- a red altar cloth
- red agate or red aventurine crystals
- a glass of mead
- a pot of honey
- ylang ylang essential oil.

Light the incense and sprinkle some of the salt around you in a circle for protection as you ask the goddess for her blessings. You can do this silently in your mind using whatever words come to you or you can say out loud:

Divine goddess, I ask you to bless and protect me as I focus on the divine light within myself as I call upon you, the Dark Goddess Maeve, for assistance. I graciously receive your sexual magnetism and magick with an open heart in gratitude. Help me to serve, help me to shine. In love and honour, so mote it be.

Maeve presides over the power of Beltane as she strides over mountains, fields and forests with staff in hand, animating all of nature and the land. She reminds you to awaken to the fullness of your true nature, to be passionate, to live, love and become inebriated with the vitality of life. As she re-ignites the Beltane fires within she touches the creative source of womb energy as a reminder of your first blood and the power of life. The energy she raises at Beltane sustains this dark warrior goddess through to the colder months of the year, when her magickal fae persona is honoured at Mabon in autumn.

Maeve's colour is blood red, which brings you in touch with your womb energy, your creative source and your chalice. As a woman you have the power of life and death, and Maeve reminds you of that. You remember Maeve with your first blood, given unto the land in honour of the life source that feeds and sustains you. To connect with Maeve and the life-force power of Beltane, place a red cloak around your shoulders to honour the life-giving powers of blood and go outside, preferably at dusk when the faeries can be seen. If you can find a hawthorn tree to work beneath then all the better.

Spread the red altar cloth out on the ground and place a red crystal in each corner and a goblet of mead in the centre along with the pot of honey. Anoint your sacral chakra with a dab of ylang ylang essential oil to enhance libido in honour of your own sexuality and awaken your kundalini energy. Say out loud:

Goddess Maeve, warrior queen,
Enchanting powers rule supreme.
Potential lovers lured by charm,
ignoring perils, pitfalls, harm.
Erotic, sexy, lusty sin,
invokes the siren deep within.
Shining queen of Elphame,
I harness the power of Beltane.
To mark our union and this rite,
drink of the mead this very night.
With fires lit across the land,
couples leap while hand in hand.
As they run through darkened wood
and find a grassy glade they should
remember well of who's around,
for bands of faeries all surround
the couple as they consummate.
The faeries cheer and seal the fate,
of plants and flowers, shrubs and trees.
While the god's upon his knees,
impregnating the mother to be
from sowing deep his natural seed.
Across the land and from the earth,

the power of life is yours to birth.
Dark mother, temptress of the land,
teach me to rise and take a stand.
Lend me the courage, build power in me;
assist my transcendence. So mote it be.

Smear honey onto any grazes or old battle wounds and allow it to heal you with its astringent properties. Drink half of the mead and pour the rest onto the land as an offering.

Signs that Maeve is around you include:

- You feel a tickling on your nose or lips.
- Your hair is tangled in knots.
- You suffer from lip blisters and cold sores.
- You feel the presence of or see faeries.
- You're presented with a golden bird.
- Birds flock to you.
- A bull chases you.
- You get easily intoxicated.
- Your sexual urges are strong.
- You wish to visit or plan a trip to Ireland.
- A new determination spurs you on.
- You experience conflict and a new sense of resolve at this stage of the dark night of the soul.

Determination will save the day when Maeve receives your invitation to draw near. She will address the balance of devious strategies, ensuring all plans are carefully carried out to your best advantage.

EXERCISES AND RITUALS TO ENGAGE WITH MAEVE

JOURNAL WORK: REFLECTION ON TAKING CHARGE

Write down in your journal the answers to these questions. What do you do to get what you want and how do you influence others to get your own way? Do you work your charm to lure others in, making them feel special so they can't turn you down, or does a sob story work for you when you want to get your way? Perhaps your tactics are underhanded and deceptive, or maybe you know how to manipulate people to make them feel guilty.

MOVING FORWARD EXERCISE

Take some seeds and hold them in your hand. With intention and focus, take your time to place a wish or desire into each seed in turn. Say out loud this incantation:

The door is closing to the past,
for future's sake it couldn't last.
The worst is gone, prepare for change;
letting go may feel strange.
Into seeds I place all hope,
and pop them in an envelope.
Send to my future self, post-haste.
Receive them well, no time to waste.
A new door opens to walk through;
I'll seize my chance and see it through.

Put the seeds in an envelope, mark it with your postal address and send it to your future self. When you receive the envelope, plant the seeds in your backyard or in a pot under a full moon at midnight to allow your dreams to grow fully into fruition.

CHARGING A TALISMAN WITH ENERGY

The more energy you give to something through your focus, thoughts, words and actions the stronger it will become. Conversely, if you don't give your time and energy to something it is unlikely to grow. Everything is energy, and it is only through focus that energy is able to build up. With that in mind, it is time to make plans and focus on your desires. Decide what your goal is, look at how you can reach it, work out a schedule, stick with it and focus on the end result. You'll find that you become stronger and more grounded as you step in the right direction of reaching for what you really want in life. Make a step today towards being fully in your power, with Queen Maeve at your side as your strength and ally.

In order to fulfil the dark night of the soul you will need to recoup and store spiritual energy.

Wise women and healers have known how to do this for centuries, using talismans and charms to hold great power, but in order for them to store the energy it had to be created in the first place. If you're feeling overwhelmed, fatigued or doubt you have the energy to go on with your journey, this quick energy pick me up will help. Sit or lie comfortably in a quiet place where you won't be interrupted and visualise a brightly coloured ball of light in your hands. This can be white or a colour associated with your desire. Place or push the light into a talisman such as a token, piece of jewellery or clear crystal while stating this invocation or just focusing on your intentions:

> *Manipulation, blessing, curse;*
> *glamour trick or something worse.*
> *Bewitching spells that work a charm;*
> *enchanting words to heal or harm.*
> *Intentions good or to devour;*
> *charge up daily, stoke the power.*

Imagine the light absorbing into the charm until you see in your mind's eye the charm radiating and pulsating with its newly charged magickal intention. Keep your charm regularly charged by placing it under a full moon each month and repeating an invocation or intention for the charm.

LESSONS FROM THE DARK GODDESS MAEVE

When you read the tale of the two bulls it shows how this dark and vicious seducer's proud resolve would not allow her to be subservient to her husband. She was never going to settle for anything less and was determined to do anything it took to match him. In fact, the plans she put in place to resolve the situation were gruesomely ruthless in the extreme; she was ambitious and knew exactly what she wanted.

Her unflinching determination is a great example of never giving up. What you want is out there, it does exist; you just have to go out there and get it. Maeve teaches you to be relentless! She never shirked her duty, and she knew how to lead and encourage her warriors. She could be harsh, jealous, vicious, scheming and domineering but she was always willing to go to great lengths to assert her rightful status. And although she was alluringly beautiful, she was always dressed and ready for war!

Hell hath no fury like a woman scorned, and the betrayal Maeve felt at her sister's marriage to her ex-husband induced her to make strategic plans to get her revenge. She had Eithne drowned even though she was pregnant. This harsh and ruthless act of jealousy certainly crowns Queen Maeve as a Dark Goddess, proving that she will stop at nothing to get what she wants. She is in charge!

Her powers of seduction are also her strength, a gift all women have if they know how to use it. However, not many understand how to fully use the energy of enticement, of magnetism, and the implication of its effects. I've used it when necessary many times, and have always known how to from an early age. However, there is a right time and a right place, and everything we do should be with harm to none. I would never betray a sister or a brother. Maeve's words to me when I met her at the sacred Hill of Tara in County Meath were to use my gifts wisely. This ancient and sacred site is the entrance to the otherworld and is known as the sacred dwelling place of the gods. The Hill of Tara is where Saint Patrick drove the snakes out of Ireland (a symbol for driving out paganism), for he knew the site was a powerful vortex of energy, and was the inauguration place and seat of the high kings of Ireland.

The dark night of the soul can seem like endless conflict, and you cannot fight effectively unless you identify your objectives and strategies in order to survive injury. Once your preparation is fully in place Maeve will direct you towards she who will help smoke out your enemies in all forms. Once you have them in your sights, the goddess of battle will greet you and lead you into war . . .

12. THE MORRIGHAN

Initiation of battle and sovereignty

A raven warns of battle cry.
Angry mists swirl through the sky.
Death, destruction, loss and woe
consumes the mind; must let it go.

ORIGIN	Celtic (Irish).
NAMES	the Morrighan, Morrigan, Mór-Rioghain, Morrigu, phantom queen, battle queen.
GODDESSES	Morgana, Macha, Badb, Nemain.
SYMBOLS	raven, crow, water, battleaxe, spears, swords, shield, fire, the colour red.
THEMES	battle, life and death, warriors, blood, boundaries, power, prophecy, magick, fords, shape-shifting, sorcery, the enemy within, antagonisers, victory, success, sovereignty.
LESSONS:	personal boundaries, claiming sovereignty, taking control.
COLOURS/CANDLES	black, red.
CRYSTALS	bloodstone, obsidian, ruby, garnet, moonstone.
HERBS/FLOWERS/OILS	dragon's blood, belladonna, red clover, rosemary.
MOON PHASES	dark, waning, new.
SEASONS	autumn, winter.
TREE	blackthorn.
FESTIVAL DATE	Samhain.

Our Celtic ancestors viewed war differently from how we now view it; in fact, they revelled in it and would call upon the Morrighan to influence the outcome of battle. As a soothsayer, foreteller and prophetess of destruction, death and victory, she is a dark goddess in her own right and is one to be feared. Her warrior self represents physical strength and the ability to protect and fight for your rights and those of others, but those who were destined to die in battle would see her washing their bloody armour in a ford before the battle commenced.

Her role in Celtic legend is similar to that of the Valkyries in Norse folklore with regard to making the decision of who would live and who would die in war and battle. Like the Valkyries, the Morrighan had the ability to predict both imminent death and victory and would arrive at the battlefield chanting an invocation, after which battle would immediately break out. The Morrighan's presence would inspire courage or instil a dreaded fear into the hearts of the warriors. She would often cause confusion and chaos in order to steer a battle in her favoured direction, and although her frightful shrieks terrorised armies she often used magick and sorcery as her chief weapons of war to determine the outcome, just as she did on behalf of the Fir Bolg, one of Ireland's indigenous tribes.

It can be seen from the story of the Fir Bolg and her decision to fight on behalf of the Tuatha Dé Danann after making love with the Dagda that the Morrighan's loyalty depends on what suits her at the time. Like many dark goddesses her natural powers of seduction ooze, as they did the day her legs were astride the river when the high king came across her and was enticed. In return for honouring the goddess the Morrighan promised to assist him and his race in battle.

On rare occasions the Morrighan would fight alongside those she favoured on the battlefield and she could be seen wielding her axe as she yelled her battle cry, which could be mistaken for that of a bean sídhe (pronounced 'banshee'), a faery who heralds the signal of death of a family member by wailing and shrieking. It is she who is in command as she rules supreme over land and livestock and demands respect as she determines the fate of all those who seek her help.

In most traditions the Morrighan is represented as a triple goddess, meaning she is made up of three aspects. Although the three aspects all identify with crows, ravens and battle, each aspect has its own contribution. As a stand-alone goddess in her own right the Morrighan carries the characteristic of each of her trio of female warriors within her; they are:

Macha, the maiden: associated with sovereignty of the land, fertility, war and horses, her name means 'field' or 'pasture'. A battle goddess and protectress, it was this aspect of the Morrighan who rained down fire and blood on her enemies. The severed heads on the battlefield were her harvest and were called the 'mast of Macha'.

Badb, the mother: associated with war and death, Badb takes the shape of a hooded crow and is known as the battle crow. She forewarns of imminent battle or death, for in this aspect of the Morrighan she is a witch, sorceress and seer who foresees the future.

Nemain, the crone: associated with the chaos and havoc of war, wisdom and magic, her name means 'frenzy' or 'venomous'. By shrieking furiously she intimidated, panicked and confused soldiers on the battlefield. This aspect of the Morrighan connects her to the role of a bean sídhe as she frightens her enemies into confusion and death.

The Celts believed that because the Morrighan was such a powerful symbol of life and birth she would revive soldiers who had fallen in battle so they could fight once more. The land after battle was considered to be sacred and was left untouched until the following day, so the Morrighan could gather the souls of those who had fallen. However, she was also known as a scavenger bird who fed from the bodies as she gathered the souls. In true Dark Goddess style the Morrighan takes offence when she is not acknowledged appropriately and immediately seeks revenge. This dark goddess should never be ignored, which you wouldn't do if you knew and understood who she is.

Carriers of magic, mystery and death, crows and ravens are closely associated with the visible and invisible and are servants of the Morrighan. Like her they have been feared for their presence, for death is believed to be imminent when they appeared before or during battle as they contain her energy. Have you noticed more crows than usual when you're out and about? If they've circled you or have cawed and called out to you, you can be sure their cry is on behalf of the Morrighan. When crows and ravens appear it is a direct invitation from the goddess of battle herself to take up your sword, for war is imminent.

The Morrighan first appears in the story of the Ulster Cycle at the great Irish Battle of Moytura, a war between invading deities: the Tuatha Dé Danann and the earliest historic race in Ireland, the Fir Bolg. They had their own laws and social institutions and established a monarchical government at the Hill of Tara, from which it is said Ireland's civilisation sprung. In true Morrighan style she cried out a prophesy of doom before the battle erupted, and used her powers of sorcery to rain down fire and blood upon the Tuatha Dé Danann so they could not move for three days and nights.

During the cattle raid of Regami the Morrighan appeared in many guises on separate occasions to the hero Cú Chulainn, the young man whom Queen Maeve's brave warriors fought. He did not recognise her when he found her stealing one of his cows and became angry. As soon as she shape-shifted into a crow he recognised her and admitted he would not have insulted her had he known who she was. She immediately prophesied his death in battle, which came to pass. On another occasion she offered him assistance in battle and also her love, appearing to him as a young maiden (in some stories she is an old hag). Foolishly, Cú Chulainn rejected her offer. In response she interfered with his next combat by shape-shifting into an eel as he crossed a ford. He lashed out and broke the eel's ribs, but she recovered well and changed into a wolf. As a wolf the Morrighan deliberately scared the sheep and drove them towards the warrior, who threw a slingshot at the wolf and blinded one of the Morrighan's eyes. Instantly she transformed into a white- and red-eared heifer and led the cattle in a stampede. Cú Chulainn fired another slingshot and the Morrighan limped away.

Soon after his victory, Cú Chulainn came across an old woman who was milking a cow. She was blind in one eye and suffered from damaged ribs and a broken leg. She offered the thirsty warrior three sips of milk, and as he took each sip in turn he blessed her. His blessings healed her immediately and the Morrighan returned to true form. The Morrighan appeared before Cú Chulainn one last time as he made his way to what would be his final battle. He was unaware of his impending doom until he came across an old hag who was washing bloody armour in a ford. At the sight of her scrubbing the blood from the clothes of warriors who were doomed to fall, Cú Chulainn knew he was to be finally conquered.

The Morrighan appeared as a raven over the battlefield, foretelling and influencing the outcome as she always did throughout a battle, until Cú Chulainn was mortally wounded. Despite his impending death he wrapped his innards around a huge a boulder so he could stand upright to continue to face and terrify his enemies. His death finally came to pass when a black crow landed on his shoulder.

Once at Samhain, during the battle of Mag Tuired against the Fomorians, a hostile and monstrous supernatural race who were later portrayed as giants and sea creatures, the Morrighan had an encounter with the high king of the Tuatha Dé Danann, the Dagda. She was washing bloody battle clothes, with her feet astride the River Unius, when he came across her and they copulated. In the throes of passion, the Morrighan promised to summon all the magicians of Ireland to cast spells against the Fomorian king on behalf of Tuatha Dé Danann.

MESSAGE FROM THE MORRIGHAN

'Those who are close to you fear your wrath. I will show you how to fight carefully, with wisdom as your tool, for it is time to reclaim your sovereignty. Don't be afraid to be dramatic, for it is okay to allow others to see that you mean business. However, you can do this in a kind and loving way, but be true to yourself and do not be afraid to place boundaries around you. Be not ruled by others, but appreciate those allies who ultimately have your best interests at heart even if you can't see it.'

SEEKING THE MORRIGHAN

The strategic plans you put into place with Queen Maeve should now put you in good stead, as you stand face to face with your demons to defeat the enemy within and all that vexes you. It is time to fight the good fight, stand firm in the face of adversity and take steps to take charge of your life as the Irish goddess of war and battle calls you to her side. This fearsome goddess is rough, blunt and violent yet she teaches you to protect all that you hold dear and to fight for what you believe is right. She will direct you towards change and help you confront the battle within. As you face your inner foe the battle to control your emotions, reactions and destructive thought patterns could well be the fight of your life. The Morrighan has yelled her battle cry to the sounds of your internal warring; the enemy within needs to be destroyed and you can only hope she has chosen to be on your side.

When you seek the Morrighan expect to be greeted by a frenzied axe-wielding warrior who shrieks and yells through the mists to warn you of battle, or she may present herself in the form of a raven or crow. Either way, her appearance is not a welcome sight for those who fear death on the battlefield, nor is her wrath. Her hostile reputation precedes her, as does her fury! She is known for her vindictiveness and weakness for revenge as she instils fear into all who cross her. This wild, war-loving goddess determines the fate of fighting soldiers and shrieks triumphantly over the losing side. She is the fearful hag of the battlefield who presides over death and destruction. She is the epitome of the Dark Goddess, and is feared for her great strength and the macabre dark traits that make her the goddess of battle.

To those who are weak of mind, who lack good judgement and self-control she is the instigator of an internal war. She will prod and provoke every irritant that lies within until she gets a reaction, and that's when the battle of the mind begins. As a dark goddess it is the Morrighan's role to make you aware of any niggles that could cause you to explode in temper and rage. Be warned, though, that when she declares war it is only those with strong minds who are able to survive the battle with negative and torturous thoughts. She will decide if your victories have been at the expense of your morals, ethics and principles and who or what was harmed in the process as she considers whether your words, thoughts or actions were necessary for your cause.

People pleasing or constantly reinventing yourself implies a lack of conviction and a fickle nature, which the Morrighan will not tolerate. Instead, like her ability to shape-shift into other forms such as crows and ravens, she exhibits the necessity of being flexible and adaptable in the face of conflict and aversion. Many do seek her out for her warrior spirit and strength of character to assist them in all matters of war and battle and to fight for their rights. She welcomes strong, independent warriors who wish to regain control of their lives and who have the determination to fight for their cause and be a champion for other people. If you're proud of your victories and have a strong sense of self-esteem, she will encourage you to be brave and will eventually lead you out from the bloodshed and turmoil of battle.

DARK GODDESS COMPARISON

In Irish the Morrighan's name was originally *Mór-Rioghain*, which means 'phantom queen' or 'great queen', with *rigan* translating as 'queen' and *mor* as 'great'; this connects her with sovereignty, for which she is much revered. However, her crone personification Nemain, according to opinion and tradition, is often also known as the Morrigu.

The Morrighan has often been mixed up with the goddess Morgana, who is probably best known for her incarnation as Morgan le Fay, the half-sister of Arthur Pendragon, who eventually became crowned King Arthur of Camelot.

REASONS FOR WORKING WITH THE MORRIGHAN

As you work with the Morrighan during this stage of the dark night of the soul she will first entice you into a battle of darkness before helping you rise up towards the light and claim supreme power. You might find yourself getting a bit feisty at this time; what you once may have let pass you now find yourself getting irritated by. You nitpick until you spark a reaction from another person, and a full-scale row can ensue as the Dark Goddess starts to become defensive within. A newfound strength will keep you defending your walls whether via verbal attack or clever tactics already honed by Queen Maeve, and the Morrighan will ask you to choose sides as she always does before battle.

The Morrighan is an antagonist who will continue to test you through all kinds of scenarios until a lesson is well and truly learned. Eventually you will get it, the moment when the same drama presents itself yet again but you refuse to play for it is your reactions that draw everything to you. Your life unfolds as a response to your reactions to the actions of others, and a particular scenario will keep coming up until you go deep within and look to see what is it within you that is making you react the way you do. This is the first step of the healing, but it may take you a thousand arguments before you realise this won't go away until you deal with it, until you take responsibility for your reactions. You are to blame; it's you that has the problem, but where does it stem from? Once pinpointed you will start the second phase of the healing and decide whether or not you will let it affect you again. You will discover that every time you think you are over it you will get caught out as the Morrighan tests you, and just when you thought that all was healed. Doh: she caught you out again!

At this stage you may find that you feel reasonably in control, especially compared with how you behaved and felt with Hel and the other dark goddesses you've met along the way. However, when the Morrighan turns up, although your sudden reactions are now sporadic and far and few between, when you are caught out they are way more vicious than ever before and all control is absolutely lost for that moment. You have become stronger in your resolve as the wheel of fortune takes you further away from rock bottom, but you could be in danger of being too powerful. At this stage you don't care who is in the firing line!

Gifted now with the Morrighan's fighting spirit, nothing can stop you from taking back what is yours but be warned, for there is a fine balance between strength and aggression and some self-control is required, and you will be continually tested as she sends a driver to swerve in front of you or someone says a wrong word to you. Without even thinking, you may burst with expletives without caring about the outcome. At this point you have no care for the opinions of others as you curse, shout and rage until you wonder who on earth you are. The old you would not have behaved in this manner, but the current you can't seem to help yourself. Deep down your blood is boiling at the unfairness of your situation, and festering resentment could invite in your inner critic's presence as old insecurities and fears follow.

Are you still listening to your inner critic? Do you hear its negativity but question what it has to say, or do you tell it to go away the moment it tries to invade your thoughts? The negativity of your inner critic enticing you to feel wretched, to drag up the past or feel resentment towards another person may never fully leave; however, by telling it to shut up the moment you become aware of its voice will disempower the enemy within. Instead of believing in what it has to say you will find yourself surprisingly disagreeing, and each internal argument you have with it will weaken its resolve. Eventually you will find you have no emotions attached to it at all, which is when the destructive voice within will get quieter and quieter until you no longer hear it.

When the Morrighan storms toward you she bids you to become aware, to be observant of your every thought, action and reaction just as a general would before battle. Each old fear that comes up unexpectedly you will have to conquer and face, with the goddess of war at your side, until they are all slain. Anger will dissipate as you cease to try controlling everything, insecurities will transform into a quiet, self-assured confidence and fears will be no more. It is time to set yourself free from hurt, anger and betrayal and let go. Be kind, forgive yourself and give yourself permission to be forgiven. Others may be reeling from your actions or you could be a target of judgement, shaming or disapproval. Soothe your wounded heart by radiating love out to those who have injured you. This is not giving them permission for bad behaviour, but instead heals your hurts. Resentment is a prison door that harbours emotional distress, while forgiveness holds the key to freedom. Make peace with your pain as you release attachment to the situation and move on.

FORGIVENESS

The key to this stage is forgiveness. Having forgiveness releases you, so don't mistake it for weakness or letting others off scot free. It brings about peace of mind and is a welcome relief from the conflict of an internal battle when you can't get past your own head. Most of us have experienced internal battles of some sorts; maybe you've struggled with conforming with society, work politics or even house rules. How did or does it make you feel? Do you find yourself having imaginary conversations with those who oppose you, getting your side of the story ready in case a particular situation arises? Do you drive yourself crazy with 'They did this or that to me', 'It's not fair' and so on? It's exhausting stuff and will give you many a sleepless night. When sometimes it is necessary for your mind to analyse, process and problem solve, the destructive voice from within will try to entice a battle and that voice wants you to fight! When the Morrighan screeches her battle cry the enemy within needs to be destroyed.

Can you imagine what it would have been like to see this bloodthirsty carrion of battle appear on the land before war as the harbinger of death? With her wild red hair blowing all around her face as she screamed her banshee battle cry, her formidable appearance would have been enough to frighten off the enemy. It wasn't unusual for the deity of war to be represented by a female, for women in those times were often warriors who would also use their feminine powers of wisdom and compassion. The mother cult of the time was expressed through battle and regenerative ecstasy, and often used magick and incantations in warfare rather than physical strength. They were respected for their power and were equal to men in rule, law and property ownership. It wasn't until Britain was invaded by more patriarchal pagan societies such as the Anglo-Saxons and Vikings and then ultimately the rise of Christianity once the Romans had left the isles that the reverence for the feminine started to decline and men and women were no longer seen as being equal. Women were looked upon as man's fall from grace and were no longer in the image of the divine, and they were thought to have little more value than that of beasts.

Many of the Celtic goddesses whose aspects derived from love were turned into early Christian saints, such the triple goddess Brigid for instance, but the goddesses who represented death and destruction were misunderstood and feared and particularly those who appeared with wild and untamed flaming red hair and wielding an axe on the battlefield. They have been disregarded or tarnished in reputation throughout history.

SEEING RED

Redheads are known for revealing their fiery side, but that may just be a story of old that has been deliberately placed into the minds of generations of people to disempower anyone with red hair. For me the colour red symbolises power, and many dark goddesses are portrayed with red hair, such as Queen Maeve and the Morrighan for example.

The colour of blood is known to represent life, but it also constitutes war, fighting, wounds and death on the battlefield. The devil has always been portrayed as being the colour red, as was hell.

A legendary leader and warrior queen of the Iceni tribe during the early Roman occupation of Britain, Boudicca fought and defended her beloved Britannia against the Romans. She inspired her people, who had once been the Romans' allies, to rebel against them after her husband Prasutagus died. He had left half of his property and lands to Rome and the other half to his daughters; however, the Romans did not honour Boudicca's husband's will and took control of all of his lands and all possessions. Rising up, Boudicca entreated her people to join with other Celtic tribes under her leadership. She led them to victory on three occasions as she wailed her frenzied battle cry with her red hair wild and untamed, destroying and ransacking the Roman forts at Colchester, London and St Albans.

Eventually the Britons lost to the Romans at the Battle of Watling Street. The Iceni dispersed after the battle, and Boudicca and her daughters were publicly punished for inciting rebellion. The Romans rebuilt and reinforced their settlements, and after the defeat occupied Britain for over 350 years. However, they took greater care in dealing with British tribes after meeting Queen Boudicca, the formidable redheaded warrior who, when the Romans tried to take her lands, fought for her cause and for her freedom despite the cost.

In many stories from history and mythology fearful characters are portrayed as having red hair so we know instinctively they are evil, and we are also taught to fear the powerful traits it seems those with red hair have. It's time to understand and heal from the red curse that has surged through the bloodlines of generations.

Have you ever been blamed for something that was out of your control? Maybe you've been dismissed unjustly from work, or perhaps you've been treated unfairly because of your sex, sexual preference, colour or status. How did you feel about such discrimination: were you complacent and permissive or did you rise up and fight for justice? I felt a new strength of power and intensity during this stage of my dark night of the soul once I had dyed my trademark long blonde hair to the brightest red I could find. It wasn't a deliberate choice, but one I feel was made for me after I connected with the Morrighan and all she stood for in my dreamtime. I needed courage if I was to fight for my rights, and it was the Morrighan's attributes that served me well. The vibration of red took dramatic effect, changing the way people behaved toward me and affecting the way I behaved. Not once did I feel like me and eventually I turned everything into a battle, as I longed to return to the gentle loving behaviours of the air sign I am.

Have you ever dramatically changed something about yourself? If so, what were the reactions of other people to you? Did you still feel like you, or did you feel even more like you? Perhaps the change made you feel uncomfortable and you wished to be how you used to be. Once a change takes place you can never fully go back to who you were, for experiences can never be undone.

BATTLES AND BOUNDARIES

Have you ever got to the point when you felt you just had to fight your corner, that enough was enough? Are you the type of person who will allow someone to walk all over you? Maybe you're in awe of somebody and believe in all they say, or perhaps you feel as though you aren't as strong as they are and protesting would be futile. Instead of playing the victim, the Morrighan calls you to stand in your strength and be exactly who you want to be. Do you want to stand up to the toxic people in your life? It is time to determine what or who is sucking the life force out of you or directing negative energy towards you. Do not be fearful; instead, be strong and turn any negativity into positive personal power. Take a stand and say 'No more!' Look more deeply into situations and don't take so much on face value. Tread carefully and keep watch for enemies who lurk in the shadows, and allow your discernment to trust your instincts and then go for the kill.

The Morrighan will help turn your natural feelings of anger into a powerful force that enhances your personal power. Instead of seeking revenge, she will help you to embrace the sacred energy of anger and show you how to use its force purposefully as you take steps to take back control. She teaches you to take your anger and turn it into something positive to fuel you to move forward, to get stronger as you load your rage and fear into a battle of will and steely nerves. It's your responsibility to combat whatever vexes you and to confront others when they push the boundaries if you wish to get your life back on track.

People do like to take advantage, and if you're a sensitive soul or are grateful for someone's help or friendship it's often hard to let them down or refuse them. However, when you are feeling at a loss and rely on others' advice their words are all you hear as you try to move forward. It can be all too easy to get lost in their words, which is when confusion sets in, but when you have your own clear guidelines, rules or limits in place you create reasonable, safe and permissible ways for other people to behave towards you. When someone breaks or goes beyond those limits the Morrighan gives you permission to respond accordingly.

Always putting others first and ignoring your own wants and needs means you are not valuing yourself. When you say 'Yes' to others, make sure you are not saying 'No' to yourself or eventually you will feel worn down, trodden on and resentful.

PREPARING FOR THE MORRIGHAN

Are you ready to purposefully seek out this frenzied and furious avenging goddess? If so, prepare for battle. From the shadows she flies and spies on your every movement, watching to see how you respond to conflict and deciding whether or not to champion your side. Once you've displayed the magickal potential of your inner warrior she will invite you to choose sorcery as your weapon of choice and will encourage you to unleash your personal power instead of fearing it, for she only favours the brave. If she perceives you as being weak and feeble and not prepared to stand up and fight for what you believe in be warned, as she may just take your head for a trophy!

You may have subconsciously called in the Morrighan on a soul level when you wished:

- to take charge of your life
- for new strength
- to be a winner
- to make a stand
- to embrace your fighting spirit

- for fairness
- for peace of mind
- another to be happier than you.

You may have unwittingly called in the Morrighan when you:

- felt the desire to dress in red
- dyed your natural hair red
- felt fear and panic
- rose up to the bait
- placed a curse or hex on another
- felt incredibly angry
- fought and argued
- suffered mental health issues
- thought everyone was against you
- wished misfortune on another
- became very defensive
- deliberately set out to cause disruption and destruction
- cheated to win
- suffered a conflict of opinion
- were furious at losing
- went swimming in a fresh waterhole or river
- took control
- screamed and yelled
- desperately wanted to win.

Turn to the Morrighan when you wish:

- for encouragement
- for revenge
- for a new challenge
- to be rid of an old foe
- for peace of mind
- for strength of mind and body
- to ignite your inner warrior
- to stand up for yourself or others

- to cast effective banishing or binding spells
- for prophetic dreams
- to understand the cause of an ending or death of someone
- to defeat bullies
- to make weaponry
- to join the forces.

As soon as she hears your invitation to come into your life, whether subconsciously or not, the Morrighan will sharpen her weapons to be battle ready and charge towards you. You will need to look sharp, for she may appear in the form of a scavenging scald crow or a ragged-winged raven, as a beautiful enchantress or a wizened old hag glorying in the death of battle.

HONOURING AND CONNECTING WITH THE MORRIGHAN

Do the following to honour and connect with the Morrighan:

- Look after crows and ravens.
- Focus on victory.
- Wash clothes in a ford.
- Yell a frenzied battle cry.
- Take control of your life.
- Dress up in armour.
- Carve arrowheads out of flint.
- Visit an ancient battlefield.
- Listen to Celtic Irish music.
- Show your respect for war veterans through donation or the giving of your time.
- Make an altar for her and place upon it crow feathers, a bowl of blood and an arrowhead.

Altar offerings to honour and give thanks to the Morrighan include:

- raven and crow figurines
- small swords or spears
- pictures of the Morrighan
- raw meat
- red wine
- skulls
- a goblet or bowl of water.

INVOCATION TO THE MORRIGHAN

To purposely call the Morrighan into your energy you will need the following, but don't worry if you are unable to get hold of all of the ingredients as your focus will determine your connection with her:

- dragon's blood incense
- a small bowl of salt
- a pin
- a red candle
- a goblet of red wine or ale
- belladonna essential oil.

Light the incense and sprinkle some of the salt around you in a circle for protection as you ask the goddess for her blessings. You can do this silently in your mind using whatever words come to you or you can say out loud:

> *Divine goddess, I ask you to bless and protect me as I focus on the divine light within myself as I call upon you, the Dark Goddess the Morrighan, for assistance. I graciously receive your strength and sovereignty with an open heart in gratitude. Help me to serve, and help me to shine. In love and honour, so mote it be.*

All's fair in love and war, but when the balance is not tipped in your favour the Morrighan will help you to summon up your inner strength and face your opposer. Call upon the Morrighan to show your commitment to her and she will ignite your inner warrior, ensuring that fairness prevails. Use the pin to scratch the word 'devotion' into the candle and prick one of your fingers with the pin. Mix a drop of your blood into the ale as an offering to her. Anoint your third eye with a dab of belladonna essential oil so you too can fly over the battlefield, in your mind's eye of course. Stand in a field or on a lawn during a dark or new moon, light the red candle and say:

Goddess of battle, of fury and fight,
protection in place, no need for fright.
Anger, fury, conflict, blame;
internal warring is your game.
Antagoniser, unhorse my mind!
Fighting torturous thoughts; unkind.
Deathly shadows twist my fate;
boundaries crossed from peace to hate.
Rise up to harness will and power.
Candle lit, burns down this hour.
Queen of witches, to you I hail,
upon the ground pour blooded ale,
in honour. Unto you I yield
and swear allegiance. Bond is sealed.

Leave the candle to safely burn down and pour the bloodied red wine onto the land to honour to show your commitment to the Morrighan. Say out loud:

Gratefully I accept the magick of you,
of protection to assist in all that I do.
Lend me the courage, build power in me;
assist my transcendence. So mote it be.

Signs that the Morrighan is around you include:

- You desire red wine.
- Everything seems to be a battle.
- You feel the need to defend yourself.
- Others verbally attack you.
- Crows or ravens follow or surround you.
- You keep seeing crows.
- You're having vivid nightmares.
- You find yourself in threatening circumstances.
- You crave steak or raw meat.
- A gash or cut won't stop bleeding.
- You become instilled with fear and panic.
- You experience a glimmer of new strength through the darkness at this stage of the dark night of the soul.

The Morrighan decides whose side she is on, for she chooses her own. If you're one of the chosen few she will reshape your life by making a weapon of you and lead you into battle. It is a great but challenging gift of rebirth and transformation that she offers, and she may demand you create sacred space for her in your life and show her the commitment she desires. As she delves deep within you searching for ferocity, steel will and a heroic heart she offers her protection, for she always protects her own.

EXERCISES AND RITUALS TO ENGAGE WITH THE MORRIGHAN

JOURNAL WORK

Acknowledging injustice and unfairness: make a list in your journal of everything that you deem to be unfair in your current dark situation. What have you had to sacrifice? How do you feel about those who have opposed you? How have you dealt with opposition and how does it make you feel now? Do you feel anger rising? What triggers you to react? At this stage of the dark night of the soul and after all that you've experienced thus far you may think you have your situation under control. It's been a while since you were suffering in isolation with Hel or kicking off when Fuamnach appeared, however, don't presume these goddesses have ever left you for they will be testing you from afar, and when the goddess of war purposefully pushes your buttons she waits to see what it is that still triggers you to react.

Setting boundaries: you can't set good boundaries if you're unsure of where you stand, so you need to identify your physical, emotional, mental and spiritual limits and consider what you can tolerate and accept. Write down in your journal what it is that makes you feel uncomfortable, upset or stressed. Those feelings will help you identify what your limits are and what is acceptable to you at this time. Of course, this may change as you are propelled further up the wheel of fortune, but for now make time to be assertive and put your personal boundaries in place.

CLAIMING YOUR SOVEREIGNTY

Light three candles – one black, one red and one white – and place them safely on your altar. Take a deep breath and close your eyes as you exhale. Imagine you're standing in the middle of an empty field at the magickal time of dusk and a thin mist hovers above the land.

Feel the earth's energy rising up to connect with yours and breathe in the gentle breeze. As it sweeps through your mind, clear pictures start to form in your mind's eye for you have been gifted with clairvoyance, with clear seeing. Your imagination feeds you images of all those who have done you wrong, of fearful situations or challenges you're fighting to overcome. Tune in to your feelings and become aware of any tensions, worries, self-doubts, rage, fury, anger or anything else that has been bubbling deep within. You are consumed with dark emotions as you say:

Attacks ensued to cause alarm,
enemies cause fatal harm.
Boiling point! Must seek revenge.
Destroyed, this act must be avenged.
Coercion forcing to conform;
enticement in its darkest form!

Sticks and stones, cruel words of fear.
Defend stand strong, won't shed a tear.
Death, destruction, loss and woe,
consumes the mind, must let it go.

In the distance you can just make out a silhouetted figure running towards you. A terrifying shriek wails across the field and the sky turns black. Hundreds of crows and ravens flap all around you as the sound of caws echoes through to your very soul. You want to turn, to run and hide, but halt when a booming and authoritative voice calls out:

Death, destruction, woe and loss.
Deep despair among chaos.
Withstand the storm to be free;
deliverance is victory!

You stand still, not daring to breathe in your terror of facing the battle you've been avoiding.

Let go of all that you hold dear.
Don't let change instil new fear.
Stand strong and watch the old decay;
a new dawn welcomes you today.

Continue to breathe deeply as you become more at peace, exhaling out any tension, worries or fears. You look up to see a cloud hovering above you in the shape of a raven. Oh, to be in the sky; oh, to fly high above the world and to soar and be free! The cloud lowers itself further and further until it reaches you and you merge completely with it. As the cloud envelops you within its form you feel your body calibrate to the energy of the raven: you have become one with the majestic bird itself. Feel your strength and fly, fly!! You rise up into the sky and become aware of your mighty wing span. Feel the power, feel the expansion as you engage with its medicine of wisdom, magick and prophecy. Your black wings take you further and further up and out to where your soul calls you to be. This is experiencing freedom!

As you soar over the battlefield, notice how the scene is very different from your bird's eye view. From your new and heightened perspective you see a strong, fierce woman waving an axe all around you in human form; it is the Morrighan gifting you her strength and courage to finish what was started. Suddenly, all those you've been battling with begin to fade from the scene. In that very moment you realise that it was old perspective who was the enemy all along and it no longer serves you. Old wounds and battle scars start to heal and your lower emotions dissolve and turn to blood as a new life force energy feeds and nourishes you. From the skies your raven self swoops down to merge into the new you. It is time to rise up and claim your sovereignty!

The Morrighan places a copper crown on your head and a black cape of raven and crow feathers upon your shoulders. Say out loud:

Honour is for what I stand.
I'll reign as sovereign o'er my land.
Authority doth rule supreme;
I'll seize my right as king or queen!

With focus and intention, leave your negativity and fears in the black candle and allow it to safely burn down. Focus your passions, fight, vigour, rage and anger into the red candle to call upon when needed. Blow out the candle and allow the swirl of the extinguished flame to wrap around you. Place your hopes and dreams for peace of mind into the white candle and blow out the flame so you can add new desires to the candle whenever you wish. Victory is yours!

Give thanks to the Morrighan by feeding crows and ravens or donating to a bird rescue charity, and place upon your Dark Goddess altar an offering in honour of the Morrighan such as a bowl of brine and blood or black and red candles to ensure she chooses to fight on your side.

INCANTATION FOR EQUALITY

Do you ever feel like the world is an unjust, cruel place? Are you overloaded by concerns about the welfare of those who have faced injustice or have you yourself been a victim of an unjust action? If so, this incantation can help ease your mind and work towards focusing energy into righteous directions:

Alluring serpents slip and slide;
secrets whispered deep inside.
All are equal, don't back down.
Master this, I'll wear the crown.
Demonised I'll never be;
Respect of who I am is key.

BANISHING RITUAL

Getting rid of negative people and energies around you is fundamental to finding your own way, and banishing rituals can be powerful tools for focusing energy on those you do not wish to stay. Focus your intentions into some black pepper seeds and place them on top of a black candle. Light the candle and say:

Beware! Be warned! Be free from harm.
Use peppercorns as magick charm.
Spite of tongue or cursed deeds,
I'll banish with my pepper seeds.
This magick is worked, with harm to none.
So mote it be. There, it is done.

Let the candle burn down to banish the person and their actions or whatever your intentions were.

MIRROR MANIFESTATION

Mirrors are considered to be a portal to the astral world, particularly when used in visualisation and spell work; think Alice in *Through the Looking-glass*. The glass of the mirror represents the psychic properties of water and the power of reflection, reflecting all that is seen and unseen, and can be used to manifest your desires. As the great queen of magick and prophesy the Morrighan knows what the Fates have in store for you and pushes you forward to cast your fears aside, to follow your dreams.

Close your eyes and take three deep breaths in and out. Light a blue candle to represent the element of water, and gaze into a mirror at dusk and say:

Mirror, mirror give me sight,
show me shadows through the light.
Reveal the one who guards me well,
that we might meet through cast of spell.
Accept, I shall, new power in me.
Mirror, mirror let me see.

Gaze into the flame and breathe deeply in and out through your heart centre. Feel the warmth of your heart as it expands to have an overwhelming, immense feeling of love. This is the time to visualise your dreams in the glass: see it all in every detail and as though it's coming true while the Morrighan prepares you for transformation. Observe and be open to your visions. Let the candle safely burn down.

EXERCISE TO RELEASE THE HURT

Place a bowl of water in front of you, hold a bloodstone crystal in your hand and say:

Crying a river, emotional flow;
harbouring hurts; it's time to let go.
Hard to forget, when treated that way;
release and be healed upon this day.
Damage is done ne'er to relive.
Write down the names of whom to forgive.
Place paper in water, holding it down;
picture their actions and watch them drown.
Bloodstone heals anxiety;
forgiveness granted, now be free!
Oh Morrighan, I ask for your power in me:
assist my transcendence. So mote it be.

Place the crystal into the bowl to hold the paper down and leave all your hurts to drown in the water until the next dark moon phase.

EXERCISE TO DEFINE BOUNDARIES

Wrap some rope around a piece of elder wood as you face the direction of north under a dark moon and say:

Limits reached, boundaries crossed;
advantage taken, respect lost.
Standing strong upon the earth,
elder, dispel to rebirth.
Wrap the rope around the wood,
binding two words, 'yes' and 'should'.
Releasing any obligation;
banishing all exploitation.
Divide and part, now draw the line.
Boundaries placed, my life is mine.

Purposefully draw a line with the roped wood in the earth in front of you, which means you have put your boundaries in place by drawing a line and making a point.

LESSONS FROM THE DARK GODDESS THE MORRIGHAN

If you feel a storm is brewing or you are being too defensive with others the Morrighan will help you to face it. This isn't a time to avoid conflict or back down. I know myself that hiding darkness in the light is unhealthy for peace of mind, and the only way to heal is to acknowledge the fight. She reminds you that with change comes chaos, which should be accepted and dealt with in order to move forward.

Although she's a fierce goddess of battle, she can assist you to take a softer approach if necessary while you build up your mental and physical strength. She will assist you to reign over the battlefield and claim your honour with the help of her gifts. This dark crone will protect you in all matters of battle, whether it's in defence, to take revenge or an internal conflict of your mind. Prophecy, magick and wisdom are the weapons she offers to lend you as you wield your axe furiously through your darkest moments. The Morrighan exists between and betwixt life and death. She dwells in the shadows and waits for you to claim your sovereignty as you walk with her between the worlds. It is time to rise up!

As the battle continues the next dark goddess beckons you with her bony finger and bids you join her if you wish to survive . . .

13. THE CAILLEACH

Initiation of survival and endurance

Born to survive, fight for life;
sufferance of tears and strife.
Darkness shadows over light,
claiming death through blackened night.

ORIGIN	Celtic (Scottish, Irish, Manx).
NAMES	the Cailleach, Cailleach Groarnagh, Cailleach Bheara, Cailleach Bheur, Beira, Cally Berry, blue hag of winter, bone mother, woman of stones, Cailleach Nollaig (Christmas old wife), Cailleach Beinne Bric (guardian of deer).
GODDESSES	Beira, Kali.
SYMBOLS	mountains, rocks, hammer, snow, grain, deer, standing stones, the land, the colour blue.
THEMES	winter, divine hag, balance, cycles, rebirth, survival, endurance, overcoming, protector of wild animals.
LESSONS	endurance, tenacity, survival.
COLOURS/CANDLES	black, blue, silver.
CRYSTALS	stones, hag stone.
HERBS/FLOWERS/OILS	thistle, heather, gorse.
MOON PHASE	dark.
SEASONS	autumn, winter.
TREE	Scots pine.
FESTIVAL	Yule.

An Irish, Manx and Scottish deity, the Cailleach is a terrifying embodiment of the crone, the old hag. Dressed entirely in grey and with a plaid wrapped around her shoulders, she wears an apron and is sometimes seen carrying a creel, or wicker basket, on her back. Her heavily lined face has a blue tinge, like a corpse, and her matted hair is long and white and flecked with frost. She holds a wooden staff in her hand, although some stories see her with a wand or a boulder and in more modern times a broom or besom. She is the divine hag who is typically portrayed as a scary, old, one-eyed witch who appears in late autumn when the earth is dying. She is the queen of winter who calls down snow for the earth to rest and restore as she spreads winter across the land.

The Cailleach is one of the most ancient spirits and she shaped the earth and created the rugged landscape of Scotland, sometimes appearing as a beautiful young maiden and at other times as a hideous old woman or a legendary giantess. Not only does she create and change the landscape, she also has the ability to shape-shift into the landscape, which was demonstrated by her stormy fight with Angus, when she turned herself into a standing stone.

The Cailleach is known throughout the British Isles and has a variety of names. She has three names in Scotland – Cailleach Bheur, Beira and Carlin – and is called Cally Berry and Cailleach Bheara in Ireland and Cailleach Groarnagh on the Isle of Man. However, in addition to these titles that are specific to geographical locations she assumes many others, including the blue hag of winter, the bone mother and the woman of stones. She is also known as Cailleach Nollaig, or the Christmas old wife, and Cailleach Beinne Bric, or the guardian of deer and can be called upon as such.

At the height of winter in Scotland it was customary for the head of the household to carve the face of the Cailleach as the Christmas old wife into a piece of oak to represent cold and death. It was thrown into the fire on Christmas Eve so that death would bypass the house during the coming year. Today it is known as a Yule Log, although you are more likely to find a chocolate version in most kitchens rather than a traditional log in the fireplace!

Despite the many variations of her name, the Cailleach's most prominent character is that of the winter goddess, who ushers in the cold, dark winter months from Samhain and maintains the cold until Imbolc, the Celtic festival of growth, new beginnings and the renewal of life, now widely marked in the USA as Groundhog Day. The name *Cailleach* weaved its way into the Gaelic language during the Dark Ages and is based on the Latin root *pallium*, meaning 'a veil'. However, *cailleach* as a word has evolved over time and its meaning is now commonly accepted as 'old wife', although its literal translation is 'veiled one', an epithet often applied to one who belongs to hidden worlds and is no stranger to us.

The Cailleach has been represented in faery tales and movies as Maleficent, the snow queen, the wicked witch and the evil queen who exudes magick and power from her fingertips. She is the old hag and other distorted versions of the crone aspect of the triple goddess. She is the dark one who spins her web of fate and teaches through deep wisdom and life lessons that so many wish to avoid, for she is the instigator of death and all you've known.

As the bringer of snow and frost the Cailleach is an original weather witch. She is the sharp, biting wind, the gatherer of black clouds and the bearer of storms. She uses weather magick to influence the outcome of battle as well as to cause chaos. She harnesses the power of the four winds to rage across the land, with gusts tearing down branches and battering gathered crops. This goddess of death is to be greatly feared, for her face is so terrifying she frightens animals into hibernation through the dark winter months. However, this is a good thing as she assures their survival, as she will for you if you ask for her assistance. There are many hands she has held through a dark night of the soul, and she has been a source of dark comfort through the bleakness.

The Cailleach isn't all bad; she has just been misjudged for her manky eye, her terrible teeth and dreadful matted hair and misunderstood for her cold and calculating actions. Just like nature, she balances her glacial destructive side. As a goddess of guardianship and magickal transformation she is naturally drawn to those who are experiencing major life changes, helping them to survive through the transition if they are bold enough to invite her in.

A crow sits upon her staff, which she uses to strike the earth to become hard and cold just like the stones she throws from her basket to create the harsh winter landscape. She is responsible for the process of dying, and even though this scary-looking grandmother is terrifying, if you are longing for some transitional relief you should welcome her presence.

In Scotland the Cailleach was regarded and revered as the mother of all deities. However, she was also terribly feared, not only for her hideous appearance but also for her temperament. Her anger was as biting as the north wind and as stormy as the harsh North Sea. Each winter she reigns as queen, but when spring blows in upon the fresh winds of the east it is a sign of warmer months to come, a time of looking forward to welcoming Angus of the White Steed, the summer king, and his beautiful queen Brid (or Bridget or Bride), who is the personification of spring and a triple goddess who appears in her maiden form at Imbolc, when the first signs of growth appear. Both were loved by all, for they were the bringers of light and bright happy days.

As winter came to an end the Cailleach was enraged to find her power passing away, and she tried her utmost to prolong the winter season by blighting early flowers such as snowdrops and crocuses with a blast of frost or raising late snow storms to keep her sacred lands hard and infertile. As the queen of winter she rules over the harsh, cold months and she used her extreme powers to capture Brid. She hid the virginal maiden inside Ben Nevis, the highest mountain in Scotland, on the night of Samhain and planned to keep her there to avoid spring from blossoming.

However, Angus, the son of the Cailleach, dreamed of the beautiful fair maiden and asked the king of the Green Isle who she was and where he could find her. The king informed him that she was Brid, and that she would be Angus's queen when he ruled over the summer months. The king warned Angus that his mother had full knowledge of the future as a seer and foreteller of doom and had hidden Brid away so that her own cold, stark reign would be sustained. On the eve of Imbolc Angus found and freed Brid from her mountainous prison. Petrified of the consequences of her release, the Cailleach sought the couple and a fight broke out. To escape a potentially fatal blow from her son, the Cailleach turned herself into a standing stone. She is said to remain in that form until the following Samhain, when she rises up once more to usher in the winter months and repeat her dark actions.

In other Gaelic folklore the Cailleach lived for hundreds and hundreds of years and never died of old age, because at the start of each spring she would journey to the floating Green Island of the west, where the only season is summer, and there she would take of the magickal waters of the well of youth. The island is said to be bright and abundant with fruits and blossoms and drifts across the Atlantic Ocean, often appearing off the west coast of Ireland and sometimes near the Hebrides and the north-western shores of Scotland. Sailors have searched for the mysterious island in vain as they steered their vessels across the ocean, but it was never found. As it lies hidden in the mist seafarers have sailed past its shores, never knowing it was nearby. Some have caught glimpses of its beauty and wonder, but for only a second before it vanished from sight and sank beneath the waters.

The Cailleach knows exactly how to reach it, visiting on the first lengthening days of light when the magickal elixir that bubbles fresh from a rock crevice, the well of youth, is at its most potent. It is vital that she drink of the waters before any birds visit the well and before a dog barks or she would turn to dust and crumble into nothingness. With one sip of the magickal water the Cailleach became young again and returned to Scotland, where she fell into a deep sleep. She awakened to bright sunshine and rose up as a beautiful young girl with long blonde hair, rosy pink cheeks and sparkling blue eyes. Dressed in a green robe and with a circlet of flowers on her head she strode across Scotland, where it was said there was no fairer goddess perceived across the lands apart from Brid, the queen of summer.

As each month passed the Cailleach aged all too quickly, reaching full womanhood by midsummer and her beauty fading through the autumn months. As soon winter returned so also did her wrinkles, and her yellow hair turned to a matted mess of white and she became an old, withered hag and began her reign of terror once more, as the fierce queen of winter.

MESSAGE FROM THE CAILLEACH

'I am the one you fear, for I am the bringer of death. I am everything you have been avoiding, yet it is I who is the answer to your wishes and dreams and the future you hope for. It is I who holds the keys to your transformation in the highest, but in return for my gift you must be brave and heroic as you face the desolation of winter and the bleakness of endings.

'Every rock, every stumbling block you face and every obstacle you conquer, I shall be waiting at the top of the highest mountain as you reach the summit for I know you have the power within and all the tools you need to step up. But do not get comfortable yet; first the biggest adventure of your life awaits you, and that is death: death to endings, of the old you. This is my transformative gift to you for completion, so allow the lonely emptiness, the barren void within to start germinating. For that to occur the process of death must begin. Let old beliefs and behaviours that do not serve the new you dissolve. As the old energy seeps back down into the earth it transmutes and transforms into the hardness of the rocks and cruel terrain of the wilds. You have nothing to fear, for I am with you. You will find me in the rugged hills, the icy glaciers, the snow-topped mountains and each hard stone. I am the bone mother, the keeper of winter, the bringer of death. Come unto me, my child.'

SEEKING THE CAILLEACH

Exhausted from what seems like an eternity of fighting the enemy, both within and without, you now find yourself in what seems like no-man's land, and just like a shield maiden with sword still in hand after battle, you survey the aftermath of destruction. There may not be many allies still standing, and deserters – those who've not stood by you or couldn't cope – are quick to disappear. As you retreat to lick your wounds the Cailleach hears your anguish in the darkness and presents herself with only one eye, matted hair and terrible teeth. She is at hand to instigate the death of all you once knew now that war is over. She is the bone woman who waits silently as you drop once more into an abyss of despair. Her bony hand will hold yours as she strips you down naked to your very core and until all illusions are broken. It's time to stop fighting, to stop the struggle and give in to her.

At this stage of the dark night of the soul change is afoot, and if you have been desperately clinging on to your old self you must understand that dying to the old will escalate you to where you truly desire to be. It is time to let go, to surrender and accept that death is never final. Try not to fear, for it is simply a portal to rebirthing into the next and glorious stage of the cycle called life, just like the changing seasons themselves.

The Cailleach is a goddess of cold honesty who won't hold back from revealing the truth, for it is only the Dark Goddess who can shed light on that which has been hidden. Only the light can be illuminated by that which is the dark; one cannot possibly exist without the other. Ultimately it is she who is the queen of disguises, and she holds the key to transformation but only if you're willing to journey with her through the darkness to confront your greatest fears. It is only the very brave who seek a bone goddess, for she is the older and fiercer sister of the crone who has been feared since time began, just like the grim reaper, as the bringer of death.

When the Cailleach appears you can be sure that death is imminent, as destruction and chaos purposefully follow her. You can expect a frosty reception and cold indifference when this hideous grandmother pays you a visit in the wee small hours. Those who fear her bitter, icy cold attributes avoid her at all costs from fear of death and the unknown; however, she is tough love just like a dear granny who has your best interests at heart and she will point her bony finger if your heart has turned to stone. With a stare she will dish out seemingly horrific promises of death and endings and she is insensitive to the heartless tasks and challenges she forces you to endure, for she believes they are for your own good.

You do need to have some genuine fear of this bone goddess who sniffs out blood and will take yours for her own. As the queen of winter she is associated with the ageing process and, rather like an alternative midwife, assists older women through menopause. She strips women of their fertility, leaving them dry as an old bone and barren and fruitless. The Cailleach also helps them to survive the physical, emotional and spiritual changes that accompany this rite of passage through into the croning years. In this case acceptance turns the magickal key for smooth transformation to occur as she takes responsibility for those under her care, for not only is she a destructor, she is a creator goddess of the land and she makes sure to always leave a portion of soft, fertile ground for the deer to graze on so they can survive her cruel reign of winter. It is the death of all she culls during the winter months that is her promise of new life to come, for in the cycle of life nature must die before it can rise up and grow again in spring. Death is necessary in order to be reborn; it is not the end.

If you are not afraid to leave your past and all you hold dear behind the Cailleach will strip you in a heartbeat of all you no longer need. Like a wicked queen, she will wave her magick wand and bestow upon you all of her gifts of extreme power and peace of mind in exchange for your commitment to her and to yourself. In order to be restored to wholeness, the Cailleach first requires you to face the coldness of the winter months to come, to retreat within, where she will reveal to you that which you've been avoiding.

DARK GODDESS COMPARISON

We've seen her represented in faery tales and movies, for she is the snow queen, the wicked witch and the evil queen who exudes magick and power from her very fingertips. She is the old hag and other distorted versions of the crone aspect of the triple goddess, and she is the dark one who spins her web of fate and teaches through her deep wisdom and life lessons that so many wish to avoid, for she is the instigator of death and all you've known. If you are not afraid to leave your past and all you hold dear behind the Cailleach will strip you of all you no longer need in a heartbeat. Like the evil queen, she will wave her magick wand and bestow upon you all of her gifts of extreme power and peace of mind in exchange for your commitment to her and to yourself. However, in order to be restored to wholeness the Cailleach first requires you to face the coldness of the winter months to come, to retreat within, where she will reveal to you what you've been avoiding.

REASONS FOR WORKING WITH THE CAILLEACH

Unless you have healed from or have broken patterns of the past you will repeat them until you are freed. Although you are experiencing a new lifetime in the here and now, your current life actually mirrors your past lives, and that includes the people you meet and love. Have you ever met somebody and felt as though you had known them forever? Did you feel an overwhelming familiarity and intense rush of energy when you met your current partner or a previous lover? If you answered 'yes' it's because you know them on a soul level.

Before each lifetime you agree on who to meet up with again, what your role will be and what you need to do in order to heal and move on. You have already met previously in other lifetimes all the people you know now: incredible, isn't it? Some are here to support you, but others will act out their previous roles until you get the lesson.

Everything that comes up for you to deal with in this lifetime is because it hasn't been resolved yet from another. For instance, you may have been abandoned by a parent; a partner may have cheated on you; perhaps you've had wealth stolen from you or been unfairly dismissed from employment; or you may have been dealt the death of a sibling, child, parent or guardian. Whatever your dark night of the soul has been it most likely will be history repeating itself and a process that needs to be healed, for the moment you can accept and move on you are released and don't have to repeat it in this lifetime or any other. Issues such as abandonment, low self-esteem or a lack of confidence will gradually disperse as you begin the healing process. Everything that is thrown at you is to help you to grow and evolve, and you cannot grow until you acknowledge and understand the lesson and then let it go.

My battle with my mother and Christianity in this lifetime is something I needed to sort out from another lifetime. But what of my father, who left when I was a young teenager: were we repeating a past life? I obviously had abandonment issues, which was why my self-esteem was so low. Of course, I didn't realise this until I had gone through the process of the dark night of the soul, but I found that the moment I took ownership I was able to start the healing process. Do you find yourself still living in the past? Do you try to hang on to the magick of yesteryear, wishing that everything could just stay as it was during happier times?

I've always loved history but I had become obsessed with certain periods in time. Whenever I walked past old Victorian houses I pretended that I was in those days, for Victorian London calls to my depths. The time periods you find yourself fascinated with are the ones you've previously lived through.

Have a think about what periods in history you are drawn to. I love the Dark Ages, including Saxons and Vikings. I'm crazy about Ancient Greece, Rome and Egypt and am in love with Tudor times and the Plantagenets, among others, but I have no interest whatsoever in World War II, for instance. My best friend and soul sister, Barbara, loves old war planes such as bombers and knows their names and sounds. She was an air hostess in this lifetime and flew the skies for more than 15 years, which connects her to a previous life as a pilot in the Battle of Britain. My greatest love is for the stage and the very first performance I gave as a little girl was in the Old Time Music Hall. I absolutely know that I was once a Victorian actress, as it's all I wanted to be when I was growing up and I performed in musical theatre well into my 30s. On a recent trip to the States we went to Tombstone: I felt more than at home there, especially in the Bird Cage theatre which is still original from the 1880s, and I sang a quick impromptu number on the stage!

Tracking into past lives can be beneficial to understanding who you are. However, if you feel stuck in the past the Cailleach will ensure that all illusions of it are well and truly shattered, especially if you've been looking back on your life with wistful delusions, having painted a perfect picture of how your life once was before your long and arduous journey of the dark night of the soul. Even getting lost in books and stories of old, drawing from them a sense of nostalgia, romanticism and comfort, is pure escapism, especially when you find yourself longing to be back in those days. It is an illusion that is not real in the present moment and will only hold you back. Likewise, understand that every time your inner critic whispers reminders of unsavoury incidents in the past, such as what someone has said or done to you, you remain a prisoner of the energies of the past. Despising or yearning for yesterday prevents you from stepping into your future; there is no way forward unless the cycle is broken.

The Cailleach will help you step out of the shadows she finds you in. As you endure her cruel and harsh terrain just to survive you may find yourself repeating destructive patterns again and again. She will teach you how to be a born survivor, to endure each lesson that is waiting to be learned. If you feel you are a prisoner of emotions to someone who once abandoned you, or treated you badly and continues to do so you may have taken out a vow in a previous lifetime to protect or look after that person. If there is someone who holds you in their power, be it a parent, partner, child, boss, friend or colleague, it is time to break free. The Cailleach will reveal old vows you have made either in this lifetime or in another, vows you may have made to always look out for someone, to look after them, to allow their disagreeable behaviour or to be subservient that will bind you – not only to the person but to repeats of circumstance.

A vow doesn't have to be made as part of a fancy ceremony or powerful declaration; it can be just a simple sentence. However, when said with sincerity and meaning a vow commits you for eternity if you truly mean it unless it is broken. If you have ever said anything such as 'I will look after you, Daddy' when you were a child, the chances are you have been looking after every significant man in your life ever since. Likewise, if you once said something like 'I'll show them how hard I work' you have more than likely been a workaholic ever since. The Cailleach will help rid you of emotional attachment as you undo the vows you made, albeit unknowingly, so you can move forward in pure love and set yourself free and step fully into your personal power.

I know that my mother was my persecutor, as she has been in this lifetime when it comes to belief systems, but I've also spent this lifetime feeling bad for her since my father left. My heart reached out to hers, and that's when I made a vow to always look after her. For her persecution of me I always forgave her, for I understood her beliefs and didn't want to cause her further pain or heartbreak, but I did eventually leave her, going to live up north and travel the world. My pagan beliefs are everything she is against; how could this be so? I felt dreadful that I had abandoned her and many tears were shed in guilt. Does this mean I had abandoned her in a previous lifetime, I wondered during a time in meditation?

I was shown differently, for it was my mother who had betrayed me in a previous lifetime. She was the one who forced me to turn my back on the old religion in favour of Christianity; she was the one who turned me in. I was hanged and came into this lifetime with terrible throat problems. My mother held me in her power and it was time, I realised, for me to break free, to undo the vows I had made in that and this lifetime in order to move forward and embrace the work I came to do in my full power. I had to be rid of my emotional attachment to the vow I had made and in pure love set myself free.

The Cailleach will call you to stand in your strength and break any vows you've made, in all directions of time, that now hold you back from being your true authentic self. She will empower you to release any guilt, shame, fear and blame, enabling you to ignite your personal power with a new sense of freedom. If you feel you need to break free from any emotions or vows you have made that are keeping you tied to the past, the powerful ceremony outlined below will enable you to break free and become empowered.

Cairns and standing stones throughout Scotland are dedicated to the Cailleach; many of the Callanish stones on the Isle of Lewis, for example, are said to be the outcome of her creative exploits, as too are many others such as the standing stones on the Isle Gigha. One such stone known as the House of the Cailleach is found at the head of Glen Lyon. A small stone structure, it is said to have been created as the Cailleach was brushing pebbles from her apron and has been a shrine to the goddess for thousands of years. During the summer months a symbolic Cailleach was placed inside the structure, which was then completely sealed up until the following winter when the cycle began again.

It's interesting how standing stones are associated with the Cailleach, for like her they hold the wisdom of the ancients in their genetic coding and can be found strewn across Scotland and across the British Isles and parts of northern Europe. They are our teachers who have stood by silently while witnessing and absorbing every detail of spent centuries. Often found at sacred sites such as Callanish in Scotland or Stonehenge in England, these gentle giants help unlock the wisdom that we hold deep within for they harbour the key to the past.

Stonehenge is shrouded in mystery and magic, but it's clear that the circle of purposely placed stones was used for tracking and celebrating the journey of the sun. Nobody really knows exactly how the builders of this megalithic site collected and moved the gigantic stones from over 240 kilometres away. There are many theories, including alien beings, the Watchers and telekinesis, but remembering the Cailleach threw rocks and boulders from her apron and basket to create the landscape clearly associates her with the standing stones, as she is of those in Argyll, Cnoc na Carraigh, Beinn an Tuirc and at other sacred sites.

Sacred sites have a powerful magnetism. These magickal spots are situated on ley lines (meridians of potent earth energy), which have a positive effect on your physical, emotional and spiritual well-being. Our ancestors were all too aware of these effects and would be drawn to these sites to connect with the mystery, the elements and the foundations upon with they stood. To this day, millions of people flock to locations such as the prehistoric site of Stonehenge in search of healing and spiritual enrichment, or simply because they feel drawn to these places without really knowing why. Thousands of pagans, Druids and other spiritual seekers join together at Stonehenge for the winter solstice to mark the longest night and shortest day of the year and to celebrate the sun's rebirth as it slowly begins to strengthen, lengthening the days in the months leading into spring. There is no atmosphere like it, and it connects people with the ancestors, Druids and magick of the old ways.

Have you ever been drawn to visit a sacred site? If you've never had the chance to visit one perhaps there is a certain place you would love to visit. Every sacred site has its own unique healing energy, and whichever one you feel strongly drawn to will help invigorate you on a spiritual level and make you feel more connected with your higher self. Even if you're unable to visit a power spot physically, you can draw on its energy and work with it on a soul level and from the heart.

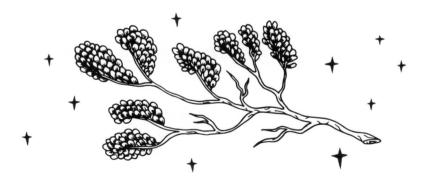

CEREMONY FOR CONNECTING WITH SACRED SPACE

Take this quiz to discover the sacred site that is best for you. By answering the questions straight from your heart and without overthinking them, you'll identify your personal connection with the sacred place that holds the particular healing energies most beneficial to you and your circumstances to help bring about more balance, an enhanced spiritual connection to assist you or help letting go of past hurts.

1. Which of the following statements best describes how you feel right now?

A. I'm feeling pulled in all directions and need to prioritise what's best for me.

B. I need to clear my head by getting close to nature.

C. My emotions are all over the place and I can't let go of the past.

2. How would your friends and colleagues usually describe you?

A. A tower of strength to all who come to you for sound advice.

B. Someone who stands firmly by her convictions, unswayed by the opinions of others.

C. Very sensitive, and someone who wears their heart on their sleeve.

3. Which of the following divination tools most appeals to you?

A. Tarot.

B. Runes.

C. Astrology.

4. How would you describe your usual self?

A. I'm a well-rounded, balanced person who knows what they want.

B. I have a deep spiritual connection with nature and love being outdoors.

C. I'm a bit of a dreamer.

5. Which of the following are you most likely to do?

A. Visit a psychic to get the answers I'm looking for.

B. Meditate in nature to clear my mind and develop my intuition.

C. Have my astrological chart read to reveal my destiny.

6. Which one of these spiritual treatments would you choose?

A. Chakra balancing.

B. Hot stone massage.

C. Past-life regression.

7. When you're having a really tough time how do you deal with it?

A. I call upon the help of spirit to view the situation from a higher perspective.

B. I retreat into nature to clear my mind and destress.

C. I sob my heart out and seek advice from others.

8. How do you prefer to spend 'me' time?

A. Gardening, crafting and baking.

B. Outdoor pursuits and activities.

C. Bubble baths, sparkling wine, reading romantic novels and watching historical films.

If you answered mostly **A** your healing sacred site is **Glastonbury Tor** in Somerset. This town is steeped in stories of King Arthur and the Knights of the Round Table and the mythical island of Avalon. The 159 metre Tor symbolises the divine feminine and stands upon the powerful ley lines of Saint Michael (also known as the archangel Michael) and Saint Bridget (once the triple goddess, and queen of spring Brid), and because of this will balance the feminine and masculine in you and enable you to harness your gifts of truth and psychic wisdom. Glastonbury's healing energies will give you emotional strength and focus so you can effect the transformation you long to see in yourself.

To connect with the Tor's healing powers, stand at the bottom holding a rose quartz crystal in one hand to connect with your feminine energy and heart centre and the divine feminine, and a hematite crystal in the other hand to connect you with your inner divine masculine energy. Invite in the magick of Avalon to heal your wounds and allow you to grasp your true potential. Leave the crystals as an offering to the spirits of the land.

If you answered mostly **B** your healing sacred site is **Stonehenge** in Wiltshire. Stonehenge calls you to reconnect with the ancient ways of the Druids and to walk in harmony and balance with nature. You know deep inside yourself that this nature connection is an authentic aspect of the true you and that the ancient standing stones are bringing you back to your soul's roots.

As you gaze at the stones feel the energy of the ancients who made the journey here before you, of the Druids and their sacred sun ceremonies, and invite the fire within your soul to reawaken. You are being called by the ancient people of this site with its connection to all the elements to awaken spiritually to the call of nature. The stones hold the secrets of the lands, and by standing in their shadow you tap into the ancient wisdom held deep in the earth, embedded there by the footsteps of your Neolithic ancestors. Before you leave, offer up a prayer of remembrance and thanks to all those who have gone before.

If you answered mostly **C** your healing sacred site is **Callanish** on the Isle of Lewis in Scotland. Your strong sense of connection to the past and the sensitivity of your soul draws you to the Scottish Stonehenge, said to be home to the Sidhe, the Scottish faeries. The stone circle is believed to have been built as an astronomical calendar, and every 18.6 years the swan constellation of Cygnus falls into alignment with the Celtic cross of Callanish. The healing energy of this site comes from the surrounding water, the element associated with the emotions. Callanish will heal you by bringing past hurts to the surface and cleansing them away. By letting go of these old wounds you will gain the emotional equilibrium you need to step forward into the life you want.

The stones are said to have two guardians: one representing chaos and one representing order. Call upon these two to combine to bring balance to your emotions and peace in your heart. Leave an offering of seeds to the birds of the skies in honour of the Cygnus alignment.

A NEW DARKNESS

Are you brave enough to allow all your past hurts to leave you in return for transformation? The Cailleach will reveal to you the truth that's hidden in the guise of family, friends, work colleagues and all you've held dear. What if she were to tell you that most of your life has been an illusion, for your perception of other people has masked the truth of the identities and intentions of others. She is the queen of disguises and holds the key to transformation, but only if you are willing to journey through the darkness to your greatest fear.

As you retreat within to lick your wounds, the Cailleach will ensure that the truth of each person who is significant in your life is highlighted. Be prepared, for you could be faced with a world you no longer recognise as you could lose everyone. This doesn't mean that those you love are going to physically die; she can only take with her those who have chosen to change form on a soul level and those whose spirits aren't strong enough to survive yet another journey through the wheel of the year. Instead, it may mean that everything you've gone through has caused the death of your ego, of insecurities that caused you to show off and big yourself up when all you really needed was to accept yourself and to love yourself. It may be the death of a relationship or the death of the past or of everything you've known.

Whatever it maybe, you can trust the Cailleach to remove what is no longer needed in order for you to experience new life. Remember that as the guardian of animals she is a protector, just like she protects the deer from being hunted down and from the cold hard winter she herself provides. Animals have no concept of life and can live their lives freely without worrying about death. Can you imagine that? However, death is all part of the cycle of life, death and rebirth, and without dying to the old new life can't come to you.

To help you with the dying process of the old, the worn and the redundant, the Cailleach will reveal to you anything that you believed was your truth and she won't hold back in showing you the reality of relationships and situations, especially if they have been based on dishonesty and untruths. You may have never been aware of someone's misaligned intentions, or you trusted the weasel words of another. When your illusions are stripped away you suddenly see the world around you for how it truly is, which is when everything crashes around you yet again. However, this time it's those who were closer to you all along who are revealed.

Those with something to hide eventually let something slip. When someone suddenly declares they are innocent of something and don't want to be held accountable or they offer their denial all too readily, they are unwittingly admitting their guilt. 'It wasn't me' rather suggests it was! Lies and dishonesty will always be found out, and when that happens you just won't know where you belong any more. Everything you once believed in was a lie, and it is in this realisation that you'll most likely wish you were the foolish person who was blinded by circumstance you were before you called upon the Cailleach. Don't despair, for this will be when the goddess of winter is holding your hand. She will encourage you to dig deep and get to the bottom of your feelings, to dig out all that's gone on before, and will highlight your behaviours and those of other people that have prevented you from moving forward towards your dreams, goals and desires. She will journey with you to the source of the problem and then together you can decide what you need to shed.

But be warned, for during this dark process you may be tempted to throw a cloak over any new discoveries, preferring to believe in the dream that shielded you from the harsh reality and truth. Be strong, be brave, and walk away, for this is the only way open to you now as you can never, ever go back. This path is one of no return. The Dark Goddess sheds light on the darkness to reveal untruths. She lifts the veil of illusions based on relationships. The crone brings with her wisdom and experience; she is the mistress of magick and divination and holds the keys to the great mystery of life, death and rebirth. However, it's not just a physical death that the crone brings with her; it can be a death to the old, the unwanted and that which no longer serves.

She certainly brought death to my door, for I truly felt as though I had lost everything that I had known. All that I believed was true, all that my life and foundations had been built upon had dissolved. I was on shaky ground, and it felt as though everything that was true had died and I needed to be restored. My whole life felt like a lie, and I was distraught and I crumbled. My dear father, who I loved and held in high esteem, who I had tried to prove myself to, who I'd forgiven for walking out on us all those years ago and who I loved without question, had just thrown it all back in my face. Every belief of love and security that I'd tried to hold on to since childhood was revealed to be pure deception, and on the very day of Yule, after I had driven five hours to see him, the veil of illusion was torn down in front of my eyes. I'd been cast aside once again, as he denied the relationship we had between daughter and father that I'd always believed in and hung on to. I was in shock, and it felt as though a very old part of me was dying. My heartbreak was unbearable and I was confined to my bed, crippled with emotional and physical pain. I was broken, and spent the entire Christmas period in solitude.

Have you ever had to face up to the harsh truth? Have you experienced your world crashing around you? How did you pick yourself up: did you sink into despair? If you wish to understand your relationship with your family, friends or partner then the truth of each person will be highlighted and you could be faced with a world you no longer recognise. Be prepared to lose everyone; the key is to have no attachments to anyone or anything. Remember the wheel of fortune: when you become indifferent to any outcome that is when you have true freedom.

THE SHADOW SIDE

The Cailleach will teach you that not everything stays the same, for it is the goddess who changes everything she touches. When you try to focus and believe in only the lighter side of life you ignore the dangers lurking in the shadows and are taught to never venture into the dark forest alone. However, this is one old crone who is so in tune with her shadow side that it is she who in faery tales is referred to as the wicked witch, the evil queen and hideous hag. She is winter itself and she presents herself at the magickal witching hour of midnight and embraces her shadow side, for she is one who knows exactly who she is.

At the heart of every tale is a battle between good and evil, which represents the internal battle we all fight from time to time. It represents our decision whether or not to do the right thing. Sometimes you will just want to scream, shout and let it all out, but instead you stuff it as far down as you possibly can, bite your lip and do what is called the decent thing and conform. What you are in effect doing is ignoring that wilder side of you that says 'No, I'm not okay with that' or 'I'm furious and want to beat the living daylights out of you!' Again, the mask is on to pretend that you are all love and light, and you smile and make the right noises to show the other person how acceptable and pleasant you are. It amuses me to watch people in conversation and hear what they are saying to pacify the other person, when I know there is an entirely different dialogue going on within. This inner darkness is known as your shadow self, and it is something you need to come to terms with.

In magick the darkness has its place and purpose and is accepted as the polar opposite of the light. However, the darkness must be confronted and faced before you can move forward into the light. You need to recognise your shadow side and that you even have one. Your shadow side is the other side of you but it is a part of you; it's the you that lives in an alternative universe. It exists in energy form, therefore it is real for as soon as energy is thought up it is birthed and can never die from that moment on. Once you have admitted you have a shadow side it is time to learn to observe it instead of ignoring it. If you feel a negative emotion come up, observe when it starts and become aware of what triggers a behaviour from the shadow side. Eventually you will be able to control it or hopefully not even consider allowing the shadow side to sneak in.

Befriend you shadow self. Learn to love it, for it is just your polarity in alignment. Learn its ways, vulnerabilities and methods so you can prevent it from turning into an explosion, or use it carefully and wisely as and when needed. It admittedly takes great skill to recognise, observe, allow and become your shadow side, but by using it and understanding where it has come from and what is lurking deep within you will be more able to call upon it when you wish to harness its power. This is exactly what the ancients meant when they taught the philosophy of 'know thyself': it's all about knowing yourself inside out, about what makes you tick or what pulls your trigger.

The dark night of the soul will take you to places within that you don't recognise. As you stumble through the wilderness, the Cailleach will reveal reactions to hidden emotions you didn't know existed. There she will wait while you discover the original wounding that led to the harbouring of such emotions. Once you've shed that part of you and healed from any hurts relating to it you will start to observe what triggers you to kick off and react negatively. She will then take you to journey deep within to uncover the true reason for your adverse reaction and prepare you for a long and arduous journey of discovery. Only the light can be illuminated by that which is dark; one cannot possibly be without the other.

Knowing yourself increases the strength of your energy through acknowledgement and subsequently your power will increase, inner or otherwise. Your self-power will be so much stronger when you use the whole of who you are. The crone is the mistress of magick, the all-powerful sorceress who summons up the power from all that she is. She knows exactly who she is and can call upon any or all of the strengths that reside in the shadows as and when is necessary. When you work with the shadow side you will be able to determine which situation calls for the use of our shadow traits and how to use them, but first the Cailleach will show you the powers you should nurture and those that should be destroyed.

RECLAIMING THE DARK

All things in nature have a darker side, and many religions teach that darkness is evil and that light will prevail. The darkness is essential when it comes to magick for sometimes you must look through the darkness to see the light, which is the purpose of experiencing a dark night of the soul. The Dark Goddess will take you to the darkest place so you may shed light on that which you are seeking. She will teach you how to draw magick from the dark mystery and to claim the power that resides in the depths of your soul. She understands you can't be all love and compassion 24/7, which is impossible. Everything is in place to support the cycle of life, death and rebirth, to bring about change, for she changes everything she touches.

The dark night of the soul can be exhausting and frightening as the perfect world you once knew caves in around you. It literally is like taking a pill that reveals a new reality, one that is so unfamiliar to you you may wish you hadn't swallowed it in the first place. However, there is no returning path once the truth has been revealed. The path is as long and arduous as you make it so don't let any stone go unturned, for this is the most incredible gift you could ever experience. The Cailleach is at hand to witness the death of all you know, and her presence is made known through your isolation and feeling of being alone. When those you trusted, relied on or even loved are exposed you will begin to question your validity and become unsure of who you really are. In this very moment the bone woman waits silently for you to drop into an abyss of despair. Her bony hand will hold yours as she leads you to face the depths of your own personal hell and as you face all of your fears one by one.

As I cried out into the darkness a pain shot through my left eye and before me stood an old lady. Her hair was matted and I noticed she had terrible teeth. I truly thought I was in the process of dying, and even though this scary-looking grandmother was terrifying I welcomed her in. I longed for the transitional relief she could offer me, even though this is the crone who is so in tune with her shadow side that faery tales refer to her as the wicked witch, the evil queen and hideous hag. However, she's also the queen of disguise, and just like a faery tale in which a fair maiden takes pity on a poor old woman, she lifts off her cloak to reveal a beautiful shining queen who rewards the young girl for trusting in the light. The Cailleach holds the key to transformation, but only if you're willing to journey with her through the darkness and face your greatest fears.

Silently she sat with me in my darkened tomb, watching as I was stripped to the very core of who I was. There I remained waiting for rebirth, until she slowly built me up piece by piece and I felt a glimmer. Not much, but enough to ignite a new light and light it into my heart. Yule is a time not only for death but also of rebirth.

SURVIVAL

Fighting to survive for so long has been a hard battle, and by now you will be worn down by the struggle. The Cailleach brings about transitional relief in the darkness of winter and helps you take your survival skills to the next level of endurance. However, this divine hag demands respect and advises a little caution as this cold, hard phase of the dark night of the soul draws in.

The glacial, sharp season of winter filled the ancient Celts with dread for it was a time of scarcity, and if they had not planned their survival earlier in the year by storing grains they could not be sure of getting through the difficult months that could for many have been a matter of life or death. It was the Cailleach who was responsible for the harsh conditions of winter, and it was she who got to decide who would survive and who she would take for her own. Just like the plants she culls at winter time, she will take with her those who are too weak to survive.

The winter solstice is a time for change, when the cycles of life and death and rebirth are acknowledged and honoured. Death is a natural part of the cycle of life, and just like the trees of her season the Cailleach will strip you to be bare, naked and vulnerable, inviting you to retreat within. It is from this dark and wallowing place of the unknown that you will feel her ghostly presence, for she is the crone, the symbol of death, destruction and decay, and death is never far away at this time of year. As the world becomes bereft of light, warmth and sustenance during the winter months, the Cailleach will take the old and infirm. Many souls choose to depart at this time of year, particularly around Yule, for it is the ultimate time of death and rebirth. It has worked out divinely perfect as I write this chapter, for I can feel the Cailleach's presence as she makes her plans to take my best friend's father, who was taken into hospital last night on the very eve of Yule. For all those who've had their loved ones taken at this time of year it's so hard, just like the frozen ground the Cailleach strikes with her staff.

My sweet granny was born with her twin sister, Muriel, in 1911 at the spring equinox, or Ostara, a time when the maiden aspect of the triple goddess breathes new life into the world. Likewise my beloved grandfather was born in 1911 at the autumn equinox, or Mabon: born, like my granny, when light and dark are in perfect balance, a time of equilibrium. Mabon is an abundant time of reaping in the harvest courtesy of the mother aspect of the triple goddess, who has blessed us with her bounty, and a time to go within to reflect on all that which has passed in the months of the year thus far. It was the Cailleach who decided to take both of my grandparents many decades later during the darkness of winter. The gatekeeper of death and transformation led them, on separate occasions, to her lair in the underworld on the day of Yule, as she had done to so many in the past and will continue to do.

In the cycle of life the death of winter at Yule is followed by the promise of rebirth in the spring. What is born dies and what dies is reborn. Winter brings rest to the earth, and it is to the earth we all return. As you work with the Cailleach during this stage of the dark night of the soul she will offer deliverance from the hardships you've endured and the death of sufferance as she points you towards newfound freedom.

PREPARING FOR THE CAILLEACH

Instead of purposefully pursuing this horrific and hideous-looking grandmother, it is she who will seek you out in the dead of night and callously bid you be witness to sudden endings and the death of what you once knew. Her sharp, beady eye will bore through your inner darkness as she searches for any traces of survival instincts that will give you the strength and tenacity you need to walk with her between the worlds detached and without feeling.

You may have subconsciously called in the Cailleach on a soul level when you wished:

- to survive
- for endurance and tenacity
- to feed and help animals survive the winter
- for the return of spring and warmer months
- for a smooth transition into cronehood
- for help to get over the passing of a loved one
- for new opportunities
- for an awakening
- for wisdom and knowing.

You may have unwittingly called in the Cailleach when you:

- didn't act your age
- had a temper tantrum
- allowed your shadow side to take control
- were out of balance
- wished your menses to be over
- were stuck in the past

- required resilience
- swam in a loch
- wished for the past to return
- relived old memories
- were afraid of night terrors
- were cold-hearted towards another
- no longer cared
- shut down all feelings
- wished for the winter months to come
- played in the snow
- climbed rocks and hills
- paddled in streams
- desired youthful looks and beauty
- wished for death
- feared ageing.

Turn to the Cailleach when you wish:

- to control your temper
- to accept the ageing process
- to heal menopause symptoms
- to understand the death of something or someone
- to embrace endings
- for pure waters
- to break free from the past
- for a new start
- to understand and embrace your shadow side
- to break free
- for relief.

As soon as she hears your invitation to come into your life, whether subconsciously or not, the Cailleach will remind you to be indifferent to life's challenges and to remain still in the eye of a storm. If you get caught up in the drama you could very well find yourself in troubled waters when this storm hag summons up a witchy wind to test your resilience and blow you off course.

HONOURING AND CONNECTING WITH THE CAILLEACH

Do the following to honour and connect with the Cailleach:

- Wear pale blue.
- Turn off the heating.
- Wear a veil.
- Become cool, reserved and in control.
- Go hill or mountain climbing.
- Visit some standing stones.
- Row across a loch.
- Collect stones from rivers in a wicker basket.
- Use stepping stones to cross rivers.
- Embrace the cold weather.
- Wear a natural hag stone as a pendant.
- Wrap up in a plaid shawl.
- Listen to traditional Scottish music.
- Dance to the sound of bagpipes.
- Walk barefoot across the land holding a staff.
- Make an altar for her and place upon it stones and pebbles.

If you wish to take something from nature for an altar or a keepsake, do so in honour of the Cailleach and she will grant her permission.

Altar offerings to honour and give thanks to the Cailleach include:

- a small hammer
- a hag stone
- thistle
- heather
- a bowl of water
- a deer figurine
- seeds
- grain
- ice cubes
- snow

- a back candle
- a silver candle.

INVOCATION TO THE CAILLEACH

To purposely call the Cailleach into your energy you will need the following, but don't worry if you are unable to get hold of all of the ingredients as your focus will determine your connection with her:

- Scots pine incense
- a small bowl of salt
- ice cubes or snow
- a dish
- small stones or pebbles
- four bones: old bones from a joint of meat or found naturally
- a yellow tea light

Light the incense and sprinkle some of the salt around you in a circle for protection as you ask the goddess for her blessings. You can do this silently in your mind using whatever words come to you or you can say out loud:

> *Divine goddess, I ask you to bless and protect me as I focus on the divine light within myself as I call upon you, the Dark Goddess the Cailleach, for assistance. I graciously receive your tenacity and endurance to survive with an open heart in gratitude. Help me to serve, help me to shine. In love and honour, so mote it be.*

Put the ice cubes in the dish and place it outside on rough terrain or hard ground. Scatter the stones around and one bone in each direction. Place the lit tea light in the centre of the dish to represent the sun. As you face the direction of north say:

> *All hail the Cailleach, winter queen,*
> *who rules o'er lands, betwixt and between.*

Bringer of snow, I'll weather your storm;
hideous features force me to conform.
Tests of endurance mean I shall survive,
promise of death aids all life to revive.
Divine hag of winter, whose face is so blue,
may deep the white snow fall in honour of you.
Gathering storm clouds I choose to ignore;
the past is behind me, I've shown it the door.
For death is now conquered, I've fought a good fight;
powers of rebirth usher in a new light.
All hail the Cailleach, seen and unseen:
to you I surrender. All hail, winter queen.

As the ice cubes melt from the heat of the lit flame it represents the death of winter and all that's gone before. Now the power of warmth and light will return to herald the coming of spring and new beginnings.

Signs that the Cailleach is around you include:

- A Bridget's cross comes into your possession.
- A fawn approaches you.
- You keep seeing herds of deer.
- You're hit by a rock.
- One of your eyes becomes sore.
- You turn blue in the cold.
- You sit on a thistle.
- The weather turns stormy.
- You find a hag stone.
- Bagpipes echo across a loch.
- A trip to the Highlands is on the cards.
- A lucky Manx cat crosses your path.
- It's snowing.
- You experience a new endurance and tenacity through the darkness at this stage of the dark night of the soul.

Perseverance will save the day when the Cailleach receives your invitation to draw near. She will help you weather the storm and survive against all odds as she nurtures and sustains you through the process of death and eradication. She will help you to flower and survive in tough conditions just like the thistle, which is considered to be both a flower and a weed and is known for its durability, strength and stoicism.

EXERCISES AND RITUALS TO ENGAGE WITH THE CAILLEACH

THE WINTER QUEEN OF REBIRTH INITIATION

The wheel of the year has yet again turned to the hard season of winter, which in magickal terms means we are in the direction of the north. The time for spell work is midnight and the colour for candle magick is black. Face north, light a black candle – for the quickest way to travel is by candlelight – and say:

Now that winter has arrived
I'll go within, deep inside.
As I reflect on all I've seen
I call upon the winter's queen,
who rules this season's frost and snow,
and so towards the north I go.
Upon the flame that lights the way,
assisted by this season's fae.

As you gaze into the flame of the candle feel a warmth wrap around you, like a magickal cloak being placed upon your shoulders. Take a deep breath in and then blow out the candle. The smoke from the extinguished flame will rise, and as you close your eyes feel yourself being lifted up. Continue to breathe deeply for a few minutes and when you are ready feel yourself being gently placed back on the ground.

You will feel hard and cold and realise you have journeyed into the true depths of winter. Naked bare trees surround you, all sparkling white with frost that glimmers in the light of the bright, full midnight moon. This really is a winter wonderland as you would imagine it to be: everything is covered by snow, coloured lanterns light the way and candy canes reach high into the midnight sky. You watch with delight as silvery, translucent faeries skate on an iced-over lake. As you look beyond the branches of the trees you notice a doorway in a huge old yew tree that stands proudly in the distance. Snow is underfoot, and you trudge with crunchy steps towards the tree of transformation and rebirth and push open the door. It opens easily and you step inside. Standing within the ancient trunk of the yew, a voice demands 'What do you see? Could it be me?'

You turn around, expecting to find someone there, and as you search and stumble through the darkness your eyes start to adjust. A cloaked figure draws back her hood to reveal a hideous old hag. You take a step back in horror, but then you take pity on the poor old woman. In your pocket you find a shiny red apple and you offer it to her, for she looks cold and hungry. As she takes the apple into her bony hand she smiles a toothless smile and says:

> *You have travelled all this way,*
> *and so you must now have your say.*
> *Tell me of that which you dream,*
> *for I'm the winter faery queen.*

Feeling a little scared, you face her and speak of all that you hope for. When you have finished she holds up her staff, and through the darkness you become dazzled by a blast of light. Tiny golden grains of light cover you entirely. She invites you to breathe them in to your very core and says gently:

> *Your wishes told are to me known.*
> *Seeds of dreams have now been sown.*

As you look to her in gratitude she nods, for she knows what is necessary in order for you to fulfil your wishes. A faery dressed in white fur approaches and hands you a black candle. As soon as it is lit you experience a lifting sensation and take another magickal ride across the dimensions. When you open your eyes you find yourself back where you started, having made your wishes to the Cailleach, the queen of winter, who always promises the gift of rebirth after she assists you through the death of that which no longer serves you.

Place upon your Dark Goddess altar an offering in honour of the Cailleach such as small stones or pebbles, a sprig of Scots pine and a blue candle to ensure your survival.

INCANTATION

> *Repeats from past hold you in fear;*
> *they keep you back when you're so near.*
> *Through veil, while thin, this very night,*
> *protection placed; no need for fright.*
> *Crone welcomes you and all you bring.*
> *Wisdom waits, now look within.*

BANISHING CEREMONY

This ceremony should preferably be performed during a dark moon phase. Place a picture or figure of the Cailleach on your goddess altar or a place that is sacred to you. Light a black candle and place it safely in front of you and say:

> *Bone goddess, I call upon you*
> *to eliminate all in my life that's not true.*
> *Devour and destroy my guilt, fear and blame;*
> *set them alight in the black candle's flame.*

Tear a piece of paper into large pieces, and write on each piece a word that represents what you would like eliminated from your life such as abandonment or self-esteem issues or any old destructive behaviours or name a situation, person or anything from the past you'd like to be released from. Take each piece of paper in turn, bring your focus to the candle and watch the orange golden light flicker on top of the black wax. Hold one piece of paper at a time safely in the flame as the Cailleach destroys and transmutes the negativity in your life until it is disintegrated. Be careful of your fingers and put any remaining paper fragments in a bowl at your feet. When each piece of paper has been dealt with, blow out the candle and say:

> By the protection of Cailleach, winter queen,
> I stand in my strength. Now I am set free,
> from vows I have made through heart or in rhyme;
> safe now in all directions of time.

SCRYING TO REVEAL THE TRUTH

Reflective surfaces have been used for millennia in magic, including scrying, to see the truth of a situation. A magick mirror is an ancient scrying tool in which all truths and the past, present and future are revealed. Magick mirrors do not lie, therefore they underline the basics of magic: that you may not always get the answer you want. However, you can be sure that whatever is revealed will always be for your highest good, as the Dark Goddess ensures your protection while the truth is shown to you.

Light a black candle and hold a small mirror close. Focus on the reflection of flame in the black glass without blinking until you go into a trance state. When you're ready, gaze fully into the reflective surface then soften your gaze so you're almost looking past the surface and peering deep into the mirror. Let your eyes become a portal to another world as you let everything you see dissolve into nothingness. Allow all thoughts to disappear and your consciousness to drift.

You may have actual visions, either in your mind or in the mirror, or you might recover previous feelings or impressions or hear the voice of spirit. Be mindful not to analyse anything; just allow it to simply come and go. You may see figures and shapes, which can be interpreted as different things, and you may see a storyline play out. Keep at it and practise, for mirror work is an essential tool in revealing that which is hidden in the shadows. Keep your magick mirror on your goddess altar or hide it away to bring out only when you are ready to work some reflection magic. Who or what did you see reflecting back to you? Perhaps you gained clarity and viewed a perspective from another angle. Use your mirror to meditate on the situation and to gain clarity. A magick mirror always reveals the answer if you are open to it. But be warned, for you may not always be shown the answer you want!

If you wish to bring a certain action or outcome into being, search for a beautiful handheld mirror you feel will support you at this time in reflecting your inner self. Paint the glass black and infuse it with the energies of the Cailleach, as well as stamping your own creative mark on it. For this you may wish to decorate your mirror with grains, small pebbles and stones to represent her or anything else that will add a personal touch. The mirror is now ready to be part of your magickal tool collection and is not to be touched by any other.

LESSONS FROM THE DARK GODDESS THE CAILLEACH

So ancient is the Cailleach that in the days when the world was young she saw land that had no water and water that had no land. She let the water loose to form the rivers and lochs and shaped the hills and glens of Scotland, and when she lifted the shawl she'd draped over the Scottish mountains they were white with snow, revealing that the Cailleach is indeed the spirit of winter. She is a bearer of storms that rage with thick snow and hard frost, and as a weather witch influenced the outcome of her battle with Angus and Brid by whipping up a storm with gusts and gales. Her sharp, biting winds were cruel to the country folk who endured her wrath and to the lands that she hardened, as nature was stripped to its very core.

Her destructive behaviour, however, was a way of being cruel to be kind, for so fearful was her appearance she scared the animals into hiding, thus guaranteeing their survival through the cold, harsh months and making her a guardian of animals and the lady of the beasts. She grows older and fiercer as her season lengthens and tries to stall the emergence of spring by destroying the growth of new life, which teaches us that without the necessary culling of new growth in winter no life can survive the harsh weather through to the following spring. Hers is a lesson of death and rebirth, and when all of her strength is spent she renews her youth in order that she may survive through the warmer months, until she can begin her hard reign of terror once again.

The Cailleach's story represents the eternal cycle of darkness and light through the changing of the seasons and the fertility of the land. She a goddess of destruction and death, and her aspects of transformation should be considered. She teaches you how to survive difficult barren periods and will keep you frozen in time unless you heal from the past and learn the hard lessons dealt to you. Only then can you move into a bright future.

You have endured the Cailleach's cruel and harsh terrain and are to be congratulated on being a born survivor. Now it is time to celebrate the re-emergence of light out from the darkness, for the renewal of life and the promise of a successful future awaits as the final dark goddess you are to meet bids you to join her in her sacred grove . . .

14. ARNEMETIA

Initiation of truth and integrity

Goddess of the sacred well
reveals a secret ne'er to tell.
Illusions shattered; now you're free.
Reclaim truth and integrity.

ORIGIN	Celtic.
NAMES	Arnemetia, Arnemetiae.
GODDESSES	Sulis, Sulis Minerva, Coventina.
SYMBOLS	water, well, grove of trees, lantern.
THEMES	healing, truth, integrity, revealing the light, sacred space, silence, retreat, exposition, secrets, hidden things, shattering illusions, transformation, re-awakening the soul, integrity, wisdom.
LESSONS	responsibility, integrity.
COLOURS/CANDLES	purple, green.
CRYSTALS	amethyst, apophyllite, lapis lazuli.
HERBS/FLOWERS/OILS	frankincense, lavender, purple iris.
MOON PHASES	new, waxing.
SEASONS	Mabon, winter.
TREE	silver birch.
FESTIVAL DATE	Buxton Well Dressing 5 July.

Arnemetia is rather an enigma, for there are no real writings of her and she is a goddess who has been ignored and misunderstood pretty much for the last 1500 years, just like Sheela-na-gig and many other deities of the old ways.

Arnemetia is the goddess of healing springs, a Romano-Celtic water goddess whose dwelling is at Buxton Springs, or Aquae Arnemetiae as the town was once known during Roman occupation. Her name contains Celtic elements within it: the letters *Ar* at the start of her name mean 'beside', 'against' or 'in front of' and *nemet* (part of the word *nemeton*) means 'sacred grove'; *aquae* means 'waters'. Thus her name is interpreted as 'she who dwells in the sacred grove' or dwells 'against, in front of or beside' the sacred grove, and it may well have Druidic associations.

The Corieltauvi, an ancient British tribe way before the Roman conquest, founded their settlement in what is now known as the Peak District, which covers an area of around 1,437 km² from north Derbyshire to the base of the Pennines, the very backbone of England. This place truly is goddess land, and glimpses of her can be caught in the rugged hills and valleys, gorges, lakes and wild moorland that sees many walkers, climbers, cyclists and other visitors visit the area for its stunning scenery. During the Roman invasion of the region in around 60-69 CE the Corieltauvi established a township at Buxton because of its natural spa. This is where Arnemetia was deeply revered by the ancient Celts and worshipped as the goddess of the grove, of the sacred waters known to cure sickness and disease that ran underground through caverns and caves. The Romans named their settlement Aquae Arnemetia in honour of her and of the warm healing waters that bubbled up from the caverns under the hills, and they incorporated their pagan worship with that of the locals. They built three public baths and a beautiful shrine to Arnemetia.

For many centuries Arnemetia's natural spring attracted multitudes of people anxious to partake of its healing waters. Prior to the Reformation it had been a pilgrim shrine and it was sacred long before the coming of Christianity. In later centuries, when Christianity took over pagan beliefs and practices, Arnemetia's well was renamed for Saint Ann. However, the cult of St Ann was not popular until the

14th century, yet the healing spring at Buxton had been dedicated to her much earlier. The name change was a typical dishonouring of pagan beliefs to ensure the Celtic and ancient goddess of the sacred grove and waters was forgotten, that she was hidden from history and from the hearts and minds of the people.

However, what is not realised is that the names Arnemetia and Ann are both linked to Anu, which derives from the goddess Danu, the most ancient of all Celtic deities. She is so old that some references have her as both goddess and god, the all-encompassing divine source. Danu is considered to be the first great mother, the divine creator aspect of the goddess who birthed all things into being and a triple goddess who takes the form of the maiden, the mother or the crone. She is an earth goddess who is associated with fertility, growth, plenty, abundance, agriculture, cultivation and nurturing of the land, as well as rivers, flowing water and the ocean.

Arnemetia is a water goddess with the magick of divine flow, which incorporates knowledge, wisdom, wealth and abundance. She is also an air goddess associated with inspiration, intellect, change and movement, and she is associated with the Irish goddess Dana and the Tuatha Dé Danann (the children of Danu). The Tuatha Dé Danann were the wise ones, the alchemists and descendants of Danu herself. When the Gaels invaded Ireland the Tuatha Dé Danann shape-shifted into little people so they could hide in the hills. They became the Sídhe (shee), the faeries and leprechauns of Ireland.

Arnemetia is a cosmic goddess who holds the secrets of divine alchemy and divine magick and reminds you that through your oneness to the divine source there really are no secrets; you are essentially one with the all-encompassing universal wisdom and divine knowledge. She realigns you with your divine truth and brings empowerment, and she reminds you that you are in charge of your own destiny and hold the power within you to realise your dreams. She assists in raising your limited self and to transcend lesser goals to your highest visions for yourself. She is the maiden, mother goddess, the divine feminine and the all-powerful crone for those who seek to realise their greatest dreams, as she encourages you to tap into her power – which actually resides in you. She is the goddess who holds a lantern to expose the light that has been consumed by the darkness. She is an enigma, a witness of secrets shrouded through the mists of time, and she exposes darkness that's been hidden in the light.

MESSAGE FROM ARNEMETIA

'Quench your thirst; nourish your inner springs. Welcome me into your inner sanctum and meet me in the grove, for I am the goddess Arnemetia of the healing springs and the sacred space you seek within. Whenever you step into this place of safety and solitude, know that you won't be challenged. Instead, you are able to heal within the seclusion and sanctity of our woodland meeting place where all will be revealed. Your journey through the darkness has highly tuned your natural sensitivity. When you feel overwhelmed or suppress emotions it's easy to withdraw from society like a hermit, to hide among the trees like I do. However, as I hold up my lantern the light streams through the dark woods, cutting through all illusions until the truth is reclaimed.

'I am the beautiful sacred shrine of the goddess hidden away within you. This place is so old and neglected, for I've never seen you visit. I have been waiting for you to come and worship me, to honour my residence within you for I am the sacred part of you; this is where I reside. It is time to be quiet and listen as I whisper my name to call you back home.

My name is Arnemetia, the one who is hidden, the goddess of the grove and sacred waters.

Come join me in sacred ritual and honour and awaken to the magick of the old ways, as I light the path towards your bright future.'

SEEKING ARNEMETIA

Still shaken from recent revelations like a child who has witnessed the death of magick at Christmas time, Arnemetia offers you calm amid chaos as she streams new light through the shadows. When you can't talk to anyone, when friends and family members don't really understand or when you've been accused of having a mid-life crisis or always creating drama or stress, you have no choice but to turn to the Dark Goddess for assistance. It was she who called you and it was she who made plans to strip you bare like the stark trees of winter until you no longer recognised yourself, until you had nobody to confide in and until you were all alone. And alone you felt. As you sought comfort you were sent you away to deal with it yourself and lick your own wounds.

Now as you seek the solace your weary soul craves Arnemetia holds a lantern to show the way through the misty waters of your tears. As you gaze upstream you see a faint yellow glow dancing in the distance as a small wooden rowing boat approaches. Facing forward stands a cloaked figure with an owl perched on one shoulder who holds up a brightly lit lantern to show the way. She has come to find you, to seek you out in the darkness, and she welcomes you into her cool embrace as she invites you into the deep reverence and stillness of her sanctuary.

When you seek Arnemetia she bids you to retreat and rest awhile within the safety of her sacred grove. Here, as majestic trees surround and guard you well, you can allow your soul to hush as you remain in the stillness of her shrine, becoming one with nature and with the goddess herself. Ancient and old, trees are the wisdom keepers and gateways to the otherworld, for the spirits of trees are multidimensional. To be one with a tree awakens the spirit within you, and you could be chosen as a custodian of the grove when you speak to or hug a tree. How often have you sat against a tree, closed your eyes and journeyed with a tree spirit?

Ever since I can remember I have always absolutely loved nature and I have always felt the mystery and magick of the seasons and marvelled at the moon phases. I am in awe of each sunrise and sunset. Nature was and always will be sacred to me, and I came into this lifetime with a true pagan heart. My father felt the same way and often when I was a child took me to an ancient grove where three giant yew trees and two silver birch trees ruled supreme; he named them the trees of power. Here we meditated and connected with the spirits of nature, for within every tree resides the medicine to help you traverse the lower and upper worlds of spirit and of the ancestors.

The silver birch symbolises new beginnings, regeneration and the promise of what is to come. It is a holder of ancient wisdom and resonates with the power of Arnemetia, who guards ancient entrances to gateways and portals and calls you back to the sanctity of stillness, to a sacred place deep within your heart, to simply listen. She is holy breath and a holy sanctuary, and she is holy intimacy and the sacred link between yourself and your soul.

Arnemetia will help you to create a special place within, a personal space of honour and reverence. She can be found in the living space all around and within the deep and sacred silence of sanctuary. She encourages you to take time out for you and not feel guilty for making precious moments for yourself. Whether it's a relaxing bubble bath, a good book or simply having a break from other people it's so important that you have your own space to reflect on things and find clarity in silence. Arnemetia encourages you to honour and respect who you are and to look back at the journey you've taken thus far. She will reach deeply into your psyche to reflect the importance of going with the flow, for she is a fresh water goddess who presides over sacred wells, streams, lakes and rivers and gives healing and blessings to those who stop to pray at them. She offers you to take a sip of her pure waters, to induce sacred communion with her and honour your sensitivity and emotions.

DARK GODDESS COMPARISON

Connected with England's River Caldew, Coventina is a British river goddess who was often depicted as a water nymph. She was worshipped around the time of Roman occupation but was honoured way before that by the Celts as a goddess of wells and springs. The only other town in Britain important enough to be given the designation 'aquae' was the Roman settlement of Aquae Sulis, the spa town we know today as Bath. It was here they worshipped their own goddess, who presided over the healing waters, sacred wells and springs. Sulis was birthed from the much older Celtic goddess Sul, the goddess of healing and sacred waters. Later she became entwined with Minerva, the Roman goddess of wisdom, and became Sulis Minerva. She presided over the sacred spring, where it was believed she answered prayers, wishes and even curses in return for a coin.

REASONS FOR WORKING WITH ARNEMETIA

As you work with Arnemetia at this last stage of the dark night of the soul she promises to light the way and guide you to return to wholeness in perfect balance, wisdom and integrity. Trying to curb your emotions is not easy if you are sensitive and tend to work from an emotional level. It's easy for you to pick up on the emotions of others and to cry a river on behalf of anyone you feel sorry for. My heart is like a huge swirling whirlpool and I've always felt everybody else's emotions, which despite being an easy way for me to read feelings when giving spiritual guidance has also been like a curse on many occasions. I was born on a Wednesday, and according to the 1800s fortune-telling poem Wednesday's child is full of woe:

> *Monday's child is fair of face.*
> *Tuesday's child is full of grace.*
> *Wednesday's child is full of woe.*
> *Thursday's child has far to go.*
> *Friday's child is loving and giving.*
> *Saturday's child works hard for a living,*
> *But the child who is born on the Sabbath day*
> *is bonny and blithe and good and gay.*
> (ANONYMOUS)

Have you ever been accused of being overly emotional or too sensitive? Are you a water sign born under Pisces, Cancer or Scorpio? Emotions run high in water signs and in those who are more spiritually inclined, for spirit works through the heart centre, the hub of emotions, so that those who are naturally clairsentient can receive intuitive messages through their feelings. In truth, sensitivity is a beautiful gift as it helps you to feel for others, to be both empathetic and sympathetic. It also opens your heart so that you are more inclined to hear the voices and messages of the goddess.

You may wish to ask the water spirits to assist you to be aware of whose feelings are affecting you: are they yours or are they those of somebody else? The art is to observe how you are feeling and come to a realisation that you are not your feelings. As the goddess of the sacred waters, Arnemetia can help you to understand whatever emotions arise and to discover where they have come from and why. You will find that with her assistance you soon act accordingly and react in different ways to situations and have a more masterful approach.

GOING WITH THE FLOW

When working with the magick of water a feminine energy is observed, for it is the receptive pure energy that naturally flows to you if you allow it that helps to manifest your desires. Contrary to current belief woman is born to receive whereas man is born to give, to provide. Over the past few decades the roles of men and women have drawn closer together in similarity: where men once went out to be hunter gathers, to provide food, safety and stability, women have now embraced that role. Instead of being in a natural receptive role, the scales have been tipped as women strive to provide and go against their make-up, as they strive to embrace the natural drive, focus and assertiveness of male tendencies. These masculine traits set a person up for success in business because their thoughts are focused singly on their goals. It's a natural progression for men whereas women can automatically think about more than one thing at a time, which makes it harder for them to be focused purely on one thing at any given time.

Empathy and nurturing are traits that are most often associated with the magick of water, along with cravings to be deeply loved and feel fulfilled. Women naturally desire to be looked after, to just 'be', whereas men like to 'do'. Women have had to strive to find their position of power by mostly abandoning their feminine energy, thus losing their innate power. Women have been left feeling unbalanced, stressed and blocked and have become rigid and lost their flow. It's time to remember how to soften and to take the path of least resistance, to go with the flow. Sometimes when you do this it may be calm and serene and at other times it will be wild and turbulent, but you should always flow forward like a river towards its destination. Men and women both have access to the energies of masculinity and femininity, which will be embraced when you are in balance. We are all born with one dominant form, either a male or female energy, and should harness that which feels the most natural no matter what your physical form is.

Women hold power and wisdom and connect to their feelings and intuition more easily than someone who is predominantly masculine. However, it's important to tap into your divine femininity in order to align with your body and heart so you can easily hear these messages. When you intentionally experience the natural pleasures your inner feminine desires you attract all that is your birthright as a woman to you. You go with the natural flow of all things and are therefore able to receive all of the good you have been asking for for so long. Everything is interconnected, so when you embrace your feminine nature you not only nurture yourself but the waters too and the planet as a whole. Instead of trying to step into masculine shoes to earn a crust or to live up to the expectations of others, you can instead draw success to yourself by harnessing your own feminine and goddess energy – with help from Arnemetia. As she holds up her bright lantern it shines forth and reveals the mysteries of hidden truths.

MYSTERY, WISDOM AND INSIGHT

Some goddesses are very well known as they have been kept alive through oral tradition and written into history through stories of old and folklore. However, like many deities of the old ways, after Arnemetia was replaced by Saint Ann she became an enigma, for the very core of who she was became shrouded in mystery. She became hidden, only to be found by those who seek the solace of her sanctuary. There in the silence of a grove deep within the woods her spirit guards the sacred streams and wells and the guardian trees that watch over them. You may have come across her, for it is her presence that is sensed in quiet moments and that connects you with your true essence. She can be found within the silence of your prayers, in the quietness of your mind and in the stillness of a peaceful heart. She is the sacred goddess of your inner sanctum who guards the truth of your soul.

Like you during a dark night of the soul, Arnemetia was stripped of everything she stood for and had no choice but to step into a place of the unknown. She remains a mystery to this day yet you will know her by her very presence. As mystery hangs in the air when she's around she asks whether you've given away too much of who you are. When you took the path of no return did you whine and moan as you processed and discussed your fall with others? Has your personal dark night of the soul become your story? Do you keep others updated with the latest tragedy or continue to rake up the past, talking of nothing else relentlessly? It is time to change your story!

As the wheel of fortune takes you further back up Arnemetia encourages you to keep an air of mystery about you, just as she has done over the centuries. Having been stripped down to your very core you are now in the wonderful place of becoming, for the Dark Goddess showed you the shadow aspect of yourself as she revealed to you everything you are not. Who were you before she stripped you down? How did you feel after every last vestige that you ever knew was taken? Who are you now that you have been stripped of everything?

No longer are you the mother, the sister, the brother, the husband, the wife, the boss, the employee you've been labelled; you are much, much more.

As Arnemetia shines light on the truth you are being given the opportunity of new life. You were stripped of everything you are not, and now she will shine the light on that which you are. In this sacred place of becoming you will find you start to have revelations as things start to click into place. Suddenly nothing will really mean anything to you, and you will start to see things differently.

Arnemetia will lend you her owl's sharp sight to see with new eyes, through misconceptions and self-deception, for the owl sees through the darkness. Take Arnemetia's owl as your companion and journey into the dark chambers within, for here lies the wisdom you seek. As the answers shine forth you will find all the advice you need to help you on your journey. You are the wise one, the wisdom keeper. Know that there is absolutely no need to seek the approval of others, for you now have all you need. When you use your insight and common sense wisdom will prevail, as you allow your optimum judgement and truths to reveal the answers to that which is sought. Stand strong in this knowledge and in time you'll find that many seek your hard-earned wisdom as you have personally experienced the dark night of the soul.

Wisdom comes across the years
to those who learn, revealing seers.
Insight strong, gifts to receive.
A wise one, true, in this believe.

Like a stage curtain torn down to expose actors who are not yet in costume, illusions will finally be shattered. You will start to see what others can't, but not only that: you'll find as you step into your truth and authenticity you're no longer able to hide the truth or accept those in authority or institutions that are forged on lies and deceit. If something doesn't ring true you will spot it a mile off, much like the little boy in the story of the Emperor's new clothes by Danish author Hans Christian Andersen.

Once upon a time there was an emperor whose only interest in life was to dress up in fashionable clothes. He kept changing his clothes so his people would admire and flatter him, and they did. Two thieves decided to teach him a lesson, one they could make money from. They told the emperor they were very fine tailors and could sew a new suit for him, but this suit would be like no other for it would be so light and fine it would seem invisible; only those who were very stupid would not be able to see his new outfit. The emperor set them to work. One day the emperor asked the prime minister to see how the tailors were getting on, but all he saw were the two men cutting the air with scissors: there was no cloth to be seen. The prime minster kept silent for fear of being called stupid and ignorant, instead praising the fabric and saying it was the most wonderful material he'd ever seen.

When the emperor's new suit was ready he couldn't see it either, but as he also didn't want to appear to be stupid he admired the dress and paid the tailors. His people lined the streets to cheer and wave the emperor in his new clothes, but all they saw was his naked body as he paraded through the town. Foolishly they cheered and praised the fabric and its colours, even though they saw nothing. The emperor smiled and waved happily to all, until one small boy cried out: 'But he is naked! The emperor isn't wearing any clothes!' Soon everyone began to murmur and then shouted out: 'The emperor has no clothes on!' In that moment the emperor realised the truth but he hid it, preferring to believe that his people were stupid.

Like an entertainer walking onto a stage into the spotlight, it's time to feel the anticipation of spring, of fresh beginnings. This turning point heralds a brand new chapter in your life: breakdowns in relationships and other challenging situations that the dark night of the soul brought had to occur in order for the good stuff to come in. It's been a long, hard slog, but now you have been given a second chance and you can throw caution to the wind and trust in the great mystery as a brighter future calls.

BECOMING THE LIGHT

The light of your inner knowing beckons you to take the steps you need to embark on a new task while embracing a positive attitude. A new gateway has opened and you are invited to step through it into an unexplored world that has been waiting for you. It's time to stop playing it safe; your dreams can only be realised if you dare to explore every avenue. Don't settle for the life that is expected of you, but instead do the unexpected. You have an important life purpose and are here to shine brightly. You have always felt different and special but life has got in the way, and even though you have felt a calling you don't actually know what it is you are meant to do. Trusting in your intuition will help you to embrace life and live it to the full.

Let's go pack, no time to wait;
the future calls, cannot be late.
A path that glitters is revealed:
follow, for your fate is sealed.
Seek, unlock the truth, be free,
and walk towards your destiny.

Arnemetia shines her bright lantern through the darkness to show you the way as you take steps to move forward into a brighter future. Now you know you understand and have embraced your shadow side it's time to recapture the light, to remember who you are in totality. Your dark time has been a vessel of your experience, bringing you growth, understanding and ultimately wisdom, but now Arnemetia holds a light in the darkness so you can see your way out of the dark forest.

The Dark Goddess taketh away, but in the new light of day she offers you a chance to rebuild a life of honour, truth and integrity as authenticity leads the way. Authenticity is about staying true to what you believe and being brave enough to express your genuine feelings and opinions. Every time a lie is told the truth is concealed, or when you gossip about your friends your vibration lowers and a dark goddess will seek you out again!

Authenticity is about presence, living in the moment with conviction and confidence and staying true to yourself in every situation while being open to ideas. *Truth* means to be sincere and loyal to that which you believe in. Having *integrity* means you follow your moral or ethical convictions and do the right thing in all circumstances even if no one is watching. Having integrity means you are true to yourself and would do nothing that demeans or dishonours you. Having *honour* means accepting personal responsibility; be prepared to accept the consequences of your actions. As long as you can look in the mirror with a clear conscience, knowing what's right isn't as important as doing what's right.

As you start to awaken your vibration will become higher, which will impact the world directly around you, and you'll find that what once appealed to you no longer does. The higher your energetic frequency the more authentic you become, and the only people drawn to you will be those who are genuine. Don't be afraid to be yourself, for you are at your most powerful when you become your authentic self.

Know that Arnemetia singled you out because she heard the call of your soul, for your desire to be the best that you can be, for your positive attitude and the grace, dignity, compassion, love and other qualities she recognises within you. Your dark journey is almost over, but not before you balance your newly embraced shadow side with the light that now shines forth from within.

Arnemetia is a considered to be a Dark Goddess for she is shrouded from the light, she is hidden in the dark. However, she also reveals light in the darkness and therefore assists you to balance both sides of dark and light. As you entwine the darkness with a newfound light that glimmers from within you step into a place of wholeness and balance. Be still, breathe and go deep into the sanctuary within. Here in this sacred place Arnemetia will light you up and restore harmony between your dark and light sides, giving you the wisdom to know when and how to use either or both in perfect balance. If ever you fall out of balance she will shine a light through the darkness and pull you back into alignment, calling your soul back home.

PREPARING FOR ARNEMETIA

Imagine this mysterious, dark figure of silence using her powers to move a small wooden boat downstream at the magickal time of dusk. With fog swirling all around, she holds up a pale lantern and you are able to make out the dark silhouette of the otherworldly nature of a grove in the distance, with mists rising up from the wetlands, as she crosses the waters to the shores of another dimension where the veil between the worlds exists.

You may have subconsciously called in Arnemetia on a soul level when you wished:

- for wisdom
- to see the truth in all situations
- to shine your light brightly
- to be integral in all you do
- to connect spiritually with trees
- to practise meditation
- to quench a spiritual thirst
- to work in ritual
- to shed light on the truth.

You may have unwittingly called in Arnemetia when you:

- sought solace and comfort
- sat against a silver birch
- collected beech nuts and acorns
- paddled in a stream

- made a wish into a well
- threw coins into a fountain.

Turn to Arnemetia when you wish:

- for relief
- for restoration
- to heal
- to shine brightly
- for balance
- to be treated with respect
- for freedom
- for completion
- to join a coven
- to work as a solitary witch
- to meet her in a grove
- to meditate with trees
- to discover the truth of who you are
- to know your destiny
- to harness your life purpose
- to change your life
- to know yourself
- to be healed and whole.

As soon as she hears your invitation to come into your life, whether subconsciously or not, Arnemetia will remind you to never doubt your abilities of focus, willpower and visualisation, for in doing so you disregard the powers of the world that live beyond that which can be seen.

HONOURING AND CONNECTING WITH ARNEMETIA

Do the following to honour and connect with Arnemetia:

- Visit a grove.
- Sip from a natural stream.

- Meditate in nature.
- Sit against a tree you are drawn to.
- Connect with the trees.
- Feed, care for or connect with owls.
- Pick out any garbage from rivers and streams.
- Go wild swimming.
- Listen to Celtic music.
- Greet the sun as it rises.
- Do whatever lights you up.
- Make an altar for her and place upon it beech nuts and a chalice of pure water.
- If you wish to take something from a grove for an altar or a keepsake, do so in honour of Arnemetia and she will grant her permission.

Altar offerings to honour and give thanks to Arnemetia include:

- silver birch leaves and twigs
- green candles
- chalices of spring water
- pictures of groves
- owl figurines
- beech nuts
- acorns.

INVOCATION TO ARNEMETIA

To purposely call Arnementia into your energy you will need the following, but don't worry if you are unable to get hold of all of the ingredients as your focus will determine your connection with her:

- lavender incense
- a small bowl of salt
- frankincense essential oil
- a goblet of spring water
- lavender and purple iris flowers.

Light the incense and sprinkle some of the salt around you in a circle for protection as you ask the goddess for her blessings. You can do this silently in your mind using whatever words come to you or you can say out loud:

Divine goddess, I ask you to bless and protect me as I focus on the divine light within myself as I call upon you, the Dark Goddess Arnemetia, for assistance. I graciously receive your wisdom and integrity as I move towards a new dawn with an open heart in gratitude. Help me to serve, and help me to shine. In love and honour, so mote it be.

Find a sacred grove or a beautiful spot in nature where you won't be disturbed. Anoint your third eye and heart chakra with the frankincense essential oil and focus on your breath as it deepens and slows its rhythm, enabling you to enter into the inner realms. Take a slow sip of spring water from the chalice, and as you close your eyes become aware of the pure liquid tricking down your throat. Follow its stream as it meanders down towards your chest, then focus on your heart for a while. As you continue to breathe deeply, imagine diving into your heart. Swim further down and down through the green swirling waters of your heart chakra until a light reveals a shrine, a beautiful well with a greenish white ceramic focal surround that bears a faint carving of a goddess.

Welcome to your inner sanctum, the holy place where the goddess resides. It is a beautiful sacred shrine that's hidden away within and is old and neglected, for you've never visited it. You hadn't even realised it was here. Take some time to care for it, to clean and lovingly restore it in Arnemetia's name, and place down flowers of lavender and purple iris in her honour.

The goddess has been waiting for you to come and worship her, to honour her holy residence in you, for she is the divinity of you and you've forgotten. Her name is Arnemetia, and when she whispers her name she is calling your weary soul back home. Chant this powerful incantation from Barbara Meiklejohn-Free's 'Daughters of Gaia' to feel Arnemetia's primordial energy and awaken the goddess within:

In a lost chamber of the world
A serpent flower she unfurled
A woman rises up Divine
Revealing herself to the edge of time
Edge of time woman Divine
Edge of time woman Divine
Reawakening the Goddess
Reawaken her anew
Reawakening the Goddess
Reawaken all that's true
In me and you, and all we do
It's true she lives in you and me
Be love, be free
So mote it be.

You can visit this holy place, this sanctuary to honour and worship Arnemetia as you kneel at the well within where she resides any time you like. She is the goddess within and now she can finally awaken your honour and worship of her. Feel her residence and allow her owl to lend its sharp sight whenever you wish to look inwards. Her name is Arnemetia, she who is hidden. Now is the time for revelation as the goddess within you stirs.

Signs that Arnemetia is around you include:

- Seeing or hearing owls.
- A silver birch wand or staff presents itself.
- A small wooden boat sails downstream.
- You can only speak the truth.
- You feel much lighter.
- The sun shines brightly through the trees.
- You come across a grove.
- You have clarity.
- You're drawn to meditate.
- You join a coven.

- You experience a sense of freedom as new light shines through the darkness, directing you out of the final stage of the dark night of the soul.

Integrity saves the day when Arnemetia receives your invitation to draw near. The beam of her lantern will expose the hidden truth as the warmth and comfort of her light bids you to retreat within for a while. Here she will restore you to wholeness in the pure solace and refuge of her potent and natural healing powers.

EXERCISES AND RITUALS TO ENGAGE WITH ARNEMETIA

JOURNAL WORK: REFLECTION ON ILLUSIONS

What illusions have shattered so far in your life? How did it leave you feeling: did you feel cheated or lied to or like a fool? What did you discover about yourself? When parents, spouses, bosses and friends are exposed you will be left feeling wretched. When Arnemetia's lantern shines through the darkness it will reveal a space in which to invite in your dreams, those who bring positivity and meaning to your life and new opportunities to become who you always wished you could be. Write down in your journal everything you wish you could be.

As Arnemetia helps you to break down the barriers take those brave steps to open your heart in order to trust and believe again so that the opinions of others truly no longer matter. Having eliminated all that's not true in your life, an empty space will now reside in you, a sacred space that has made room for the goddess within to thrive and come alive. As the scales fall from your eyes a whole new world awaits as the Dark Goddess gently shows you who you once were, how far you've come and who you can become: a whole new you! A whole new world awaits.

EXERCISE TO REAWAKEN THE GODDESS AND GROVE WITHIN

Close your eyes and take a deep, deep breath in and out. Feel your body relax further as you continue to breathe deeply in and out and feel yourself sink down, down into the earth. In your mind's eye see a silver cord connecting you to the heavens above as you travel down further and further through the darkness and here you stop, in the dark chambers of what appears to be a cave. You know there is an exit somewhere, but it does not yet reveal itself. Embrace yourself as you rest in this womb of black velvet, safe in the darkness of the earth's belly. Become aware of the darkness around and listen to the heartbeat of the mother, of Mother Earth who nurtures you and tells you that it's okay, that it's safe.

Thump. Thump. Thump. Thump. Listen to the beat as it takes you deeper within. Here in the darkness you become aware that this is where the magick begins, this is the place where you can really be you. In this safe haven of you, allow yourself to really feel who you always knew you were. Remember when you felt magickal, when you had a thirst for knowledge and when you knew your power. What took that away? Who stripped you of that belief?

What disempowering actions or whose words echo through you, telling you that you are no good? This has contributed to who you are *not*.

Breathe the earth's healing energy into your heart and allow it to cleanse away the pain. Be willing to allow the healing to carry away the fears of being used, abandoned, rejected, controlled, persecuted or in other ways that hurt. Allow the fears from any lifetime to be dissolved, and exhale them back to the mother. As you breathe to the rhythm feel the mother's heartbeat, and feel her loving energy releasing the fears as they lift completely as your heart expands to its natural loving self.

You see a spark of light. As you go towards this light you feel a warmth and find yourself in a chamber that has been hidden through the mists of time. Have a look around: do you feel a sense of sadness, of loss and neglect? In the centre of the room is a large stone tomb. You walk over and peer in: there lies a body that is the very image of you, beautiful, serene and at peace. This is your inner mystic, the essence of who you truly are that has lain dormant for centuries and centuries. As you watch you notice signs of stirring: it is time to awaken, to come fully alive.

Lean over the body and kiss the lips of your mystic being self. As you do, you feel the rush of energy flowing through the whole of your body. As you release the kiss just stand for a moment and allow the awakening. The vital energy surges through you and you feel every part of you come alive as each cell, each vessel and every particle becomes alive with the healing vibration of magick. Breathe it in deeply as you resonate with the natural gifts of your mystical self. This is a time to receive. Allow yourself to be willing to accept these gifts that are your birthright and fully embrace your natural and very powerful ancient wisdom, knowledge and healing. Be still as they integrate on a full cosmic level.

As you stand in the chamber feel the energies surge through you and become aware of all that surrounds you, a connection to the entire universe. Your mystic twin steps out of the tomb and stands in front of you. Feel the magnetic force between you both and listen to what is now being said, knowing that an answer to any question you have will be revealed. Your mystic twin moves towards you and slowly you both merge. Welcome the mystic being once more to you as you become one with each other and with the all. See yourself expanding out, becoming one with nature – out into the skies. You are the twinkle of the stars; you are the glow of the moon; you are the power and the magick in every step you take, in all that you see, touch and are, awakening all and lighting the way.

Now that you have re-awakened the natural mystical powers that have lain dormant for many centuries it is time for you to put them to use. The ancient mystics worked with the flow of the universe and recognised that when we operate in this way we abundantly receive all that we need to survive. Many famous mystics walked this path and showed us the way, but sadly this was misconstrued and was turned around to become a form of control that would instil fear into the masses in order to prevent anyone tapping into their inner mystic.

The energies on this planet are changing and cannot support anything that is no longer in alignment or harmony with the natural world, which is why there are breakdowns in society and large corporations have been allowed to expand on the back of lies and collective control. The truth is finally breaking through, and Arnemetia has stirred and awoken the mystic within.

You find yourself in a beautiful place in nature. There is a path ahead, which you follow. It takes you to a sacred grove in the middle of which you see huge standing stones that make up the walls of an ancient burial chamber with a grassy roof on top. As you enter this sacred site you become aware of the energies of the many ancient and once honoured deities. You know you have been here many times before and you feel the magick coursing through this place. Surrounding and protecting the grove stand huge, powerful trees of different kinds: oak, ash, elder, yew, beech, willow, holly, hawthorn, sycamore, elm and many more. You feel the call from one of these keepers of wisdom and walk towards the tree that has chosen you. As you stand before it, feel your strong roots attached to the earth. Stand strongly in your power and say:

Arnemetia, I call upon you:
awaken and assist in all that I do.
I invoke your magick to connect us as one,
by alluring enchantment, united, it's done.

Feel your power rising and stand in this new strength. With a blast of light Arnemetia appears before you. You have worked with her in many lifetimes and you know each other on a deep soul level. Your relationship is still strong, for it is only in recent incarnations that you as the self has forgotten. Allow Arnemetia to remind you. Take some time to connect, to ask questions, to listen and be still. Walk to the burial chamber and through its entrance. Here you find yourself back in the darkness; how long you remain in here is up to you. When you have learned well a light glimmers in the distance and an exit is revealed. You push your way through the darkness, push, push and push: it's a struggle. Finally, you make it and light shines all around you.

As the sun greets you it highlights the path you are to take. Borrow its strength and warmth as it shines favourably upon you. Feel the thrill of experiencing something new and the anticipation of how it will evolve. Go explore, investigate and pursue adventure as you discover the whole new you that you weren't even aware of before your grim encounter with the Dark Goddess.

Place upon your Dark Goddess altar an offering in honour of Arnemetia such as a lantern to light the way and a purple candle to represent wisdom. Give thanks to her for shining light on the truth and highlighting the path through the darkness to your soul's awakening.

WATER-CLEANSING RITUALS

The element of water is symbolic for spiritual rebirth and renewal, purification and regeneration. It is the source from where you were birthed, the amniotic waters of the womb. The healing power of sacred waters enables you to let go of your ego self so you can throw caution to the wind and dive deeply down within to uncover the core of who you truly are. Your wisdom and perception are enhanced as you learn to go with the flow. Arnemetia offers to soothe and wash away any negative emotions and to seek out your sensitivity. As old hurts are washed away emotions are released, enhancing your natural vitality and positive outlook.

There are many ways you can connect with water for healing and cleansing. Drink a glass of water, blessing it with your intentions before you do so by saying:

Magick of water, of rivers and streams,
cleanse my emotions, flow through my dreams.
Soothe away hurts, help me to heal;
health is restored, I'm whole now to feel.
I give thanks for this magick most gratefully
and accept this healing most graciously.

See in your mind's eye the healing liquid light as you swallow, and consciously follow its stream as it slides down your throat and through your body. Imagine the water as a strong golden healing light seeking out any darkened areas within you that need to be lit up and allow the purification and cleansing to begin. Focus on restored health on every level: physical, mental and spiritual.

Other ways to cleanse and heal with the purity of water include:

- Visualising golden healing light purifying and cleansing you in the shower as the water washes over you.
- Rejuvenating and reviving your spirit by soaking in warm sea salt baths.
- Splashing about in puddles, dancing in the rain and eating a healthy diet of water-based fruits and veggies, including seaweed.

- Bathing in an old tin bath or in a pool at midnight under a waxing moon, within a forest clearing, to connect with the magick of the sacred grove and its swirling waters, the source of all life.

Emotions tide-healing ritual: the energy of water is considered to be receptive. Imagine the tide pulling back, taking with it any negativity aspects from you that you may have picked up from another person's emotions. As the water draws towards you it gifts you with prosperity and positivity. For ultimate psychic protection and healing benefits, imagine yourself being encased in a beautiful hard seashell such as oyster, scallop or conch.

WALKING THE SPIRAL EXERCISE

Upon the original foundations of Arnemetia's temple in Buxton is a spiral pattern that people can walk around; many priestesses of the goddess used to worship her by walking the spiral in a meditative state. At the centre of the spiral was the holy of holies, where prayers and offerings were made to her. Practise walking in this way by using a stick to draw a spiral in the dirt and walk around it, and do it in focus and dedication to Arnemetia. At the centre of the spiral drink a glass of water in honour of her sacred spring or use your power finger (the index finger of your dominant hand) to dab the water gently on your heart as you say:

> *I give thanks for this water so it may impart,*
> *connection and healing to open my heart.*
> *I connect with the light, welcome unto me.*
> *By the power of rivers, of streams and sea,*
> *so mote it be.*

LESSONS FROM THE DARK GODDESS ARNEMETIA

Arnemetia is a goddess of healing springs, a Romano-Celtic water goddess whose dwelling is at Buxton Springs. The Corieltauvi, an ancient tribe long before the Romans came and ruled Britain, worshipped her at her sacred grove, and it is said that those who drink of her waters can be cured of sickness and disease.

Arnemetia teaches you that it is not enough to seek power for power's sake, that you must accept the responsibility that comes with it. All good witches know that consequences are attached to spell casting, candle magick and any other magickal workings they may undertake. The universal law of cause and effect is the law of three in its purest form and teaches you that if you perform any action that causes a result, that result causes an effect that influences all of creation in some way. Arnemetia looks to those who come together as a coven and all those who choose to work as a solitary to act with integral responsibility. See yourself as being a high priestess or priest who undertakes a deep awareness of the possible effect of all things, of the results of all thoughts, words and actions magickal or not, and treat all that you do with respect and reverence – and that includes yourself.

Arnemetia holds up her glowing lamp to shine light through the darkness, to highlight the goddess within and any inner work still left to examine. As you walk with her between the worlds she inhabits the space where the magick grows and spirits reside, calling you to engage in deep and sacred spiritual work that heals and empowers not only yourself but the world around you on every level. She will encourage you not to hide any more as you face up to who you really are. Your authentic self will no longer wish to cower behind the mask that has concealed your soul, for your desire to fit in with the world around you will fade and your heart will embrace the truth that Arnemetia will reveal.

15. GODDESS AWAKENING

A path that shines is now revealed;
follow, for your fate is sealed.
Goddess of darkness sets you free.
Now walk towards your destiny.

Going through a transformational process of awakening, such as the journey of the dark night of the soul, seriously changes your life – for the better! But it's rather like swallowing a pill that tears through the veil of illusion. Once you have had all that you think you are, all that you think you know, stripped away to be replaced by a much older and ancient knowledge, wisdom and magick then you are ready to embrace your soul's knowing. As your dark journey comes towards an end, the transformation your soul craves has already started to rise up. If so, you may be able to identify with some of the following signs of experiencing an awakening.

AUTHENTICITY AND TRUTH

Having built up and worked towards goals for your future, it may all seem to be a bit false now. You're not sure what your beliefs and values are any more and you may have come to the conclusion that you've been influenced by the beliefs and ideals of others. Being true to yourself is most important and you cannot bear liars. You hate faking it and refuse to wear the old masks that used to present you as someone else. You want to be completely authentic now, and can't bear those who are egotistical or show-offs.

SOCIETY

You'll find you can no longer abide frivolous chit chat. You prefer for someone to get straight to the point to avoid lengthy conversations that leave you feeling restless and frustrated. Conversations that don't fulfil you will seem pointless and you'll soon notice that many people are unable to speak with truth, meaning and soul. Success, materialism and work targets mean nothing to you. You have no desire to meet social expectations and would rather not take part in the facade of daily life. As social contact reduces you may find you lose touch with old friends. Surprisingly, they will fall away naturally as new people enter your life who resonate more with your newfound interests and passions.

EMPATHY AND COMPASSION

As you awaken so too will your empathy, and you now find it hard to cope with the intensity of your feelings. You find you've developed a deep compassion for others as your attention is drawn to the perceived afflictions of the world. Be careful not to stuff down your emotions with addictive substances such as sugar, alcohol or drugs to numb the pain; instead, try to observe whether the feelings you're experiencing are yours and, if not, ask the unicorns to light up those people or situations who need healing.

ALONE TIME

Whereas once you may have been a party animal and the centre of attention you now prefer to hide away. Craving solitude is a natural part of awakening as you start to experience the introverted side of your nature. Time alone is just what your soul craves as you enjoy the silence of your inner sanctum.

MEANING AND PURPOSE

Endless questions about your life purpose arise and you may begin to read spiritual and self-help books to feed your soul. Sudden concern about completing your destiny has priority as you take steps to understand the reason why you're here and what you were born to do. Having worked hard for years to get qualifications and build your career now feels insignificant to you. You no longer feel fulfilled and desperately crave something with more meaning, something that satisfies your soul. You wish to make a difference in the world, and your job just isn't cutting it.

NEGATIVITY

Although you may have once enjoyed a good gossip in the past, you find it almost impossible to join in such conversations. You understand the karmic law that what goes around comes around and would not wish harm on anyone, whether it's verbal or physical. The expectations of others is lost, as is your interest in conflict and drama, and you refuse to engage in anything that causes negative outcomes. You are more able to observe your own flaws and are doing your best to keep your opinions positive and upbeat.

ANXIETY AND DEPRESSION

Often the shock of so many rapid changes can leave you feeling rather unstable. Periods of depression or bouts of anxiety are absolutely natural as you adjust to the new you and the completely different way you view the world.

INTUITION

As your energy levels rise to the higher frequency of light you start to become aware of your inner voice and begin to trust it to guide your decisions. You become drawn towards eating a cleaner, healthier diet such as one that is plant based, and find that your intuition really starts to hum as your energetic vibration heightens.

SYNCHRONICITY

Serendipitous occurrences and déjà vu experiences increase as you notice the signs, symbols and omens that present themselves as signposts to direct you in life. When you understand their meanings and take action accordingly life becomes receptive and its gifts flow more easily to you.

WONDER

Everything seems magickal and fascinating. Suddenly miracles are everywhere and you feel joy from the simplest of things as you embrace the wonder of life.

LOVE

You begin to love yourself and allow your barriers to break down, enabling your heart to love others without expectations and conditions. You understand that we are all interconnected and are all fragments of one love, and you wish to help make the world a better place. You want everyone to understand and feel the wholeness and yearn to make the world a better place.

You have journeyed through utter darkness with only the Dark Goddess for unwelcome company as she stripped you of all you knew. She heard your soul's call to embrace the wisdom of the crone and you had no choice but to accept her invitation and welcome her in. Now, having walked with the Dark Goddess, perhaps you are no longer fearful of her for it was she who had been your only friend, even though she led you to desolation. It was your deep, silent wishes and desire to spiritually evolve, to live as your authentic self, that brought about your dark experience.

Through your long recovery you were forced into dormancy just like trees in winter. For the trees, dormancy is much more than a period of suspended animation; it's part of their survival as nature gears them up to be ready to produce new life in spring. Now you can finally see the trees in among the darkened forest, and just like the trees at the beginning of each year a stirring of new life will get your creative juices flowing and give you utter clarity for the first time in a long, long while. Once I had been rescued and eventually raised from the lowest depths of despair my vibrational frequency was lifted to new heights. Suddenly I was infused with inspiration, and words poured out of me as though a light had been switched on. I had a million ideas streaming through my head, and for the first time in ages I was writing again.

The Dark Goddess takes you to the depths of an abyss, to your own private hell. It's her gift of death and rebirth, but through these grim teachings of hers you will emerge stronger and wiser, you will become whole and complete and light and dark in perfect balance and know yourself perfectly. Just as she had done to me the Dark Goddess will strip you down to your bare bones until you no longer recognise who you were, and you will lose your confidence after having been betrayed, ignored and bullied and everything else that contributed to the darkness. But still you soldiered on, never once retreating, for all along something within pushed you and egged you on to keep going. It was the Dark Goddess, for she knew that the moment you had nothing left she would be able to start building you back up again bit by bit to restore you to your highest potential. Now new opportunities will present themselves and doorways will open up to you: ones that are in tune with your soul.

You will find that the depths you sank to are no longer accessible, for the worst is now behind you and access is denied. Try not to search for old feelings and emotions as you process your journey; instead accept all that has gone before you as you look forward to new life. A fresh day is dawning, and the only way for you now is back up. The weight of worry, doubts and fears and a lack of self-worth will lift, leaving you to feel only freedom and no longer bruised. All that has vexed you in the past will disappear and you will not be bothered any more; in fact, you won't even think about it as your mind finds peace after its ordeal and you move forwards with newfound strength. Finally the shrouded veil will be raised as the sun comes out. The illusions of how you saw your family, friends, career and your own life will be shattered, for it is the Dark Goddess who reveals the reality and the truth behind the pretence. Integrity is key to your relationships now, without the need for any masks. It would be impossible for you to fake it as you've stepped into a new reality that is no longer just virtual.

To stand in and reclaim your full power you need to know how to draw from both your shadow side and the light as and when is needed, but only in perfect balance and knowing. The Dark Goddess's gift is for anyone seeking to obtain self-mastery in order to move through life with greater understanding of themselves as a whole, and it is the greatest opportunity you will ever have. The goddesses have both a shadow side and light side but they know when to use either and how to use them when necessary. Of course they often went to extremes, but what their stories teach us is that everything has a consequence and the lesson to be learned is to be aware of everything you do. Become conscious of every thought, word and action and remember that whether you are female or male the Dark Goddess resides within you. She remains an ally and offers to hold you in love and balance as you take your final steps towards wholeness. The light is shining through now, but the bond between you will never cease.

CREATING AN INNER GODDESS GROVE

It is time to create an inner sacred space, a goddess grove, so you can call upon the strength and attributes of your chosen goddesses whenever you reach within. This will be your personal sanctuary, one in which the goddess can reside. Decide what it is you require at this time and take a good look at the archetypal gifts each dark goddess you've already met can offer you; these attributes are listed in the appendix. If you feel drawn to explore other dark goddesses that may be part of your culture or philosophy you can also check the appendix. For example, you might invite Cerridwen to reside in your mind, for she offers inspiration, or you might ask the Morrighan into your heart to defend your personal boundaries. Choose what you need at this time.

Visualise a cloak of light being placed around your shoulders. Pull up your hood and imagine you are standing in the centre of a sacred woodland grove, but instead of trees surrounding you there is a circle of the most powerful deities of the divine feminine. They offer to reside within you if you will but ask.

Who will you invite to step into your *heart*, to be the instigator of love and influencer of relationships, including one with yourself, and to assist with your emotions?

Who will you invite to step into your *throat*, to influence your communication, your voice, truth and words?

Who will you invite to step into your *mind*, to instil clarity, inspiration, control, balance and peace of mind?

Who will you invite into your *soul* to be your guide, to direct you towards your life purpose, your soul's quest, and to complete your destiny?

Take your time, and choose wisely.

Once your goddesses are in place you will have all the tools you require to journey through your own dark night of the soul. As you allow the goddesses of your choice to integrate within you will be gifted the attributes and strength of the triple goddess, for you are the maiden, mother and crone as you walk between the worlds of light and shadows while holding the energy of both dark and light in balance, knowing and wisdom.

JOURNAL WORK: REFLECTION ON YOUR SHADOW SIDE

Now that they've been exposed, make a list of all of your shadow traits you've come to recognise along the way. Be honest and don't judge yourself or feel any shame, which is a dark trait in itself. Instead, claim them all, for they are a part of you and should be acknowledged and not ignored. If you ignore them your shadow side will become darker, explosive and uncontrollable.

Understand that your shadow side works hand in hand with the Dark Goddess herself. Each Dark Goddess aspect has her own archetypical behaviours traits she uses as and when necessary. As you look at each of your own shadow traits in turn it will match that of a Dark Goddess, and you will understand who has been influencing you. For instance, if you have inner anger it is the Morrighan who is influencing you to fight, or if you have a victim mentality and blame others for your woes you can be sure that Fuamnach is running the show.

Take a moment to go within to uncover your shadow side. When you've written your list of traits, write the name of the Dark Goddess who is associated with that characteristic next to each. Now you know who has been truly walking with you! Quietly ask the Dark Goddess whose archetypical character matches your shadow side to safeguard those traits for you, to keep them locked away within for now. Only borrow these darker qualities when the situation arises for you to use them again; however, you must be in mindful control and balance. Which Dark Goddess is working with you? Who will you call back? Which Dark Goddess will you say a final farewell to?

AFTER DEATH COMES REBIRTH

After stumbling around in the dark without light to show the way you'll emerge transformed, whole and fully equipped to embrace your life's mission, for it was the Dark Goddess who challenged you. Dazzled by her offer of transformation and powers of extremity, you had unwittingly invited in death: death of the old, a funeral for the former you that the Dark Goddess, in her many aspects, had prepared you for. Your old self had to die in order to become reborn, just like the phoenix, and rise!

Very soon you will be longing to never react to another person's negative energy and projections again as you welcome back your natural empathy, sensitivity and kindness and start to feel from your heart centre once more. As you begin to see through the eyes of love your joy and radiance will be reflected in others. Some won't bask in your new light when they see how strongly you are shining, but you will discover who is open-hearted and not guarded.

A sense of peace and serenity will become truths for you now as your heart grows stronger and more open. Peace is like a sacred grove within from which you can draw nourishment as you become healed and whole. Practise acts of peace. Be strong, be free and be blessed as you take steps to practise peace in some way each day. Allow your feminine wisdom to surface as you cherish the power of the goddess within.

The Dark Goddess made sure that you experienced yourself as the opposite from who you truly are, for how can you know who you are until you become who you are not? Now as the wheel of fortune makes its way further to the top you are ready to call the goddess back into your heart, for when you tap into the beauty of the divine feminine you become fully in tune with your sensitivity, enabling you to know how to express your emotions in balance and opening your heart from being guarded. If you feel ready for your heart to be healed and restored say this powerful invocation, which can be used every day at morning or night to invoke the power of love and the goddess within to keep your heart open to wonder and fulfilment and all your soul craves:

Goddess in me, of feminine beauty,
guide me to seek the love within me.
Goddess of love, of passion and lust,
I ask that you help me to rebuild my trust.
My heart has been broken, I suffered deep pain
I ask for your healing, for love I'll regain.
Goddess in me, of feminine beauty,
guide me to nurture the love within me.
Oh, to awaken the goddess within,
to embrace my gifts of deep feminine.
In your honour I sing and I dance
as I feel my heart open to love and romance.
Goddess in me, of feminine beauty,
show me the truth within me.
And now I see that the love within me
reflects the pure divinity.
Within my heart it doth reside,
and shines forth and is seen within my eyes
Goddess in me, of feminine beauty,
guide me to honour the love within me.
As I grow stronger I am able to see
that it matters not that 'I' becomes 'we'.
I focus on wisdom, on kindness to all,
and the goddess of love ensures I am whole.
Goddess in me, of feminine beauty,
thank you for the divine love within me.

As your vibration begins to lift you may feel an affinity with the magickal pathway of the old ways, having felt the call since childhood. The old ways call with a purpose to awaken you up to the days when magick abounded, when humans and the natural world respected each other and worked together in harmony to ensure balance in all things. The goddess has sounded a great alarm to stir each of us from our deep slumber, for it is time to wake up and acknowledge that the keys to existence are belief and realisation, to understand that this is a world of duality of darkness and light. The pathway of the Dark Goddess is uncertain but necessary if you wish to become the greatest version of yourself. There will perhaps be pitfalls and great losses, but you can be assured that wherever she leads you it will ultimately be for your highest good, even if you are kicking and screaming most of the way.

It is only now after my transformation through the darkness that I realise I had been living with the Dark Goddess all along. I was to meet my very own Maleficent, who pushed and tested my every button until I finally got it, until I no longer reacted, until I became indifferent to the outcome and until I could stand in my full strength and power. Together the Dark Goddess and I work hand in hand in, strength in strength, as we stand united both in the beauty of the light and the power of the dark, in wisdom, knowledge and love. I thank her from the very depths of my soul, as I do all those perpetrators who played their parts, which they did to perfection. Without them I would never have experienced the long, dark night of the soul, which led me ultimately to my salvation.

Thank you for joining with me through these pages and for trusting the process as you took a personal journey with the Dark Goddess. You may find that she takes you further, or she could have a few mini dark nights set up for you to experience. My dark journey seems to have gone on since childhood, with different aspects healed along the way and new dark situations arising. You may experience something similar until your journey's end, so use this book as your survival guide and a tool to navigate through the darker times.

The Dark Goddess will continue to test you, but now you will recognise who she is when she greets you. So, for instance, if you feel loss at any time you will know Baba Yaga is beckoning you into her wooden lair, or if you start reacting in defence you'll realise it is Fuamnach who has pushed your buttons while the Morrighan defends you. The dark night of the soul is a long and arduous journey and is not for the faint hearted who wish to believe only in the lighter side of life, thus being only half of who they are. When the shadow is revealed a process of understanding and forgiveness enables you to embrace the parts that serve you that you can call upon as your strength as and when you need it. It is only the Dark Goddess who can shed light on that which has been hidden, for only the light can be illuminated by that which is the dark.

When your soul called upon the Dark Goddess you had no idea of the trials and tribulations you would face. As you were to find out, you had no choice but to say goodbye to friends you'd known for years, and family members were revealed to you as those you no longer recognised. Through challenges such as depression and illness, the lesson learned was that life became all the more precious. As you dealt with infliction your prayers became stronger, and gradually through facing your pain and fears your body was given an energetic overhaul as you witnessed the death of all you knew until you had nothing and had to start all over again. You were thrown back to the beginning, but now you were aware you were starting from scratch but really from the next rung of the ladder.

Nobody held you, sympathised with you, dried your tears or congratulated or praised you. This was your path to walk alone, and desperately alone you walked and felt every misery of isolation. All the while the self voice from within continuously criticised and condemned you, encouraging you to leave, to go back to your old life and ways and to where you knew you were safe and loved. You felt the very force of the Dark Goddess as she pushed and pulled you to your limits of despair, yet you carried on as though she were dangling a golden carrot before you: the future you desired. You could almost see it and taste it, and all the while you never knew when you would see the brand new day you desperately hoped for. But at last the dawn appeared when you least expected it.

The lessons have been learned. You had been stripped to the very core of who you were and slowly the Dark Goddess has built you up piece by piece. You survived her initiation and now she is proud to call you her servant, her high priestess who has walked through the darkness and emerged, transformed into the light and holding the energy of both dark and light in balance, knowledge and wisdom. No longer are you paralysed by any fears, for now you are fully confident and strong in all that you do and know exactly who you are. You are to be congratulated for taking the path of no return with only the Dark Goddess for company and you made it through to the other side, to a place in which only truth and reality can exist. This is your new playground.

The archetypal traits of the Dark Goddess exist in a part of every one of us and are found only within the shadows. She will help and assist you to uncover and hone your darkest secrets, to shed light on any illusions, and she has prepared a journey that is unique to you. When you dedicate your life to standing fully in your power and embracing the magick of the old ways you'll find that the overall outcome will be beyond what you could ever imagine —and it's guaranteed you will meet some powerful goddesses along the way! The Dark Goddess has a personal invitation for you to walk with her for a while and embrace the dark offerings that will serve you best. Wherever you are in the world she is waiting for you to accept, if you dare . . .

You are very blessed indeed, for you were chosen especially by the Dark Goddess to experience a rebirth, to be transformed magickally into your very own happily ever after. May the Dark Goddess bless you as she takes you on a path of no return towards your highest potential.

For death completes you.

So mote it be.

Flavia Kate

APPENDIX: DARK GODDESSES AND THEIR ARCHETYPICAL SHADOW TRAITS

Arachne, archetypal 'exhibitionist' of Greek origin: Arachne was a most gifted weaver who challenged Athena. Talent she had, but her attitude left much to be desired, and when she realised this she took her own life in shame. Athena brought her back as a spider so Arachne could do what she truly loved: weave forever more.

Aradia, archetypal 'defender' of Roman origin: Aradia was the daughter of the deities Diana and Apollo and was known as the goddess of witches because she was sent to teach people, especially the poor and oppressed, how to perform witchcraft and magick and to be their defence against oppression, exploitation and ridicule.

Arnemetia, archetypal 'critic' of Celtic origin: Arnemetia was a water goddess whose sacred grove can be found at Buxton Springs (St Ann's Well) in England. The Corieltauvi tribe worshipped 'she who dwells at the sacred grove' long before the Romans came, on the valley floor where two springs meet together, and those who drank of her waters were cured of wasting disease and sickness.

Baba Yaga, archetypal 'thief' of Slavic origin: a supernatural goddess who dwells in the forest, Baba Yaga was of the forest itself. Children in particular were warned not to venture off, for she would ensnare them and they would be lost to her forever. She was very crafty so some people actively chose to seek her out for advice, and she would then decide whether to help or hinder.

The Cailleach, archetypal 'survivor' of Gaelic origin: one of the first revered goddesses on record, the veiled one resided high on clifftops and was associated with wet and windy weather. She endured all things, outliving those about her and epitomising the circle of life through the seasons, for without her enforced dormancy on earth there could be no energy left for the spring and summer to follow.

Cerridwen, archetypal 'rescuer' of Welsh origin: Cerridwen's first-born son was so hideous that she concocted a potion in her magickal cauldron of inspiration, Awen, to make him a poetic genius so he would be valued in some way rather than ostracised for his appearance. Sadly, her servant accidentally drank the potion and she devoured him as punishment.

Chang'e, archetypal 'obsessor' of Chinese origin: dogged in her pursuit of becoming immortal again and returning to the heavens, Chang'e swallowed too much of a special pill. She got stuck halfway and become the goddess of the moon, where she now dwells with only rabbits for company and is destined to forever look to the earth and heaven, contemplating all she left behind.

Deer Woman, archetypal 'temptress' of North American origin: the Deer Woman lures men of ill morals into the woods never to return; young adults and prepubescents are warned about her. She can be banished through the use of chanting and tobacco, and spells she casts can be broken by looking at her cloven hooves. Sightings of her are a sign of personal transformation or a warning.

Diti, archetypal 'avenger' of Indian origin: Diti wanted a son more powerful than Indra, who had killed her previous children, but Indra used a thunderbolt to splinter the foetus into many pieces, creating the Maruts. Diti was instrumental in the partitioning of India into Hindu and Tamil, north and south India, to gain control and autonomy over the gods.

Eingana, archetypal 'shaman' of Aboriginal origin: known also as the Dreamtime snake, Eingana is the primordial goddess of the Dreamtime and is the mother of humanity and all of the water animals. She bestows on all she has birthed health and longevity sustained through her invisible, mystical umbilical cord, which is attached to every living thing. When she cuts the cord the creature dies, so her demise would mean the death of us all.

Ereshkigal, archetypal 'blackmailer' of Sumerian origin: Ereshkigal passes judgement on the deceased and famously threatened the king of the gods himself that she would bring all the dead back to life and release them unto the world unless her lover Nergal was allowed to stay and rule with her. She got her way.

Erzulie, archetypal 'collector' of Haitian origin: clever, cunning and multitalented, Erzulie managed three husbands who provided her with a lavish and luxurious existence. She embodied all ages of the goddess and welcomed offerings of cakes, alcohol and jewellery in return for protecting or avenging those who suffered at the hands of the greedy, promiscuous, selfish or irresponsible.

Fortuna, archetypal 'gambler' of Roman origin: Fortuna is the goddess of chance, and is regarded as being the bearer of prosperity and increase. However, she is indifferent to any outcome and does not care either way if she raises someone up or throws them down. Frequently she was an oracular goddess consulted in various ways regarding the future.

Fuamnach, archetypal 'obsessor' of Irish origin: Fuamnach, versed in all things Túatha Dé Danann, was so jealous of her husband's second wife Étaín that she plotted to remove her using magic, including transforming Étaín into a butterfly so she would be blown away. Her attempts failed, and she eventually lost her head as a result.

Gaia, archetypal 'manifestor' of Greek origin: Gaia is the earth as we know it, a living, breathing, life-giving and life-ending entity, but she is not without her boundaries or her limits of creation for just as new things, ideas and life come forth to be birthed so, too, do old, tried and tested things eventually return to her, keeping the balance just so.

Guabancex, archetypal 'antagonist' of Haitian origin: Guabancex enlists the help of other gods to deal out hurricanes, earthquakes and other such disasters of nature. However, she doesn't release these storms willy-nilly and won't stand for neglect of the appropriate zemi worship and offerings or general disrespect of her awesome powers to manipulate the elements.

Hekate, archetypal 'guardian' of Greek origin: Hekate is the goddess of magic, witchcraft, the night, moon, ghosts and necromancy. She was the only child of the Titans Perses and Asteria, from whom she received her power over heaven, earth and the sea. She became the embodiment of the triple goddess and had far-reaching powers and a wealth of wisdom.

Hel, archetypal 'hoarder' of Norse origin: Hel has authority over nine worlds, administering board and lodging to those sent to her and those who die of sickness or old age. This black and white mistress of the underworld liked to accumulate the chattels of those who she received, hoarding their wealth and keeping her treasures secret so no one could steal from her.

Hine-nui-te-pō, archetypal 'sceptic' of Polynesian origin: Hine-nui-te-pō turned her back on the light and fled to the underworld after she discovered that the father of her children was also her own father. Unable to live with the shame she felt at this betrayal she embraced death and became its goddess. She is salvation and the chance for all to be reborn, literally through her body.

Inanna, archetypal 'seducer' of Sumerian origin: the goddess of sex, war and political power, Inanna was the original version of the goddess Ishtar. Her powers of seduction knew no bounds and enabled her to win over hearts, minds and entire realms.

Inara, archetypal 'trickster' of Hittite origin: Inara is the goddess of wild animals, becoming at one with all manner of beings from dragons to mortal men in order to trick them. During a special feast she lures in the dragon Illuyanka, enlisting the aid of Hupasiyas by becoming his lover. When the dragon is drunk he is tied up and slain, thereby preserving creation.

Isis, archetypal 'martyr' of Egyptian origin: Isis was worshipped as being the ideal mother, wife, protector of the dead and patroness of magic. She was instrumental in the resurrection of Osiris, restoring his body to life after having gathered the body parts that had been strewn about the earth by Set.

Itzpapalotl, archetypal 'purifier' of Aztec origin: this obsidian butterfly is a fearsome warrior goddess who ruled over the paradise world of Tamoanchan, where humans were created. She was the patron of the day and of women and children who died in childbirth. To pass through her kingdom is to be cleansed of all ills and be reborn again. As a star demon she sometimes did this by devouring people during solar eclipses.

Kali, archetypal 'destroyer' of Indian origin: as an embodiment of time, Kali devours all things. She is irresistibly attractive to mortals and gods and represents the benevolence of a mother goddess. Her dark skin, which is symbolic of eternal darkness, has the potential to both destroy and create.

Lilith, archetypal 'egalitarian' of Mesopotamian origin: Lilith was Adam's first wife and was created as an equal, but she fell out with Adam when she insisted on equality. She left Adam and Eve was then created from him. Lilith was created in God's feminine image and can be seen as being the first lady of creation and as such on a par with man.

Ma'at, archetypal 'judge' of Egyptian origin: the daughter of Ra and the wife of Thoth, Ma'at decided whether a person would successfully reach the afterlife by weighing their soul, in form of the heart, against her feather of truth, and was the personification of the cosmic order and a representation of the stability of the universe.

Maeve, archetypal 'leader' of Irish origin: Maeve is a most determined goddess who gets what she wants – victory in battle and the conquest of men. Her name means 'intoxicated woman', and she was associated with substances such as mead and mind-altering herbs. Ancient kings of Ireland married her when they came to the throne so she would bestow her powerful gifts upon them.

Maman Brigitte, archetypal 'redeemer' of Haitian origin: this goddess of justice who guards over cemeteries is one of the most powerful in voodoo beliefs. A figure representing her is the first female buried in every voodoo cemetery, so that those laid to rest may – Maman Brigitte willing – be redeemed of their sins or the sins inflicted upon them.

Medea, archetypal 'deceiver' of Greek origin: Medea was a gifted enchantress who unscrupulously used her powers to help Jason, the leader of the Argonauts, obtain the golden fleece from her father. She married Jason and used her magick powers to help him; however, when her powers and deceptions finally failed her and Jason deserted her for the daughter of King Creon, she went on a murderous rampage, including killing her own children by Jason.

Medusa, archetypal 'narcissist' of Greek origin: this Gorgon would petrify anyone foolish enough to meet her gaze, which she actively encouraged; her reign ended when she was finally decapitated by Perseus. So legendary was her power that depictions of her head appeared on buildings and shields to ward off evil spirits and physical harm.

Morgana, archetypal 'enchantress' of Celtic origin: this goddess incarnated as Morgan Le Fay in Arthurian legend. She studied under the great wizard Merlin and is a healer with herbal knowledge. She shape-shifts into ravens and crows and is also known as the queen of the faeries, and she is the gatekeeper to the magick of the old ways.

The Morrighan, archetypal 'warrior' of Celtic origin: the Morrighan is a complex goddess who is blunt, rough and violent and has the ability to take animal form as a crow, raven, cow or wolf. She was worshipped most as the battle raven, who determined whether a warrior walked off the field of battle or was carried off on his shield.

Nemetona, archetypal 'hermit' of Germanic origin: primarily worshipped across Germany, France and England, Nemetona guards over sacred groves of trees wherein the soul became hushed and calm and was at one with nature and the goddess. She was linked to Rigonemetis, the king of the sacred grove, who is also associated with Mars.

Nuba, archetypal 'miser' of Chinese origin: this green-clad goddess of drought descended from heaven to aid her father, Huangdi, during a mighty battle against the wind god Feng Bo and the rain god Yu Shi. Her drought power denied their victory, but instead of returning to heaven she ran off to wander the earth, causing droughts and famine wherever she went.

Nyx, archetypal 'confider' of Greek origin: the primordial goddess of the night, Nyx is a figure of such exceptional power and beauty that she is feared by Zeus himself. She is the mother of all of the creatures of the night, including vampires, lycans and werewolves, and all can go to her to find comfort and respite and bare their souls in confidence.

Oya, archetypal 'reaper' of African origin: Oya symbolises the first and last breath of life. This primordial deity of immense power and influence was linked to both the Niger and Amazon rivers, yet more often than not it was the fiercest of winds that heralded her presence. She was the compassionate guardian of the unborn, who after death she delivered to the other side.

Pandora, archetypal 'gifted one' of Greek origin: created by the gods as the first mortal woman, Pandora was gifted with many talents, including a jar. Releasing the lid of the jar unleashed disease, plague and misery upon the world, and Pandora got the lid back on just in time to save hope; however, by that stage the cycle of death and rebirth had been established on earth.

Pele, archetypal 'transformer' of Polynesian origin: in addition to being recognised as the goddess of volcanoes, Pele is also known for her power, passion, jealousy and capriciousness. By devouring land and bringing forth new land in equal measure, she heralds significant change.

Penthesilea, archetypal 'perpetrator' of Greek origin: this queen of the Amazons is fearless and determined. A great warrior, she accidentally killed her own sister while hunting. Unable to reconcile with what she had done and plagued by guilt, she took to war against the mighty Trojans in order to immerse her thoughts in battle and finally succumbed to Achilles.

Persephone, archetypal 'victim' of Greek origin: Persephone was carried off to the underworld by Hades without struggle and appeared to be willing to fulfil her function without question. Unlike most goddesses, she is of a very subservient nature.

Pythia, archetypal 'teacher' of Greek origin: this oracle of Delphi held court at Pytho, the sanctuary of the Delphinians that was dedicated to Apollo. She was highly regarded, for it was believed that she channelled prophecies from Apollo himself while steeped in dreamlike trances.

Rán, archetypal 'ravager' of Norse origin: Rán is the darker, more destructive side of the sea's nature and she makes no bones about it. Using her alluring beauty, incredible strength and magickal net, her hobby is collecting souls to populate Aegirheim, in particular those of seafaring men.

Sedna, archetypal 'outcast' of Inuit origin: Sedna is a beautiful maiden who was ostracised when it was believed she had been impregnated by a wild animal. Her father took her out on the water to throw her overboard, but she clung to the side of the kayak so tight that he cut off her fingers. They became sea creatures and she was immortalised as the goddess of the sea.

Sekhmet, archetypal 'rebel' of Egyptian origin: the powerful one is both a goddess of war and healing. Depicted as a lioness, the fiercest hunter known to the Egyptians, Sekhmet's breath formed the desert. She protected the pharaohs, and when called she would rise up and lead them in warfare.

Sheela-na-gig, archetypal 'warrior' of Irish origin: Sheela-na-gig, who appeared as a lustful hag, was hailed as the goddess who granted kingship. Most men would refuse her advances, except for one man who accepted. When he slept with her she was transformed into a beautiful maiden who conferred royalty on him and blessed his reign.

Skadi, archetypal 'underdog' of Norse origin: Skadi is a giant warrior goddess associated with bow hunting, winter and mountains. She was wife first to Njord and later Odin, but is most noted as being responsible for punishing Loki as atonement for his verbal and sexual abuse of the goddesses by physically scarring him and brutally killing his son.

Scylla, archetypal 'drama queen' of Greek origin: Scylla haunts the rocks of a narrow waterways; ships that sailed too close to her rocks lost men to her grasp and appetite. Her voice is likened to the yelping of dogs. She is the nature of treacherous waters and stormy, violent seas and rocky shores made flesh.

Tiamat, archetypal 'controller' of Babylonian origin: Tiamat predated all other deities and dwelled in the oceans. She gave birth to the first generation of creation beings: dragons and serpents. Upon her death her body was used to form the land and sky, ensuring her influence over all beings that inhabit earth, and she lives on via the forces of nature, which are under her control.

Uzume, archetypal 'persuader' of Japanese origin: using song, dance and a trick of mirrors, the multitalented goddess Uzume is the only deity who could lead the great sun goddess Amaterasu out of a severe depression and back to her heavenly responsibilities, ensuring the return of light to earth and the fertility of crops.

ACKNOWLEDGEMENTS

To Barbara Meiklejohn-Free, a dark goddess in every way: my dream maker, soul sister and partner in all things magickal. You witnessed my tears, frustrations and outbursts as I came face to face with each dark goddess yet again for the purpose of this book. Thank you for holding the space, for listening, for your wisdom and for being a big part of my dark journey and transformation. Thanks too for letting me 'borrow' your lyrics for 'Re-awakening the Goddess' in dedication to Arnemetia, who welcomed us both many moons ago into her sacred grove in Buxton.

To Tigger, my prince in shining armour, whom the goddess brought to me upon my transformation with her eternal promise that dreams do come true.

To Lisa and the super team at Rockpool, thank you for believing and trusting in the vision and for being brave enough to invite the Dark Goddess and her journey of transformation to birth into the world through these pages. I am honoured and extremely grateful for all the hard work and dedication you've invested. What an awesome edit, too, and nobody can beat you guys when it comes to design and artwork. You truly do rock!

Note the following websites for those who endorsed this book:
Ronald Hutton: www.bristol.ac.uk
Olaf Nixon: www.OlafNixon.com
Barbara Meiklejohn-Free: www.spirit-visions.co.uk
Lynne Franks OBE: www.lynnefranks.com, www.seednetwork.com, www.theseedhub.club

ABOUT THE AUTHOR

Bestselling author Flavia Kate Peters, who is known as the Faery Seer, is an hereditary witch and high priestess of Arnemetia and of the Morrighan. Recognised as the UK's leading elemental and ancient magick expert, she teaches her professional certification magickal courses at the College of Psychic Studies, London and is a regular presenter on the mind, body, spirit and pagan circuits.

Flavia is a working medium and clairvoyant and has appeared on TV and BBC Radio. She regularly graces the pages of *Spirit & Destiny* magazine and is a columnist for *FAE* and *Witchcraft & Wicca* magazines. Her authentic approach makes her a most sought-after wisdom keeper, and her mission is to keep the magick of the old ways alive!

WWW.FLAVIAKATEPETERS.COM

WWW.SPIRIT-VISIONS.CO.UK

INSTA: FLAVIA_KATE_PETERS

OTHER TITLES BY FLAVIA KATE

WITCH'S DIARY

Reclaiming the magick of the old ways

Flavia Kate Peters and **Barbara Meiklejohn-Free**

The *Witch's Diary* will awaken the witch within and help you discover the freedom to express who you truly are.

This practical guide will show you how to harness the magic of nature, reclaim your personal power through the discovery of ancient wisdom and embrace the feminine divine. You will journey through the year, learning to work with the forces of nature through spellwork, incantations, rituals, sigils, age-old recipes and charms that use herbs, candles and crystals.

This is a must-have magickal tool for anyone who has a love of the natural world and wants to bring the power and magick of the old ways into their everyday lives.

MAGICKAL MERMAIDS

Harness the power of the mermaids to create an enchanted life

ISBN: 9781925682434

It is time to reap the magick and abundance that has been bubbling under the surface and dive right in to stir the siren within, to uncover the inner treasure that is waiting to be revealed …

Faeries of the seas, mermaids are alluring elementals who help to ignite your own sensuality and seductive powers, whether male or female, and harness your natural powerful manifestation abilities.

MAGICKAL UNICORNS

Harness the power of the unicorns to create an enchanted life

Flavia Kate Peters

ISBN: 9781925682441

Discover the path of ancient magick and lore with *Magickal Unicorns*. Learn to awaken, connect and heal with these magickal creatures as you shift your personal energy to a different realm.

Wishes, invocations, meditations and easy to learn spellwork all feature in this book, enhancing our natural magickal abilities to bring healing and balance into our lives.